THURSDAY'S

CHILDREN

Their school betrayed them.

Their teacher defended them.

Their struggle continues today.

ELISABETH PENDLEY

Library of Congress Control Number: 2021902745
ISBNs: 978-0-578-86381-8 (pbk); 978-0-578-86433-4 (ebook)

IN THE GHETTO (The Vicious Circle)
Words and Music by Mac Davis
Copyright © 1978 Sony/ATV Music Publishing LLC and Elvis Presley Music
All Rights on behalf of Sony/ATV Music Publishing LLC Administered
     by Sony/ATV Music Publishing LLC, 424 Church Street, Suite 1200,
     Nashville, TN 37219
All Rights on behalf of Elvis Presley Music Administered by Songs Of Kobalt
     Music Publishing and Songs Of Steve Peter
International Copyright Secured All Rights Reserved
Reprinted by Permission of Hal Leonard LLC

AQUARIUS (from Hair)
Lyrics by JAMES RADO and GEROME RAGNI
Music by GALT MACDERMOT
Copyright © 1966, 1967, 1968, 1970 (Copyrights Renewed) JAMES RADO,
     GEROME RAGNI, GALT MACDERMOT, NAT SHAPIRO and EMI U
     CATALOG, INC.
All Rights Administered by EMI U CATALOG, INC. (Publishing) and
     ALFRED MUSIC (Print)
All Rights Reserved
Used By Permission of ALFRED MUSIC

OOH CHILD
Words and Music by STAN VINCENT
© 1970 (Renewed) KAMA SUTRA MUSIC, INC. and FRANTINO MUSIC
All Rights Controlled and Administered by EMI UNART CATALOG INC.
     (Publishing) and ALFRED MUSIC (Print) All Rights Reserved
Used By Permission of ALFRED MUSIC

CONTENTS

DEDICATION

To the Thursday's Children in my classroom
And to all of their children and grandchildren,
Most likely Thursday's Children every one of them,
And to the Thursday's Children of today and tomorrow,
Deprived, even now in the history of the Republic,
Of the education they deserve,

This book is dedicated.

AUTHOR'S NOTE

IT IS FIFTY YEARS since I sat down at my desk with an electric typewriter, a ream of onion skin typing paper and piles of notes that I wrote each day as I taught at Johnson Public School 123.

I often think of my class of twenty-seven, Thursday's children. I want everyone to know their story: the racial tension that undermined their education, the dilapidated school building and lack of supplies, the indifference of many school teachers and administrators, and the seemingly insurmountable task faced by these children to change their life through education.

The names of the adults were changed, including my own. The names of the children remain the same. Even after all this time, I can see their faces clearly. The harshness of the language spoken then is faithfully recorded here.

This is a snap shot in time of a newly integrated elementary school in the rural south in 1969. I leave it to you to determine if the schools today are any better at meeting the needs of Thursday's children.

MONDAY'S CHILD

Monday's child is fair of face,
Tuesday's child is full of grace,
Wednesday's child is full of woe,
Thursday's child has far to go,
Friday's child is loving and giving,
Saturday's child works hard for his living,
And the child that is born on the Sabbath day
Is bonny and blithe, and good and gay.

MOTHER GOOSE

CHAPTER 1

Johnson Public School 123

IT WAS DECEMBER 1969, fifty years ago, when I walked down that dirt road. The red brick building was older than I expected. With a letter missing, the sign read, "Jonson P.S. 123." It was surrounded by a high fence topped with rusty barbed wire. The brown earth was littered with papers and bottles. Finding the gate, I followed the broken concrete sidewalk to a battered green double door and pulled it open.

Inside, the tiny front office was filled by a large black woman who stared at me. As my eyes adjusted to the dimness, I noticed a young black girl sitting at the typewriter. She did not look up.

"Is Mr. Rufus Carter in, please? I have a 10:00 appointment with him."

Mrs. Black waited a long time before answering. First a shrug, then, "I don't know wheres he at. But you can sit there and waits if you want." As I sat down on an old folding chair, she mumbled, "I guess he somewheres in the building."

The secretary did not try to find Mr. Carter. Instead, she munched a handful of chips from a bag in her bottom drawer. I watched her curiously and thought of a huge spotted frog on a lily pad. Her eyes bulged, and the chips turned to flies.

1

My image was shattered by the sound of gum popping to the rhythm of the typewriter. "Son of a bitch." Nadette, the typist, cursed at a mistake, yanked the paper out, and crumpled it. I noticed files and papers stacked all over the desk and shelves. An old half-eaten sandwich and apple core sat on the window ledge.

As I waited, the gloom of the building pressed down on me. The smell of lunch hung in the air. I saw no children in the hall outside the open door, but their noise throbbed erratically through the halls. Screams punctuated a child's anger. A torrent of high-pitched words, "I ain't. I ain't. You bitch. You ain't gonna—" was cut off by a door slamming, then more shouts and footsteps running down metal stairs.

A middle-aged black man strolled into the office. From the looks of the women toward him, and then toward me, I guessed this was Mr. Carter.

The office clock snapped to 10:20. "Mr. Carter?"

"Yes?"

"Lisa Evans." He looked puzzled. "I called you about a teaching vacancy."

"Oh. Yeah."

I followed him into his small, cluttered office. The pockets of his suit coat sagged from holding his hands. The legs of his trousers hid most of his brown shoes. He sat down hurriedly behind an old, wooden desk, sifted through some papers, found a worn red rubber band to stretch between his fingers, and cleared his throat. "Well, Mrs. . . . *ahh.*"

"Evans," I said.

"Right. Well, you knows, I was looking for an older, more experienced teacher. You is too young. You young teachers can't control these students. Now what experience does you have that would make me wants to hire you? Has you ever taught in a disadvantaged school like this?" He enunciated "disadvantaged." "Why, from the looks of you, I doubt you can handle a black class. You being so young and all, what you know about discipline? Discipline is real important. I demands quiet, well-behaved, learning children. Yes, indeed. I do."

He didn't look up to see if his words made any impact. His fingers stretched and snapped the rubber band. Abruptly, he stopped his rapid-fire questions. Silence filled the room.

"Well, I—" but he interrupted.

Realizing he had forgotten a vital question, he sat forward in his chair, snapped the rubber band, and spate out, "You being white and all, are you prejudice? I ain't putting up with no up-pity white folk." Then he leaned back and fished in his pockets for his smoking tobacco, pipe, and matches.

Momentarily speechless, I stammered, "Sir, for the past two years, I taught third grade in an award-winning public school in Maryland in an affluent suburb of the District of Columbia. It was a self-contained classroom of thirty-five children. I also taught smaller groups in reading and social studies. The second year I was grade chairman, responsible for helping two first-year teachers."

He looked bored. Rocking on the back chair legs, he tamped his pipe one last time and lit it. The smoke floated toward the open window. "Well, now ain't that a coincidence," he said. "The position I am filling is a third grade. Teacher's white and young and she ain't never taught before. Sure can't handle her class. Why I has to go down there and shut them up, they is so loud I hears them in my office."

As he spoke, he leaned forward and shuffled some papers together. I was surprised that none of the forms I completed at the county education office were on his desk.

"No, I never taught in a disadvantaged school. I think I am up for the challenge, though, and if the job is offered, I will certainly accept it."

He stared at me and cleared his throat. "Well now, Mrs. . . . .

ahh. You ain't the only one applied for the job. Been couple of others. They is older than you, more experience, you know. Course now, they ain't taught third grade."

With that comment, he pushed his chair back and stood up. Leaning forward, he waved his hand at me in dismissal. Hurriedly, I continued, "Even though I have only taught two years, I never had discipline problems. My first class was quite large. I feel confident that I could teach this third grade."

Mr. Carter obviously did not believe me. He looked directly at me for the first time. I knew he saw a slightly built girl with wide green eyes. I blushed at my attempt to look older, with my modest knee-length skirt and white buttoned-up blouse and my long blond hair tacked in a bun at the back of my neck. He smiled. "Oh really, Mrs. Evans?" His smile broadened and then disappeared, leaving his face expressionless. He stood and looked out the window.

Hastily, I added, "My students behave because they are treated fairly and know what is expected of them." The silence and the pipe smoke hung in the air. "Mr. Carter, could you tell me the size of the class, please?" I paused, expecting an answer. "Also, what are the hours the teachers work? And the school lunch policy?" I started to ask another question, but he interrupted me.

"Can't rightly say how many in the class." Exasperated, he turned from the window and answered my questions tersely. "Ain't no more than thirty, I suppose. The day is 8:00 to 4:00." He puffed on his pipe and then continued, "But the children come at 8:30 and leave at 3:15. Now about lunch time. This here is real important. You got to sit and eat with your class. I wants them taught proper manners, so they ain't laughed at. You got to teach them how to eat right." He sat down with an air of finality and seemed quite surprised to have his pipe smoking interrupted by one more question.

"Mr. Carter, what are the rules about playtime? I think it is really important to take them outside often."

"Well, there ain't no scheduled playtime, but I guess you can take them out." He picked up a paper from the top of the stack and began reading it. He did not look up when I stood to leave.

"Mr. Carter, when does the third grade vacancy begin?"

"Monday. But don't you forget now. Several others already been interviewed. Don't get your hopes up."

"Goodbye, Mr. Carter. Thank you for your time."

"*Umm huh*," he grunted.

Closing his door, I stepped into the outer office. The gum-chewing typist stared at me and the head secretary popped her eyes. I nodded at them both and said goodbye, but neither of them spoke.

Curious about the school, I started down the dark hallway. The harsh bang of a metal classroom door convinced me to retreat. Turning around, I saw a small patch of blue sky through a broken windowpane. Several more steps took me past the office to the double doors through which I had entered. I stepped into the warm Florida sunshine. A soft breeze played with an errant strand of hair. I pulled at a few hair pins and my hair fell to my shoulders.

I sighed, convinced that the interview had not gone well. Opening and closing the school gate behind me, I stood out in the road. An old black man shuffled toward me. His head was rimmed with tufts of gray hair. His clothes hung loosely on his thin frame. His bloodshot eyes and uncertain steps convinced me he was headed home from the corner bar.

The rest of the day I thought of Johnson P.S. 123—the tension in the air, the sounds of invisible children, the harsh bang of the metal door, Mr. Carter's hostile comments. To my amazement, the phone call came the next morning. I accepted the position immediately and set up a time on Thursday morning to meet the teacher who was leaving and see the children I would inherit.

Excited about teaching, I pulled out boxes of teaching supplies I collected in the last two years. I found books I thought the children would enjoy and unearthed my favorite teaching tools: stories, poems, puzzles, maps, posters, pictures, and word cards. I fantasized about play-acting or conducting science experiments or reading stories about heroes. I remembered sitting in the middle of the floor at my school in Maryland, surrounded by teaching supplies. I imagined a sunny classroom filled with lively, interested children. "Good Morning! I am Mrs. Evans. We will learn many things together this year."

I was delighted to have another teaching job. I always wanted to teach. As a little girl, I listened to stuffed bears read and taught wide-eyed dolls the alphabet. Later, younger neighbors and their pets joined my class. Excited about the thought of a new classroom of children, I smiled. I was about to do what I loved most: teach.

When I returned to school on Thursday, I ran into Mr. Carter as I struggled through the heavy double doors. He was coming back from the cafetorium (as the dual-purpose cafeteria and auditorium was called) with a coffee cup in his hand and sleep clouding his eyes.

"Good morning," I said cheerfully. He looked at me suspiciously, searching for my name.

"Mrs. Evans," I reminded him.

"Oh, yeah," he nodded. Gesturing with his cup, he led me down the dark hallway. The wall clock erroneously displayed

6:15. All the classroom doors were closed, but I could hear children shouting.

We stopped at a gray metal door and he banged on it. The noise from the classroom rushed at us when a little girl opened the door and peered out. Seeing Mr. Carter, she darted back inside. Her pigtails, tied with different colored ribbons, bounced. Mr. Carter motioned for me to enter. After I stepped past him and inside, he closed the door. The noise swirled around me. A small group of children was in the back of the room. A few were reading. One boy was crawling across the floor. Two boys stood beside a young woman seated on the only chair on the rug as she feverishly corrected their papers. The other students, who were supposed to be working quietly, were in various stages of hysteria. Three boys were whooping loudly, running up and down the aisles, bumping into desks, and knocking off books. One boy pounded the boy behind him with his reading book and a very plump girl practiced blowing pink bubble-gum bubbles. Then a scuffle began over a pencil. Meanwhile, four little girls stood by the windows and giggled. A large boy in a bright green shirt drummed on the desktop with pencils, his head nodding approval to the rhythm. A little boy with scabs on his scalp slept in the front row.

I stepped away from the door and walked slowly to the front of the room. My red dress attracted attention. The giggling girls turned to watch, the bubble-gum chewer's bubble burst and lodged in her tightly curled bangs, and the boy stopped drumming on the desk.

Their teacher stood up and screamed, "Shut up. All of you!" It was difficult to hear her. She moved forward, grabbed the crawling boy, lifted him off his hands and knees, and shoved him toward his desk. She stepped over some coats that were on the floor and yelled again, "I said sit down and shut up."

As she reached the front of the room, she looked at me and nodded hello. I was startled at how unwell she looked. She was very thin. Her face was pale with dark shadows under her blue eyes. She motioned to her desk chair, and as I sat down, she yelled, "It is time to go over spelling."

Angrily picking up the pointer, she shouted each word written on the board, "Barn, farm, year." Few could hear her. The aisle racers had not stopped, but finally did when she punctuated a sentence with, "Sit down. Now!" and walked toward them swinging the pointer. Several girls and one boy had their spelling books open. The noise finally lessened as she finished going over the spelling.

"Next, we will have handwriting." Pandemonium began again as more than twelve children leapt up and ran for the pencil sharpener in the back of the room. She sat on the edge of the table and waited as the group of children pushed and shoved, straining to sharpen their pencils. No one hurried back. Finally, the lesson began.

They liked penmanship. The children worked slowly, feeling the roundness of "O." Occasionally, pencil points broke under the strain. Then the desks shook as children ran back to the sharpener. The grinding noise cut into the back of my head. Their teacher wrote each letter on the board because there were no wall posters. After each letter, she leaned against the edge of the table, exhausted.

In the relative calm, I was able to look objectively at the classroom. There were twenty-six desks in the room, so I guessed there were twenty-six children. It was stifling hot, but no windows were open. The windows, a few with cracked panes and two boarded, lined one side. The front of the room was blackboards. Opposite the windows were bare bulletin boards. The back of the room held a sink, several closets, and a long rod for coats. The rod was empty. Instead, the coats were on the floor, over students' heads or on the backs of their chairs. The room had a sour smell, intensified by the steam heat. The walls were a drab, dirty green. Several missing light bulbs added to the grim reality of the room. I began to write down several items to bring—a small clock, hangers, air spray—but was interrupted by the noise of children pushing, shoving, and finally bursting out of the door, their teacher trailing behind.

I followed and watched them run down the hall and disappear around the corner. I caught up with them at the door of the music teacher's room where a toothless black woman filled the doorway, her graying hair clamped with a barrette to the back of her head. Mrs. Williams's harsh, shrill voice screamed, "Shut up! Hey, you two, who do you think you is?" She bellowed at two boys who tried to push past her into the room and shoved them back. "I ain't gonna let you monkeys in here. No, sir. Not till you quiets up, and that the God's truth." Then the gray door closed.

Finally, with the children in the music room, we headed for the teachers' lounge to get some coffee.

"Oh, I am Mary Ann Jenkins."

I smiled at her. "Lisa Evans."

She blew on her coffee, put it down on the table, and walked the length of the teachers' lounge. Putting her elbows on the ledge, she looked out the small, split windowpane. Her voice was soft when she spoke, "This is my first year of teaching. I always wanted to teach, you know." She turned and looked at me. "I just love children." Her blue eyes filled with tears. Quickly she brushed them away. "But I can't stand this anymore." Her hands fluttered and tugged at her short, straight hair. Her voice wavered when she continued, "Some of the teachers are real sweet and helpful but some are . . . you know . . ." She stopped and started again, "But you don't have to worry about Mr. Carter. All the teachers do what they want."

She offered to mark the desks with the children's names and list what chapters they were working on in the books.

"I'm sorry I disturbed the class this morning, Mary Ann."

"Gosh, no. You didn't. They are always like that. You know, real active. Everything distracts them." Abruptly she walked to the couch, put her feet on the low table, and drank her coffee. I heard the plumbing gurgle, the Coke machine clank, the clash of the xylophone, and the music teacher's strident voice drown out the children's singing.

She continued, "I plan to get married soon. Nothing formal. Just a few guests. I don't even have my dress yet, and it's in a few weeks."

All too soon, the noise in the hall convinced me that the music lesson was over. Since they misbehaved, the music teacher put them out early. Miss Jenkins planned to let them watch an educational television show that morning. The class charged up the stairs, shoved into the film room, and banged chairs against the desks.

Two boys fought over the same seat. "Hey, boy, that my seat."

"You bastard. It ain't. I got it first."

"Miss Jenkins, he gots my seat."

"Stop right now. Everyone find a seat. Get away from the windows. Sit down, Nicholas. Dexter, stop fighting!" yelled Miss Jenkins. The boy who was asleep earlier was missing. I didn't remember seeing him at music, either.

Much to Mary Ann's distress, the television set was broken,

as well as the film projector. The full horror of having to go back to the classroom showed on her face.

"Why not take them outside for a few minutes?" I suggested. She looked at me strangely. "I guess I will. Sure glad you mentioned it. I couldn't stand going back into the classroom." This time the class did better lining up, forming a ragged line. Surging ahead, the children pushed and slid down the steps and dashed out the door into the sun.

I stared at the playground. The brown clay was gouged with deep ravines. A dead tree leaned against the barbed wire fence. The playground equipment consisted of one rusted metal ladder missing a few rungs and a broken jungle gym with a frayed rope that had broken off above the boys' reach. There were no swings. There were no balls, bats, jump ropes, basketball hoops, or hopscotch lines. I looked at this young teacher as she sat on the steps to watch the children.

"Thank you for your help." She smiled wanly and looked away.

My head throbbed as I walked up the dark hallway, pounded by the children's noise and the disciplinary screams of the teachers. The harsh voice of the music teacher bellowed the same song to another group of noisy children.

Outside, the sunshine and the quiet of the street were a relief. As I walked down that dusty dirt road, I looked past the small gray clapboard houses and saw Mary Ann Jenkins's slumped shoulders and sad eyes, and I wondered if she ever would teach again. I knew taking a class mid-year would not be easy, but the lack of any discipline at all was unnerving. I resolved then and there not to end as she had. No longer dulled by the chaotic surroundings, I made plans for that crucial first day. I was imagining myself teaching 26 third grade children.

My husband, Paul, attracted some attention that warm Friday afternoon as he strode ahead of me past the office, a huge box of books balanced effortlessly on his broad shoulder. Softly singing Elvis Presley's comeback hit, "In the Ghetto," he moved boldly down the dark hallway.

And his hunger burns
So he starts to roam the streets at night
And he learns how to steal, and he learns how to fight
In the ghetto (in the ghetto)
Then one night in desperation
A young man breaks away
He buys a gun, steals a car
Tries to run, but he don't get far
And his mama cries

Paul stopped at the door of my classroom. I waited until late afternoon to claim the room. Paul made several more trips to the car and each time reappeared with more cartons of equipment and supplies. Then, sitting on top of a desk, he looked out at the barren playground.

As Mary Ann emptied her desk and the file cabinet, I put 26 hangers on the clothes rod in the back of the room, each with an unfamiliar name: Felicia, L'Angela, Angela, Danny, Sandy, Edward, Nicholas, Cecil, Nanci, Kelvin, Tanya, Jack, Sharon, Tynetta, Sylvia, Larry, Jeffrey, Shirley, Barbara, Billy, Marjorie, Jimmy, Sandra, Patricia, Dexter, Eric. Weeks later, Curtis joined the class, changing the class number to 27.

Finally, Mary Ann walked over to us. "Well, I'm ready to leave now. I told my class this afternoon that I wouldn't be here on Monday and that a new teacher they would like will take my place, but, you know, they just didn't care." Hesitating, she smiled sardonically at us and added, "Oh yeah, some of them cheered." She turned, picked up her purse, looked slowly around the room, and said, "Good luck."

Inheritor of twenty-six unruly children, I opened the boxes and unearthed treasured items from my previous classroom in Maryland. Paul and I worked well as a team. His cheerful presence and positive attitude reassured me. Desks and shelves were scrubbed. The children's desks named and rearranged. No amount of encouragement would stop a leaky faucet, though. I discovered that the sour smell came from a tiny bathroom shared with another classroom.

All my teaching books were arranged on a shelf, and the storybooks were placed on a table, awaiting new readers. The walls were covered with posters. Snoopy declared that even he washed his hands as he sat roguishly over the sink. A bright orange poster announced the wonderful world of books. A huge world map filled the middle bulletin board with felt symbols of Christmas around the world proclaiming the first week's social studies unit. A moon map and colored NASA photographs filled the science corner. A Picasso poster was tacked up alongside a poem with stick figures for counting. Handwriting letters were stuck above the blackboard. After pulling staples out of the blackboard and taping my name on the door, I was ready.

When I closed the door, my name looked back at me and I smiled. Paul and I walked down the hallway together and out into a night, clear and starlit. I spent the weekend with thoughts of Monday. My nerves were beaten back with a quick review of my plans. Regardless, on Sunday night, I lay sleepless and excited.

CHAPTER 2

An Auspicious Beginning

ONDAY'S GRAY SKY fit my first impressions of
P.S. 123. As I looked at the heavy rain clouds from
my classroom window, I heard my tiny alarm clock
tick loudly. Turning away from the window, I checked to see
that each desk had a puzzle. In my last classroom, the children
enjoyed having puzzles, poems, word games, or stories waiting
on their desks. They often looked at their morning work before
hanging up their coats.

Standing in that dark hallway outside my door, I heard a
heavy shuffling sound. A large woman, her hair puffed around
a plump face, came so close behind me that I felt her heavy
breathing move my hair. "Welcome, Mrs. *ahh* Evans," she said
as she read my name from the door. "Welcome to P.S. 123." And
then she laughed. "How long you planning to stay?"

"Good morning," I said, but she did not stop. Her bedroom
slippers shuffled down the hall and I could hear her mumbling
as she climbed the stairs at the end. In five more minutes,
classes would begin. The clock in the dark hallway, wrong as always, announced 5:20. When the bell rang, a group of children
burst through the door, pushing and shoving and yelling and
tripping each other.

"Good morning. You will line up quietly against the wall." I
took them by surprise. They did as they were told.

Repeating the simple request until all stood waiting, I looked at them solemnly. Some had no coats. At the front of the line, a little girl's knit hat hung limply over one ear. She wiped her runny nose on her sleeve. They leaned against the wall and watched me. It was difficult to believe these were last week's rowdy children.

With instructions, several walked in, hung their coats on the clothes rod, found their desks, and sat down. This was repeated by small groups of their classmates until the entire class was seated and the door closed. They looked at each other and then at the classroom. They did not seem sure it was Friday's room. Whispering, they pointed at the new posters. Snoopy made them smile.

I walked to the front of the room. "I am Mrs. Evans." Their roving eyes locked with mine and the whispering stopped. "I am so pleased with the way you came into the room. That was very well done!" A few children looked pleased but most just looked sleepy. "Now that you know who I am, I would like you to introduce yourselves to me. Just stand by your desk and say your name."

One at a time, they stood and spoke their names. Dexter was the plump, moon-faced boy. Jack was tiny and blond. A shy little girl, L'Angela, made me think of a spring violet. Felicia was tall and thin. Danny stuttered his name. Next was sturdy Cecil, self-assured Eric, dainty Nanci . . . until all were introduced. There were 26 third graders—20 black children from The Projects across the street behind the playground and 6 white children who were bused to school.

Before we pledged allegiance or read the prayer or sang or collected lunch money or took attendance that day, we talked about class rules. "How many of you rode in a car yesterday? Why did your car stop at the corner?"

"Flat tire? No gas? Stop sign?" offered the children.

"What would happen if there were no traffic lights or stop signs?"

"They be a big wreck." Cecil made that sound exciting.

"Are wrecks good?"

"No, cuz you get bunged up!" shouted Jack.

"Yes, you're right. So there are rules to ride in a car, rules to play games, and rules for school. Can you think of some good rules for school?"

"No running in the halls."

"Yeah. And no fighting," said Sandy with a big smile.

"Raise your hand?" shouted Felicia.

"And no gum chewing."

"No talking."

"Where is there to be no talking, Nicholas?" I asked.

"Everywhere!" yelled Nicholas cheerfully.

"Well, shall I write down no talking in the halls? How would that be?"

"Okay!" yelled Nicholas again, but he looked disappointed.

I added times to use the pencil sharpener to the list. At the bottom, I wrote in big letters, "ALWAYS DO YOUR BEST!"

"What does that mean?" I asked.

"Means when I does my best, I gets a home run," boasted Cecil.

We discussed each rule and the children decided which ones were the hardest to remember. Then I explained the work on their desks and that the directions were on the board. Many had no pencils, so I rented pencils. If not returned, they owed me a job like cleaning the chalkboard.

I took a paper airplane from Jimmy, awakened the sleeping Edward, moved the desks of two whispering girls, and put a large black plastic comb and a pair of scissors into my desk drawer. Quiet descended on the room. Eric, heading for the pencil sharpener, received the first of the grim looks I'd practiced over the weekend. It worked! I almost gave myself away by smiling. He returned to his desk and found another pencil.

While they worked, I filled out the teacher's daily attendance register and collected lunch money. In my other school, attendance was done in the office and lunch money collected at the door of the cafetorium. I had no trouble with the attendance record, but I soon learned that collecting lunch money was an art. Many paid for the week. Seven had no money and no lunch. Three had "free" lunch. Others brought their lunch. Two little girls only bought milk and the rest gave me their precious 20 cents for lunch that day. Their pinched faces and faded, torn clothes made me wonder how they could afford to pay one dollar a week for lunch, especially with several brothers and sisters in school.

That thought was pushed aside for the moment with the struggle to put the right amount of money in the brown envelope. I checked again to be certain that they all would eat lunch that day and looked up at the class. Several little girls stared at me, but when I looked at them, they hastily retreated into their desks. I noticed a few daydreamers, and Edward was sleeping again. This time I let him sleep. No one finished the assignment. I took the second paper airplane away from Jimmy.

I walked by their desks and as the arithmetic puzzle was finished and corrected, harder problems were given. Many still counted on their fingers. Patricia, however, answered 18 out of 20 simple addition and subtraction problems incorrectly. This nine-year-old was not sure how many units were in each number. Later, we began by counting her fingers. By the end of January, she was convinced there were ten. Meanwhile, another child, Dexter, could add perfectly but was totally mystified by subtraction. Jeffrey and Kelvin tried to sneak out to the bathroom. I brought them back to their seats. Then I took a third paper airplane from Jimmy and added a grave warning.

Remembering the chaos last Thursday, when they headed to the music room, I started to line up the class early. The schedule varied each day: today was P.E., tomorrow was music class, and then repeat. After two attempts to line up, the children were quiet. They walked as far as the corner without pushing or shoving, but after Jimmy tripped Eric, we went back to the room. The next well-rehearsed try took them down the hall, past the office, around the corner, and down to the end room for P.E.

An enormous man waited by the door. One hand rested a Coke bottle on his large stomach and the other held a cigarette. He grinned at me. "Hey there, I'm Ozell Lewis. Welcome to P.S. 123." Although it was not too cold to go outside, he waved the children into his smoke-filled room. I learned later that they sat there for the next 20 minutes while I enjoyed a cup of coffee in the narrow teachers' lounge that was dominated by the noisy red Coke machine.

A sturdily built young woman pushed dark hair from her large gray eyes as she opened the lounge door. She grinned. "You sure look comfortable! How you doing? Is there any way I can help?"

"Hi. Really, the morning is going well."

"Gee, that's great. You couldn't be having much trouble. I didn't hear any noise. First time in months! Her class was really wild. Felt so sorry for her. You know, I tried to help but it just wasn't enough. Nobody else gave her advice or anything, and she really wanted to do a good job. Saw you walking to school this morning. Are you looking for a ride to work?"

"Yes, I am. I live in the Lincoln Apartments."

"Well, I have to go by your apartment every morning, so I'll just pick you up tomorrow, by 7:45 or so—okay with you? I like to get to school early. There is so much to do."

"Thank you! That is really wonderful. I certainly appreciate it."

"Oh, gotta run. I can hear my class. You know, I'm right across the hall from you, so if you need help, just come and get me."

"Yes, I will. Thank you."

Then she laughed. "Say, my name is Maggie Stevens."

"Lisa Evans." We both smiled.

"See you tomorrow," Maggie said and dashed out into the hall.

I liked her immediately. Her friendliness had certainly brightened my day. Checking the time, I decided to wait for the class at Ozell Lewis's door.

After returning to my room, we worked on language and spelling until lunch. Besides practicing simple sentences, the most important lessons were in raising their hands, not fighting, staying out of a classmate's desk, and remaining in their seats.

"Mrs. Evans, Dexter done got my pencil!" shrieked Felicia.

"I ain't." Dexter glared.

"You gonna get whopped, boy. You just wait," she shrilled.

These skirmishes surprised me. Their short attention spans limited the time spent on any topic.

The line for the cafetorium made it with only one practice. We then waited 15 minutes in the dark hall with four other third grade classes for the doors of the cafetorium to open. The children eyed me carefully, then elbowed each other, stepped on their classmates' feet, or banged their heads into the wall. They looked embarrassed when I caught them. The noise from the other classes was deafening.

It was worse in the cafetorium. All seven third grade classes ate together. I started to sit with my class, but a third grade teacher grabbed my arm and steered me to a tiny teachers' table in the midst of the roaring children. Each of the teachers shouted her name at me.

"Is it always like this?" I asked.

"Worse on Fridays."

As I looked at the crowded cafetorium, I noticed that the majority of the children were black.

"You won't believe what happened this morning," Hilda said. "You know the one kid, Cedric? Who can't even write his name? Well, he brought a worm to school and was running around scaring all the girls. He threw a tantrum when I took it away. He claimed it was his pet! Then, you know, he threw books, overturned his desk, and cursed. Well, I sent someone to the office to get Mr. Carter, but he never did come." No one looked surprised.

"Well, that's nothing," said Debbie.

I never did hear her story, though, because I walked over to my class, took an empty milk carton they were tossing at each other, and reminded them of the good table manners we discussed. I went back to finish my lunch. Hilda showed me teeth marks. Fay Morris shouted at a little girl who walked up to her with a complaint. "Shut up and sit down. I hate, hate, hate, hate this job," she said. I looked at each of them. The looks of desperation reminded me of Mary Ann Jenkins.

After that lunch, I was relieved to be closeted in my room. Excited by the clamor and confusion of the cafetorium, the kids were noisy. Banging on the wastebasket, they stopped and looked at me. "Class, I want to speak with you, but you will not be able to hear me if you are talking too." Many stopped talking.

"Dexter?"

"I ain't doing nothing." Dexter sulked.

"Most of you were well behaved in the cafetorium today, but let me remind you that there is no food throwing, including milk cartons." Jeffrey, Kelvin, and Cecil grinned. "When you finish eating, you may talk quietly but you must stay in your seats. If you need anything, please raise your hand and I will help you. Now, I want to tell you about a new game. The table or tables that are the best behaved will earn a brightly colored tablecloth for one week, and everyone at that table may have an extra dessert."

"Wow," said Billy.

"Hey lady, what you do if we all be good?" asked Sandy.

"You will all win!" And we all laughed.

I picked out a story, sat down near Dexter, and began to read. They loved to listen to stories. Jimmy didn't make any airplanes and Edward stayed awake. The story had such a good ending that they all giggled.

"What did you like about that story?"

"The boy."

"Why?"

"He cool man, you know?"

While phonics and simple reading papers were worked on, each child read to me. Four of them read from a third grade book: Nanci, Eric, Larry, Sandra. The others ranged from second-grade reading level all the way to Sandy, Danny, and Nicholas who were stumped by simple words like "at," "he," and "the." I finally went through the alphabet and found that 12 year-old Sandy and 11 year-old Danny had spent five years in school and did not know their letters. How could that be possible? I gave each of them one letter to learn for Tuesday.

Next was playtime. I wrote the schedule on the blackboard that morning with the time in brackets so that every visitor would know what we were studying and when. That was another P.S. 123 rule. I was never required to post a daily schedule before.

"Playtime? We ain't never had no playtime before," gasped Larry.

"We going outside tomorrow, too?" demanded Eric.

"What we going do outside?" whined Nicholas.

"Well, class, first we will exercise, then do relays, then have free time." They stared at me in disbelief. The line of 26 tiptoed past the office and around the corner to the schoolyard.

They giggled at me as I exercised with them. "Hey, look at Mrs. Evans. She sure look funny."

Cecil and Eric headed the relays and I checked to make sure the runners touched their marks. The air was filled with shouts and laughter.

"Hey, hurry up."

"Come on, why you so slow, boy?"

"I ain't slow."

"You is."

"Aw, we ain't never going win."

When they scattered for free play, I realized that no other class was outside. I had not seen any children from my window all day. I wondered why the other children were kept inside.

The rest of the afternoon passed without problems. We talked about Christmas and I told them what children did in Holland. We followed the ribbon from the picture of the shoes to the country of Holland on the world map. Then we read about it together and they shared crayons to color the picture of wooden shoes.

"I is glad I get a stocking full. Ain't no room in my shoes."

"Yeah and what about the switches to whip bad kids?" added Eric.

We reviewed the class rules before they went home. Each child solemnly said goodbye, marched past me and out the

door. "Goodbye Jimmy. No more paper airplanes tomorrow."
He nodded.

The girls smiled at me and chorused, "Goodbye, Mrs. Evans." The remaining children nodded at me and I nodded at them, until only Dexter was left. Two fights, shoving in line, kicking stones on the playground, and yelling in the classroom kept him behind.

"Dexter, do you remember the rules the class made this morning?" He stared at me and sulked. I tried again. "Do you know why you are here?"

"Didn't do nothing." Then he added, "He hit me too. How come he ain't here?"

"Did he hit you after you kicked rocks at him?"

"*Uh-huh.*" Dexter nodded.

After reading the class rules he had forgotten, he turned to me and, with a perfect Northern accent, said, "Goodbye. See you tomorrow." Then with great dignity, head held high, he walked out the door.

I was at the sink when I heard Paul outside the door. Mr. Carter walked down the hall to meet him. I heard my husband say, "Yes, she is a fine teacher, one of the best."

Mr. Carter cleared his throat and looked at me. "Well now, we'll see about that. You seems to be doing pretty good. I ain't had to come down and quiet the class once today."

"You never will, Mr. Carter," I said.

He stepped into the classroom, looked around, grunted at us, shoved his pipe in his mouth, and strolled back up the hall.

I picked up some papers, the register, and several books. Then I put the clock in my purse and locked the closet and classroom door.

"Well, how was your first day?" Paul asked.

As we walked up the hallway, we passed Mr. Carter lounging in the office doorway. He took the pipe out of his mouth and laughed. "You taking all of that home? My. My. My."

As I lay in bed, impressions of that first day rushed through my mind: sights, sounds, smells, noises. I tried to sort out all the children, but three cousins were mixed up together in my mind. One after another, their faces appeared: Felicia trebling "America the Beautiful," L'Angela and her beautiful handwriting, and Jimmy, the airplane maker–daydreamer. He had grown this year. His arms and legs exceeded the ends of his clothes. Then there was Danny with his vacant, pale blue eyes; 12 year-old Sandy wearing his bright green shirt and sour expression; Edward ill and asleep; and all the rest—Dexter, Nicholas, Cecil, Nanci, Sandra, Marjorie, Kelvin, Tanya, Patricia, Jack, Sharon, Tynetta, Sylvia, Larry, Eric, Jeffrey, Shirley, Barbara, Billy, Angela.

My mind jumped erratically—painfully thin legs, booming cafetorium noise, sour bathroom smells, no supplies. "You watch out for him. He's a bad one!" "Sit down, Dexter." "I hate, hate, hate these kids!" Then it jumped to broken playground equipment, off-key singing leaking into the hallway, the relays led by Cecil, laughter and giggles at the end of a story, ugly red teeth marks on Hilda's arm, dark hallways, broken windows, gray overcast sky, cold winter air, barking dogs, pipe smoke, and burning garbage. "Welcome to P.S. 123."

Yes, "Welcome to P.S. 123" with little red ants in the classroom carpet and the tension, teachers openly grabbing, shoving, striking children, "You little brat I'll learn you to talk back" and then a resounding slap and a torrent of curses. Finally, "Dexter, if two and two are four, then what is four minus two?"

As I fell asleep, my dreams turned into nightmares. I

wrestled with nonsensical symbols in the teacher's register, collected 20 cents from hollow-eyed, hungry children, and corrected spelling tests, reading tests, math tests—piles and piles of paper. Dexter, Jeffrey, Kelvin, and Nicholas sulked. Cecil had a tantrum. The plumbing in the sink burst and water gushed onto the rug. The red ants grew to giant size. Mercifully, I finally woke up. The second day of teaching dawned as gray as the first.

CHAPTER 3

Christmas Week

THE CLASS WAS EXCITED about Christmas. Restless but resigned, time went slowly for all of us. I started chat time after lunch.

"What about your Christmas? What do you do that day?"

"I get lots and lots of presents."

"No way, girl."

"Do so!"

"This year I wants a new doll, a bicycle, and clothes."

"Not me. I don't want no clothes. I wants marbles, skates, and a watch. I got me a bicycle last year."

Edward muttered, "I wants food. Lots of food—chitlins, fried pies, greens, ham. Yeah, I stuff myself." No one else said a word.

When I suggested making Christmas cards for their friends, the idea brought silence and sullenness. That surprised me since all my former students loved art. The problem was solved by giving them a choice of quiet storybook reading or making Christmas cards. A few girls cut out and glued Christmas shapes, and I helped with the words for their greetings.

To increase the excitement of Christmas week, the sixth graders staged a play Tuesday morning in the cafetorium. Although we were invited, no start time was announced and no bells were rung. A white-sheeted angel knocked on my door and informed me that the pageant had begun. We were late! It is difficult to enter a crowded auditorium unobtrusively while escorting 26 children. Much to my chagrin, the actors stopped and waited for us to be seated.

"There my cousin Jim. Hi, Jim!" yelled Nicholas.

"*Shh.*"

The play began again. Mary and Joseph saw an angel, the same one I saw at my door, and they were looking for an inn. The soft Southern accents made the spoken words difficult for me to recognize as the Scripture I had heard so often. A lone aluminum star hung limply from the ceiling (and forgotten, it would remain there until June).

As the story unfolded, the rest of the sixth graders sang Christmas hymns. My class, uninvited, joined in, but when we realized no one else was singing, we stopped abruptly.

The curtain rose for the second act. The stable appeared. Black Joseph lost his sheet and black Mary held a startlingly white doll. Students milled around on their hands and knees as cows and donkeys, and one child folded up in the corner was a camel. The music teacher pounded out more carols on the badly tuned piano.

In the third act, the Wise Men found the stable, Mary and Joseph, and the baby. They offered gifts, and the curtain dropped as the cast sang "Joy to the World" and "We Three Kings." The applause was enthusiastic.

When the director, Mrs. Dickson, stood up to take a bow, I recognized her as the same woman who startled me the first day in the hall when she lumbered past my classroom. After that, Mr. Carter walked to the front of the cafetorium, and I was surprised to hear boos, whistles, foot-stomping, and catcalls. Mrs. Dickson yelled at them and finally they were silent.

"Ahem," Mr. Carter said, "now then. I wants to thank Mrs. Dickson and her class for doing such a fine job, real entertaining. I wants to apologize to Mrs. Evans. Here now, where is she at? This here is our new third grade teacher." He pointed over the heads of all the others toward me. "Like I says earlier, I wants to apologize for not calling you to the play on time. That there won't happen again. Well now, we got business taken care of. I wants to wish you boys and girls a real fine Christmas and . . ."

I did not hear the rest of his Christmas speech. The teachers had turned around and with them their classes, and all began to flow noisily around me and out the door. Seeing them all together for the first time, I realized there was only token integration at Johnson P.S. 123. Very few white students were in the cafetorium that morning. All like my six, were bused to school. Racially, the teachers appeared divided equally between black and white. I wondered if this school were previously an all-black school, providing a "separate but equal" education that was declared unconstitutional by the Supreme Court of the United States years earlier. Could this be the cause of the tension, the stares, the hostility?

Knowing that the children needed exercise, we tiptoed outside for 10 precious minutes of free play. Four third-grade classes were taught in the annex, and my class watched as those children walked across the playground and disappeared behind the gray doors. Once again, we had the playground to ourselves. The girls climbed the rickety jungle gym and perched on top, chattering like a small flock of brightly colored birds. The boys, led by Cecil, began tumbling on the clay. Handstands, flips, and somersaults—their legs had built-in springs. I clapped, cheered, and said, "You are really good. That's wonderful!" The boys looked down at the ground and shuffled their feet, but the tops of their heads looked pleased.

"Aw, that ain't nothing." Cecil grinned and the tumbling that followed was even more amazing than before.

We spent the remainder of the morning writing a letter. The class decided to write to Santa.

"Mrs. Evans, I don't know where I lives."

"Hush up, girl. You lives by me."

"I can't spell no street," complained Felicia.

As I spelled the street for them, I noticed that most of them lived on the same street that was behind the playground, an area called "The Projects."

Later, when the children lined up for lunch, I reminded them about the cafetorium rules and the contest. The wait in the hall seemed endless. I waved to Maggie who was eating with her class. Just as I remembered that Mr. Carter specifically told me it was my responsibility to teach the children table manners, Fay dashed over, grabbed my arm, and pulled me toward the teachers' table. Fay was looking especially festive, with a fake poinsettia tucked behind her ear. Hilda, the tall blond teacher with teeth marks still visible on her arm, looked tired.

One of her boys was throwing food. Hilda rushed over, yanked him out of his seat, and slapped him several times. Then she stuffed him back into his chair. Debby, a small, short-haired matronly woman, was philosophical about the school, the noise, and her class. She calmly admitted to paddling her students. She shrugged and said, "What else can you do? You can't reason with them."

When I asked them about sitting and eating at the tables with their students, they groaned. Fay cursed, "God damn, you won't catch me eating with them. I'm no glutton for punishment."

Hilda said, "Don't worry about it. Carter never comes into the cafetorium to check."

Sitting so I could see my students, I watched them glance at me several times. I wondered how well the cafetorium game would work. Only two tables, Nicholas's and Jack's, were noisy, but no one was throwing food or fighting.

The teachers were all talking about Christmas vacation and the play that morning. Fay thought it was "hilarious." Before I could comment, she was interrupted by several students, all talking at once. "He hitting me." "She took my hot dog." "Can I go to the bathroom?" "I don't feel so good."

That afternoon, as I began their math work, there was a loud knock at the door. A tall, stately, well-dressed black woman sauntered slowly down the aisle to the table in the back of the room and sat down. The children stared at the stranger and started talking. With difficulty, I finished explaining their math problems and helped Cecil, Sandy, and Nicholas individually.

Then I walked back to talk with my unexpected guest. The class was restless. "I am Mrs. Evans. May I help you?"

"Yes. I know." She stood, and in a loud voice said, "I am Mrs. Miller." I wondered if she were a parent who wanted to meet the new teacher, but then she hissed, "I am Mrs. Miller, the *curriculum coordinator*." Was she really talking in italics? I turned away from her and faced the class. No one was working. The girls were giggling, talking, and rummaging in their desks. Nicholas reached over to stick a safety pin in his neighbor. Kelvin and Jeffrey were out of their seats and strolling aimlessly around the room. I feared chaos.

"Are you here to evaluate me?" She stared at me and sat down at the table, apparently planning to stay.

The noise increased and several more boys were out of their seats.

"Mrs. Miller, I have only taught this class for one full day. I would certainly appreciate it if you would come again after Christmas since your visit is distracting the children today." I was not prepared for her reaction.

She knocked over her chair as she stood up. "Well, I never. How rude!" Stretching to her full height, straightening her wig, and pulling her shoulders back, she shook her notebook at me. The woman was furious! She was sputtering and then shouted, "I don't have to be here. I am a very busy and important woman. I am the CURRICULUM COORDINATOR." She stomped to the door and yanked it open. In a stentorian tone, she declared, "Good day, Mrs. Evans," and then slammed the door behind her.

The children stared. The boys scrambled to their seats and the girls stopped giggling. They had just witnessed their second performance of the day. I quickly forgot her visit and would not see her again until after Christmas vacation. The second teaching day dragged on and the children, weary after six hours and forty-five minutes in school, left the classroom silently.

As the week plodded on toward Friday, there were a few highlights: Dexter spent an hour on Wednesday at his desk in the hall for being totally uncooperative. Danny vomited in class and was sent home. Nicholas finished a spelling worksheet. I found a brand new Xerox photocopier buried under broken science equipment and torn reading charts in the storage room next to the teachers' lounge.

Mr. Carter came in while I was staring at the photocopier. "Now, Mrs. . . . . a*hh* . . . if you knows how to use that there thing maybe you could show us sometime?" He beamed when he learned that I knew how to use it, adding, "It been here for quite a while but ain't nobody used it." He waved at me and left.

I also found the speech teacher, and learned that it was her first year. She saw Danny once a week for fifteen minutes. I wondered how such a schedule would help him. He stuttered badly and often repeated simple phrases.

On Wednesday, Felicia and Marjorie got into a fight on the playground—pushing, scratching, and pulling hair. I overheard the end of the argument.

"Marjorie, you is a bastard."

"Ain't."

"You is. My ma says so."

"I ain't," she yelled and kicked at Felicia.

"You can't be no bastard, girl," said Sandy. "Only boys."

Undeterred, Felicia shouted, "Then you is a girl bastard."

After a lengthy lecture on name-calling and how hurtful it was, Felicia sat down, sucked her thumb, and twisted a pigtail. Marjorie sulked and stuck her head inside her desk. They took their schoolwork home. Marjorie smiled at me and then skipped down the hall. I thought she would make an excellent actress. I had never seen a child change moods so quickly.

Each day, several of my students went to the special reading teacher, Ida Mae Lee, a frizzy-haired woman of 50 whom the children all disliked. Two perfectly rouged circles on her white cheeks and a garish red line of lipstick decorated her powdered face. Her clothes were extremely tight. Leaning toward me, she drawled, "What do you think of my girlish figure?" and then patted her stomach and smoothed her hair.

Her instructions to me were quite explicit. "Now, you send me only your slow readers, those who can be helped. Don't you send me any of your non-readers like Miss Jenkins done. I don't want to waste my time." So Sandy, Danny, Cecil, Edward, Jeffrey, and Nicholas were ignored, as they had been ignored for the four or five years that it had taken them to get to third grade.

At that point, I realized that reading would be difficult to teach to this class. Their reading range varied from fourth grade level down to A-B-C letter recognition, with every conceivable level in between. As I planned work for each reading level, my task was made even more difficult by the lack of books. There were three primers. I needed at least twelve! The remaining books were third-grade readers. When I asked in the office about books, Mr. Carter was evasive. "You has to make do. There ain't no more. Miss Jenkins didn't complain."

Besides the lack of reading books, there were no phonics charts, word cards, picture charts. In fact, there was nothing to teach reading on an individual basis. I decided to use library books. The whole class looked amazed when I said we were all going to the library, but that did not compare to the surprise I received or the surprise we gave the librarian. Mrs. Wilson, a heavy, chain-smoking, pasty-skinned woman, shrieked, "Good heavens. How many do you have here?"

"Twenty-six."

"Oh no, no, no, Mrs. Evans. No one brings the whole class at one time." She was kind enough, though, to make an exception for me that day. The children were seated and a few of them found books right away. I planned to help each one find the right level while those who waited worked on a phonics paper. When I looked at the primary section, I found only third through sixth grade books and some fiction for seventh or eighth graders.

"Mrs. Wilson, would you please show me the primary level books?" She hauled her great bulk off the stool and lumbered over to the window.

"These are the easiest books we have." She pointed to six or seven second grade books. "And we're not even supposed to have these."

"No picture books? No primers?"

"Oh no. The children at P.S. 123 are in the third through sixth grade, so we have third through sixth grade books."

I guess there was some logic to that, but knowing how far behind my class was in reading, I knew that the upper grades could not be any different. "But most of my children can't read third grade books."

"*Shh.* I wouldn't admit that if I were you!" Turning, she hollered at several of my students, "Don't touch those magazines." Facing me she explained, "Why it will take me an hour to straighten them." As she bustled away to guard her extensive selection of magazines from the children, she called over her shoulder, "You might try the book warehouse or the reading supervisor."

The special reading teacher was not the answer. The library was not the answer. How was I to teach them to read? I was disillusioned and frustrated. I thought of my other classrooms, of the shelves lined with books, of the closets brimming over with charts, vocabulary cards, workbooks, phonics kits, of the reading specialists ready to assist—all of that to teach children who already knew how to read.

Thursday was the morning of the teachers' Christmas breakfast, a tradition at P.S. 123. In the cafetorium at 7:30, teachers gathered in various states of alertness. One especially peppy group hovered around the music teacher as she pounded out familiar carols. Their rich voices filled the room and mingled with the smells of bacon, grits, eggs, and coffee.

As I waited, I met the last two third grade teachers—there were seven of us. The first was Mrs. LeBlanc, a short, grim, wrinkled woman with unkempt mousey red hair and a rumpled housedress. She was not pleased with the breakfast or the singing. "All this nonsense," she snapped. "Why, I have been teaching more than twenty years, not here of course, and I never saw no need for a Christmas breakfast." From her sour expression, I wondered if she had enjoyed any of those years. Politely backing away from her, I bumped into Mrs. Madison, the only black third grade teacher. Her beautiful knit outfit, Christmas pin, and perfectly styled hair were quite a contrast to Mrs. LeBlanc.

Suffering from arthritis, she leaned heavily on a cane. In a pleasant voice, she said, "I am just down the hall from your room. If I can help, please ask. Isn't this a lovely party? So nice of them to do this for us." Smiling and nodding, she limped over to the P.E. teacher, Ozell Lewis. She chatted with him until breakfast was served.

Since few teachers had arrived on time and the cafetorium ladies were not ready with breakfast, the party ran late. A pine branch decorated with dollar bills and stuck into a clay pot was given to Mr. Carter. "Thank you, ladies. Thank you kindly. I plan to plant this here Christmas money tree and hope for another crop."

Hearing sounds of children yelling and running through the halls, I stopped listening. I wanted him to hurry and finish his speech. Fifteen minutes later he said, "Now girls, I want you to be real firm on these kids. I don't want none of them running wild. Keep your Christmas parties simple, hear?" And with that, we were excused to our classrooms.

I ran. The children were sliding and shouting in the hallway outside the locked door. Dexter was hitting blond Sandra, who was crying loudly. Several were sitting on the floor and Nicholas beat his head on the door. Only five little girls and Eric were standing patiently in line. All the disorder stopped abruptly when they saw me. They scurried to get into line—knit hats, pencils, and paper scattering on the floor.

"Dexter! Stop that at once! You may never hit another person. You could hurt her. Do you understand me?"

"Yes, ma'am," he muttered.

"Have you apologized to Sandra?"

"Sorry," he growled. Her wailing ended abruptly. Sandra looked at him with wide blue eyes and smiled.

After the rest of the class entered the room, Nicholas was reprimanded for making so much noise. He pouted the entire morning. Never have I seen a child so adept at sulking. His lower lip protruded, his forehead furrowed, and huge storm clouds sat on his shoulders. If only he concentrated this much on his classwork.

Later that day, we talked about Christmas celebrations around the world and each of them decided what country they wanted to visit.

"I likes Holland 'cause I put out my dad's shoes and he gots big feet!"

"I wants to eat a yule log."

"I likes the Russian lady best," said Nanci.

"No, you don't. You just wants to be different," sneered Felicia.

"Mrs. Evans, is we going to have a party? Everyone else is."

"No, we are going to do something different."

"We ain't having even a little party?" asked Larry.

I don't think they believed me. That Friday they came to school expecting candy, cookies, and Coke. Knowing that the slightest change of pace upset the entire class and that my control over their behavior was, at best, superficial, I did not want to end the week with an uncontrollable party. When the other third grade teachers realized my class would not have a party, they told their class and threatened to send their students to my room to work all Friday afternoon if they didn't behave. No one came.

Although there was no party, the afternoon was pleasant. A Christmas story of magical animals kept their attention. Then I told them the story of the Nutcracker Suite and played some of the music. They loved the sugar plum fairy, the magic tree, and the nutcracker, but not the mouse king. We played the music again and they all played a part: Nanci, the dainty sugar plum fairy; Cecil, the Nutcracker; and finally, Larry volunteered to be the mouse king.

Extra playtime was a treat too. They tiptoed down the hall and out into the blustery wind and empty playground. It was colder than I thought Florida could be.

"What you wearing, Mrs. Evans?"

"A cape."

"How come you wear that?"

"It's my warmest coat."

"Where your arms be?" asked Cecil.

"It ugly. I don't like it!" said Marjorie and then she ran off to join the other girls.

Later we enthusiastically sang Christmas carols with Felicia leading the group. She trilled loudly and waved her arms.

As they left that cold, gray afternoon, I shook their hands, gave them each a candy cane, and wished them a Merry Christmas. They were quiet, overwhelmed with the thought that vacation had begun at last.

I watched as Eric rushed down the hall, with Dexter close behind. Nanci and Barbara held hands. Tynetta sucked her thumb. Patricia stooped to pull up a sock. Jimmy pulled out a crushed paper airplane. Coatless, Edward shoved his hands in his pockets. "Merry Christmas," whispered L'Angela. As I watched each child round the corner and move out of sight, their images became etched in my memory. I silently vowed to teach them everything I could in the months ahead. I thought about them often during those days I spent in Wyoming on Christmas break.

CHAPTER 4

Gray Cold

CHRISTMAS DAY WAS COLD AND CLEAR. In Wyoming with my Marine Corps husband, Paul, and his family, the vast western sky was cloudless across the snow-covered high plains. The distant snow-capped mountains stood silent vigil and the land was quiet. The wind played with the snow, pulling the flakes into higher drifts across the driveway until bald brown spots appeared where the snow had been. As I stared, the brown spots grew larger, and the winter grass expanded and swelled into the brown clay playground at P.S. 123. Many times during my Christmas vacation, my thoughts returned to the school and its children.

Listeners to the stories of Dexter or Edward or Nicholas were incredulous. It was difficult for them to cope with the harsh reality of children who fell asleep in class, who cursed proficiently but were childish enough to enjoy sucking their thumbs, who did not have twenty cents for lunch, and who came to school on Monday mornings without breakfast or a coat. I do not know if they believed that the roof leaked, that two of my classroom windows were broken and boarded, or that the plumbing and heating systems were as faulty as I described. I mentioned having no reading books, no paper, no art supplies, no chalk or playground equipment, but by then, my family and friends had blocked out this uncomfortably dreary story that did not, after all, affect their children.

My nephews and niece never tired of stories about the class and my students.

"Tell me again about the one who sleeps."

"What did you do when Dexter threw a tantrum?"

"Is Patricia the one who can't count?"

"Aw, I don't believe that. I could count when I was four," interrupted my youngest nephew.

I told them about the angry look in Sandy's eyes, the hatred written across Jeffrey's face, the wild cafetorium lunches with seven third-grade classes screaming, fighting, and eating together. As I looked at them, I understood why this school was so foreign to them. I had taught in schools similar to the ones they now attended. Such conditions would never be allowed. My nephews and niece, well-fed, sturdy, active, intelligent, raised in an environment my students might never see, were educated in schools completely unlike P.S. 123.

Then I thought of my students—their thin arms and legs, torn clothes, runny noses, and pinched faces. Their only hope was education. If they could learn basic addition and subtraction and fundamental reading, my months with them would be well spent.

Thinking about my former classrooms and the closets brimming with supplies, I decided to create the missing teaching aids. I spent the remainder of Christmas vacation making a clock to help them tell time, arithmetic flash cards for simple addition and subtraction, paper rulers, wooden blocks to recognize letters and then build words, picture cards for phonics, sheets for reading skills, and a fluffy, red yarn ball for playing indoors.

As I worked on these teaching tools, I remembered the tension in the school. Its weight pressed down on me as I waited for Mr. Carter for my interview that first morning. It filled the office and pushed against the back of my head, not just the secretary's rudeness but her stares of suspicion and distrust. The tension lurked in the poorly lit hallways and permeated the teachers' lounge. It glared at me through the curriculum coordinator's anger. I had never taught in a school where such a cold gray feeling was present. Why did Mrs. Dickson's booming welcome continue to echo in my mind? She had spoken to several other teachers before reaching the stairs at the end of the hallway but none had answered her.

When my patient listeners realized that some of the less disciplined boys were 11 or 12 and my height, they became concerned for my safety. I tried to reassure them, but they responded with gruesome stories of teachers being knifed, beaten, or shot. Their fears were somewhat alleviated when I agreed to pack an old, inch-thick yardstick. Its commanding appearance and thunderous crack when slammed against a chair or wastebasket would add dramatic flair.

I had so much to teach my students, and I was very impatient to begin. Finally, without my prodding, Christmas vacation ended, and the January school days began. It was cold in the P.S. 123 school building that Monday. I shivered as I waited in the hall. The tired wall clock stopped working over Christmas, and its hands were folded permanently across its face at 7:10.

I greeted my students with smiles and cheerful "Good mornings." "Hello. My, you look pretty. What a nice warm sweater. Did Santa bring it to you?" Many looked at me sleepily and entered the classroom slowly, quietly, as if drugged. The effort to hang their coats made them yawn. They shuffled to their seats and waited.

"Hey man, who steal my desk? You take my desk, boy? I bust in your head." Nicholas could not find his seat and the look of confusion on his face was erased only when I led him to it. Felicia's constant coughing made me turn toward her. Her bluish face and sunken eyes startled me. She wiggled in her seat and pulled up the collar of her coat, which was gold corduroy with a thick gold fur collar, wooden buttons, and a gold belt. Even her knit hat was new. She coughed until springtime.

Edward wore a warm new sweater that day that I never saw again. He covered his flaking scalp with an arm and slept fitfully.

Wearing their hair in tight ringlets, several of the girls had new cotton dresses. Nanci, Patricia, and Sharon brought new Barbie dolls to school and hid them in their desks. The dolls voiced no objections to being placed in my bottom desk drawer during school hours, nor did they visit our class again.

Eric's two new yellow pencils were lined up at the top of his desk. He absorbed the instructions for the morning work from the board, and as his lips moved, I could tell which words he read. He then began the assignment before the others, and when finished, read or came to me for more work. Unfortunately, his industrious attitude and well-behaved actions soured most of his classmates. Eric's mother was a librarian and his father a day laborer. I knew he had been told many times about the importance of education. Even his well-scrubbed appearance and clean clothes contrasted sharply with some of his classmates. Since this attitude was so unlike Cecil's or Jeffrey's or Sandy's, Eric had only one friend, Billy. Billy had short brown hair and big blue eyes. Eric and Billy were inseparable. Eric would sometimes help Billy if he could not do an assignment. They shared candy and competed to see who would finish first and constantly whispered across the aisles. They could not play together after school, for Billy was bused home and Eric walked home alone down the dirt road behind the school.

With the children seated, the morning ritual began: The Pledge of Allegiance, a patriotic song, a Bible verse and prayer, reading and explanation of the board work, attendance, and collection of lunch money. The children reacted slowly that day. Most had not brought their lunch money. The air was filled with coughs and sneezes. The room stayed chilly and the wind slipped through window cracks to tease papers off their desks.

They were fond of board work, but it took them a long time to copy lessons written in chalk. Their efforts sometimes produced strange sentences and misspelled words. With their numerous reading levels, some children had difficulty understanding the directions. Unfortunately, the scarcity of books and ditto paper and the erratic health of the ditto machine made board work necessary. They rustled papers, chewed their pencils, and laboriously copied their assignments.

Later, we began our daily talk. The children enjoyed these discussions, and in preparation, several propped their heads up with their hands or slumped into the seats. That first school day in January, I asked them if they had made New Year's resolutions. They looked at me curiously. Only Nanci and Eric had ever heard of them. "Why for I want to make one?" asked Sandy. "Is it something to eat?" The class giggled. Both Sandy and Edward were excellent comics. After watching Sandy pretend to eat a resolution, Eric and Nanci explained what it was.

"Like a rule to make you be better," said Nanci.

The class thought about being better. "Like me. I going to be a better baseball player," said Eric.

Several girls thought of being more helpful, but they all agreed with Cecil when he said, "I going to be the best there is!" As I was writing these resolutions on the board, Jeffrey and Kelvin began making faces and throwing paper wads. Without turning around, I told them both to stop. The class was so quiet that I turned to look at them. They were staring at me. Kelvin and Jeffrey looked surprised. "Hey, how you do that?" sputtered Kelvin.

"I could see you. Jeffrey, please throw the paper wads into the waste basket."

"But you ain't looking at us. How you know that?"

"You got one of them magic eyes like on TV?" The class looked impressed and a little scared. I could feel them looking for the magic eye under my hair. They whispered about it whenever I corrected someone's behavior without turning around. Every time I thought of Jeffrey and Kelvin and their wide-eyed surprise, I smiled. Knowing where each sat, I could sense their activities, but that was not magic—just a few years of experience.

To help the class gain confidence and enjoy responsibility, I explained a poster called "Snoopy's Flying Aces." Snoopy had taken time out from chasing the Red Baron to visit the class. On the poster, classroom tasks would be listed for the week. The children were pleased to be selected for jobs and did excellent work. There were line leaders, song leaders, board washers, paper passers, P.E. leaders. Other duties were added to the list. They liked Snoopy in his flying hat and goggles and were excited about their jobs. With the children picking the next week's workers on Friday, everyone had at least one turn a month. I was delighted that the idea was so well accepted. Dexter was a very conscientious worker, and his behavior slowly improved because of the attention he paid to his jobs.

That day, the line leaders, feeling very important, led the procession to music class. Mrs. Williams greeted them at the door, scowled at two of the boys, and hit Nicholas in the back of the head for walking so slowly.

During my 20 minutes of free time, I tried to find the school nurse. It was imperative that she see Edward and Felicia. The clinic was a bare, cheerless, drafty room with dusty, dead, and dying plants lined up on the windowsill. The nurse was not there.

"Mrs. Black, could you tell me where the school nurse is?" She blinked at me and then slowly said, "She only come on certain days." She turned her back on me and shifted more papers on her cluttered desk.

"Which days will she be at P.S. 123?"

"Well, now, I ain't too sure. Maybe Tuesday, maybe not."

I asked to see the principal and was told that he was busy. I waited at the counter. She looked up and glared at me. "You still here? I'll go see if he talk to you." She walked slowly to his door, opened it slightly, and put her head inside. "Mrs. Evans here to see you."

"You go in now but don't stay long. He busy."

Mr. Carter was smoking a cigar that morning and counting money on a battered adding machine. I waited until he counted a row of figures. When he looked up, I said, "Mr. Carter, I am concerned about two of my students. They need to see the school nurse as soon as possible."

He seemed amused. "Well now, Mrs. Evans, there's nothing I can do. They has to see the school nurse."

"Yes. Can she make a special trip?"

"Oh now, surely that ain't necessary. If they gets to feeling poorly, they can go to the clinic and lay down." He nodded at me to indicate that I was dismissed and returned to his adding machine. As I left his office, I wondered why he had hurriedly covered the sheet of figures he was adding.

I spoke to Edward after music. "My head hurt, Mrs. Evans. I don't feel good." The rest of that day he slept on the little cot in the clinic and Cecil, his friend, checked on him hourly. His report was notable for its brevity: "Sleeping!" he would announce importantly. This continued for two weeks even though I put more notes in the nurse's mailbox and wrote several notes to Edward's mother. Mr. Carter was so unconcerned about it that I decided not to ask him again. Instead, I made frequent office checks to ask about the school nurse. I also tried to locate her at the county office.

We spent the rest of that morning reading. The dittos I made over vacation were invaluable. I decided to teach cognitive skills by reading a story to the entire class and then by working with each student individually or in small groups, reviewing the skills and having each read to me orally. Then we would discuss the story. This system was especially difficult since only five children could work independently. The lack of primers and second grade books was aggravating. When they finished, they looked at phonics cards or old magazines. Some of the boys worked with blocks and made several words.

As I worked with the class that morning, I felt that I was running a three-ring circus. It was difficult to meet each child's needs, and having them all complete their assignments together was close to impossible. Excusing Cecil's temper tantrum and block throwing, Dexter's taking of Sandra's book with resultant screams, and Felicia's sleeping through the assignment, the morning session did not go too badly. It infuriated me that these children did not have the equipment they needed to read. I was determined to find more books. I wondered if more books would be enough, though. Perhaps an entirely new reading program was needed.

I felt tired as we waited in that dim hall for lunch. The thought of eating in that noisy cafetorium did not appeal to me. I remembered teaching previous years, arriving at 8:30 a.m. and leaving at 4:00 p.m. with an hour for lunch without the children. At lunchtime I was free to eat, relax, or work. This pleasant daydream was interrupted by a howl of anguish. The howler was in Mrs. LeBlanc's class. She was nowhere to be seen and he was being crushed into the wall by a heavier classmate. After I separated the two boys, my class was finally allowed into the cafetorium and filed in quietly to their seats. Jimmy bumped into Jack on the way in and dropped his tray. After helping him find the broom, I sat down with three other teachers. The cafetorium was quieter than usual. "Are your classes as sleepy as mine?" The teachers nodded and talked about Christmas vacation. Debbie and Hilda went home. They both asked about my trip west.

"God, am I ever hung over," said Fay. "The kids' noise drove me wild this morning." She paused and crammed part of her sandwich into her mouth. "Why the hell did I even come back here?"

After lunch, the children were tired, and as they rested, I played a record of *Aesop's Fables*. Their favorite characters were the camel and the fox. If I had crayons and paper, they would draw pictures, but there was no paper for art and they had to bring their own crayons.

Watching the children as the record played, I noticed that several of them had difficulty understanding the narrator, for he spoke quickly with a British accent. I was concerned that the children would not be able to understand my northern accent, but found that speaking slowly and clearly greatly helped. Fortunately, I did not have any difficulty understanding them.

When the record ended, I asked, "What do you think of animals that can talk?"

"No animal can talk."

"A parrot can too talk," Larry pointed out.

"Yeah. But ain't no fox can talk," Jack said.

"Would you like to meet a talking animal, Tynetta?"

"Yes, ma'am," said Tynetta.

"I would keep him for a pet," boasted Jack.

"What about the ending of the story?"

"Yeah. I guess so," Eric said. "It was kind of like church."

"Yes. Very good. Fables always have a moral or a rule at the end." We talked about the story a bit longer and then they drew their favorite animals on the blackboard.

"That ain't no fox, girl!" laughed Kelvin.

"You mind your own, boy," L'Angela snorted.

We decided to go outside, but it was too cold to stay long. The air felt refreshing. The boys chased after a threadbare tennis ball and the girls clustered together, singing and repeating over and over a dance about a little Dutch girl.

The brown clay playground had cracked with the cold, the jungle gym bars were too frozen to climb with mitten-less hands, and the sky was gray and filled with dark clouds.

Beyond the six-foot wire fence at the end of the playground was the dirt road that led to many of their homes. A junkyard sat along one side of the fence. Thankfully, trash was not burning that day. New basketball posts lay on the edge of the playground and rested there that entire school year. Occasionally they were used by some to sit on after jumping rope or running. Again, it was obvious that no other class was outside.

Dexter and Nicholas had difficulty playing with their classmates. Both would bully others until a fight nearly began, then they would run away laughing. When their behavior became too obnoxious, they stood by me and watched the others.

They were too noisy going outside, so before they came back in, I warned them, "Class, noise in the hallway will mean less playtime tomorrow." The line became quiet and well-behaved. As we filed up the hall, we watched a fourth grader get thrown out of his classroom door, into the hall. His teacher, Miss Bernardo, a short, broad Italian woman with graying hair and protruding teeth, followed. An amazing confrontation ensued.

"Now, what makes you think you can act like that?" she screamed. "I won't put up with you any longer, sassing and clowning." She spoke so quickly that all her words ran together. It was difficult to understand her, but obvious she was voicing her disapproval.

All the time she screamed at him, he screamed back. "You old hag. You ain't gonna tell me what the hell to do. I ain't going back in there and you can't make me, you mother fucker. Don't you touch me!" She held a short ruler and whacked at him ineffectively. He tried to grab the ruler but missed.

"I have had enough from you. You're going to the office."

"I ain't and ain't no way to fucking make me, you white whore."

My children stared at Miss Bernardo and her misbehaving student. Sobered, they returned to the room, quietly hung their coats, and found their seats quickly. Several eyed the thick yardstick propped against the blackboard.

They copied addition and subtraction problems from the blackboard. As they worked, small groups used the drill cards with me. Many of the children needed individual attention. Patricia had forgotten her numbers over the vacation. So I counted her fingers, and she counted mine. We counted twenty! I'll always remember the look of triumph on her face when she counted to twenty and had no fingers or thumbs left over.

Dexter could not subtract, or perhaps would not. I worked with him daily. Then, I checked all their papers before we ended the afternoon with spelling. The non-readers had their own spelling group, enjoying the extra attention besides learning to spell most of the simple words correctly. The others worked in their third grade speller. It was obvious that the children were tired. The day had been a very long one.

Dexter, Nicholas, and Cecil did not leave with their classmates that afternoon. Dexter and Nicholas could not leave because of their playground antics, and Cecil was in because of his refusal to cooperate during reading. I spoke to each of them individually and each decided to write the class rule that he had broken. As I was speaking with Dexter, Nadette, the typist from the front office, knocked on my door. "Mrs. Evans, where is you? There's a teachers' meeting and it already begun. Mr. Carter don't like teachers to be late." I wondered why I had not been told about the meeting. It annoyed me that I would not be able to carry through on disciplinary measures.

"Well, gentlemen, you will have to write the rules ten times at home. I must go to a meeting. I expect your behavior to improve tomorrow." They nodded solemnly and hustled down the hall.

It is impossible to enter the teachers' meeting ten minutes late without attracting attention. Mr. Carter stopped speaking, and the faculty stared as I sat down with pencil and paper, ready to take notes. I noticed Mrs. Miller, the curriculum coordinator I met before Christmas, and decided to speak with her after the meeting. On my left was Miss Bernardo, the fourth grade teacher I saw in the hall. She seemed extremely nervous. She twitched and wiggled and tore a sheet of paper into tiny pieces.

The meeting just started and for my benefit, Mr. Carter repeated what he already said. I looked at him objectively. He looked older than I first thought. His hair was gray at the sides. His baggy coat and loose trousers were well worn. He held a pipe in one hand and gestured with the other. His topic was discipline.

"Now, there is something wrong with a teacher who can't control her class. These are children and they know when you don't love them, yes indeed. They need all the love you can give them. Now, I know some of you don't love them and that you treat them bad. Well, I'll have you know that there ain't no such thing as a mean, bad child. Why, that's just a child who ain't loved. Now then, some of you come to me with discipline problems. You should be able to handle your own problems. After all, it's your fault if you have problems in your class. Why should I have to handle your problems, anyway? I am the principal and a very busy, important man." He cleared his throat. "Now as far as discipline, well, you can't hit a child ever. You'll get the law on you for sure. And don't you send them to me to hit 'cause I won't hit them. I don't believe in hitting kids, no sir, I don't. I have seen some children being put outside the room. I don't like that. You can't see them if they is outside the room."

Timidly, one first-year teacher raised her hand. "Could you suggest some methods we could use?"

"Well now, I ain't thought of none, but I am going to ask the disciplinary committee to consider these here problems and to give a report on discipline at the next meeting."

The room was very quiet. Several lit cigarettes as they waited. I wrote down some of the things he said. "Report cards are coming out soon and I don't want you to give no Ds or Fs. After all if a child fails, it is you who has failed." He added, "If a child fails a test, then the test is too hard or you ain't taught the subject. There ain't no reason for Ds and Fs.

"Some of you ain't taking door duty, and kids is inside the building before it's time, running around in the halls. I want the building and grounds committee to look into the problem." I had heard of "door duty." For a week from 8:00 to 8:30, a teacher stood by a door to make sure that the children did not enter the building. I had no idea where to find the door duty list and I resented the entire idea. That time was necessary to set up the classroom for the day. I watched him light his pipe, puff on it awhile, check his list, and begin again.

Before I realized it, my hand was raised and I started to

speak. I noticed a ripple of surprise in the seats behind me. "Would it be possible to keep the doors locked until 8:20 since all the teachers enter through the front door?"

Mr. Carter looked bewildered. "No," he said. "Well, I don't know," he added. The matter ended there and for the rest of the year, teachers stood guarding the doors from an early invasion of children.

Another teacher asked if the children should be let in if it was raining or cold. She stopped lamely mid-sentence. It became obvious to me that he did not encourage questions. "Well now, I haven't thought about that," he admitted. "The committee, for *ahh*, the committee, *umm*, will have to figure that out." I was amazed that after five months of school, he did not know what to do in inclement weather.

Asking questions made him nervous. Puffing furiously on a dead pipe, he finally stuck it back into his pocket and rushed through the remainder of his notes. "Something will have to be done about this here cafetorium noise. Well, that is the problem of the lunchroom committee. They will have to handle it."

"May I join that committee?" I asked.

Mr. Carter was pleased. "Surely you can, Mrs. Evans."

My idea would make lunch more pleasant for everyone, or at least I thought so. I mentioned it to the faculty. "I know it is difficult to reprimand a student with food in your mouth, so why not have several teachers patrol the cafetorium for a week and then eat quietly in the teachers' lounge the other weeks?" My idea was appreciated by the teachers, but Mr. Carter looked dubious. "No, I don't think that works. I think the teachers should eat with their children. After all, it is up to you to teach them manners. I couldn't let you eat in the teachers' lounge." I wondered how many other teachers noticed that he never appeared in the cafetorium during lunchtime.

Next, he chastised the teachers for not handing in behavioral objectives. In fact, he fished out a slip of paper from his coat pocket and read off the names of the teachers who had not done them. "Now ladies, this here is state law. You must hand in behavioral objectives every Monday and I must turn them all into the state legislature and they will read them and you will be graded on them. Now, Mrs. Evans, you must hand yours in tomorrow."

After reading off the names of the delinquent teachers, he launched into another tirade about teachers who do not do as they are told. More cigarettes were lit and with the windows closed, it felt as if the tension was building behind the smoke screen.

"And about P.E. time—I noticed that some of you is taking your children outside. I am against playtime. The class needs all their time to work. You all tell me how far behind they is and then you go and waste good learning time by going outside for unsupervised play. The day is short enough with all you is teaching. I don't like helter-skelter playing. Someone might get hurt. Beside, they get organized P.E. twice a week and some three times a week. That is enough. And don't forget this girls, recess is forbidden in this county."

It was 4:20 when the meeting ended. I knew it would take the rest of the evening to sort out his statements. I started by making Mrs. Wilson, the 250 pound librarian, climb upstairs to give me a copy of the county's policy book since the one in the office could not be used by the teachers. I also found the two-page behavioral objectives form and the formula for writing them.

Unfortunately, the curriculum coordinator had already left by the time I arrived at the office. I wanted to invite her into my classroom that next week. I have never enjoyed people walking in and out of my classroom unannounced, as it always disrupts the children. I thought if I asked her to come at a specific time and prepared the children, the class would be more receptive.

I wanted to find the county rule forbidding playtime right there in the hall, but I decided that was a bit too obvious. I had never heard of a county that had abolished organized playtime. Certainly the idea of not taking the children outside every day made me feel desperate. How could these children with such short attention spans work through a six-hour-and-forty-five minute day?

As I waited for Maggie by her car, I skimmed the small book for recess policy, but I could not find a statement forbidding recess. As a matter of fact, the county only demanded five hours of instruction a day. With twenty minutes spent for lunch, my class could play for more than one hour and still be within the restrictions of the county. I had no intention of staying outside that long, but I decided to continue taking my class out for one half-hour, at least until Mr. Carter spoke to me personally. The idea of keeping children inside for an entire school day seemed cruel and heartless. I knew that time outside helped my class a great deal. The children were less restless and much more willing to begin work again.

Having made up my mind to continue organized playtime and remembering that he said I could take them outside during my interview for the job, I picked up the sheets for behavioral objectives and read the formula:

Prescription For Writing A Behavioral Objective

Write goals

Goals must contain:

A domain, cognitive, affective, psychomotor

An instructional variable-content

The psychological objective-students

Example: To provide experiences for increasing speaking and reading vocabulary of third grade pupils

Add to the E 1

E 1 tells how you are going to measure the pupils' performance.

_____ as measured by teacher's observation of pupils' usage of words relative to discussions.

Then apply E 2

E 2 tells how many pupils are able to demonstrate the proficiency and points out the time involved.

_____ at the end of the year, 50% of the children are able to discuss field trips, current events, and readings from the library intelligently.

I had no idea what Mr. Carter was talking about when he mentioned behavioral objectives, but after seeing the sheet and reading the formula for writing them, I did not believe that the state legislature had so little to do that it would read more than forty behavioral objectives from each teacher and then grade them!

I remembered that several of the teachers copied theirs out of a book in the library and handed them in every Monday to the office. They said Mrs. Black just checked their names off in the office and they never saw the objectives again. Copying word for inane word out of a book did not make sense.

That evening I wrote my own goals: teaching self-control was first on my sheet. How can anyone teach unless the children are listening? The goal was reached when there were fewer fights and tantrums. Under equipment, I put down what I wanted to use but did not have, and I included subject areas I covered in class with the page number, if I had a textbook to use. Finally, I decided the students would be evaluated by class participation and individual review rather than written tests. I wondered just how valuable behavioral objectives were and decided to make multiple copies of the sheets and hand in the same objectives each Monday until these goals were reached.

Still pondering these ideas, I returned to my classroom that next morning. The room was cold, but weak sunlight filtered through the dirty windowpanes. I hurried to the second floor to use the ditto machine. Those dittos were necessary for the reading lessons. I noticed that the new unused photocopier was still pushed into a dusty corner on the floor. Much to my despair, the ditto machine did not work. The old cylinder had come loose and ate the paper as I fed it. And if that were not enough, the fluid was used up. Eventually I did fix the machine and by searching through the cabinets, I found a new can of fluid. I would have dittos for reading after all! The precarious health of the machine made me more determined to have reading books for my students.

I met Mr. Carter at the bottom of the stairs and decided to ask him again about books. "Well now, I don't rightly know where you could get more reading books. I guess you will have to make do with what you have. You have third grade books, Mrs. Evans?" When I nodded, he visibly brightened. "Well, good. You teach reading from them. Don't you know with all your fine schooling that it hurt a child's ego to have him read first or second grade books? That ain't good. They will think they is stupid. You let them read third grade books." I did not know how to make him realize that a child who could not recognize letters could not possibly read a third grade book. I did not try.

Asking Mr. Carter for books had not worked. I decided to try Ida Mae Lee, the special reading teacher. Since her room connected with mine through the bathroom, I thought it would be easy to borrow several books just for the reading period. But she refused to lend me any books, even though her shelves were lined with readers, and she taught no more than eight or ten children at a time.

"Oh my, no, honey. I need all these books. Yes, indeed, every last one!" Instead, she generously offered to let me have an old phonics chart with pictures so outdated that I was not certain what some of them represented. I could not decide if it were better than nothing at all and accepted it. The monstrosity mildewed in the back of the room for several months while the children played recognition games with the pictures. Some of the initial sounds could be applied after the pictures were identified. Finally, we decided to make our own phonics chart. Each child drew a different picture or found a picture in a magazine to represent a sound.

That teaching day was not unlike the first, nor unlike those to follow. Dexter was scowling when he arrived at school. His mood did not improve during the day. Because he could not play with the others, he lost some of his morning playtime, and his refusal to try five subtraction problems kept him after school in the afternoon. Jeffrey and Cecil had a fight over the pencil sharpener. Jimmy pestered Eric until he began to cry while we waited in line for lunch. Nanci was sure that Kelvin had her missing dime.

"I know he gots it, Mrs. Evans."

"How do you know, Nanci?"

"'Cause he got a dime and I don't."

It became apparent that talking to these children was not enough. Many of them had little or no concept of fair play and could read or explain the class rules but not follow them. I began to wonder what a teacher did when reasoning did not work with her students. Most of the children when corrected would talk back, make faces, or grin! Any one of these responses was annoying. As their inappropriate behavior continued, minutes were added to an after-school stay. No child in my former school ever wanted to stay in school after their classmates left for the day. But I soon learned that the children at P.S. 123 loved to stay after school . . . the later the better!

Reading that day was without tantrums. I had to find books for the multiple reading levels. I decided to find the reading supervisor after school and ask her for books.

Although the children had scheduled P.E. that morning with Ozell Lewis, he did not take them outside. Instead, they played a game for a few minutes and then sat quietly in his room while he smoked cigarettes. I took them outside that afternoon. First, we did exercises, then relay races, and then circle ball with a ball one of the children had brought to school.

We talked about cold lands that January, which seemed especially appropriate since the classroom was poorly heated and it was freezing outside. We found Alaska, Iceland, Lapland, Scandinavia, and the Swiss Alps on the map. I showed them pictures and articles that I brought back from a trip to Europe. We sang songs native to these countries and drew pictures to hang on the bulletin board with paper I bought. I borrowed films from the public library on these different countries. That day we went to the film room to see one of them.

The small room was directly above my classroom, with no curtains or shades on the windows, so films were hard to see on sunny days. By mid-afternoon, some of the children were so tired that they put their heads down on the desks and slept through the film. When it was over, we talked about it and then returned to the room. Tynetta had fallen asleep during the film and did not wake up even when the others were in line. Although I patted her gently, she still did not awaken. Sharon stayed to wake her, as it was departure time for the children who rode the buses.

That afternoon, my plans to keep Jimmy, Cecil, Jeffrey, and Dexter after class were thwarted by another unannounced meeting. This one was with the curriculum coordinator for all third-grade teachers.

I was on time for this meeting and waited for several other teachers to appear. Mrs. Miller stood at the desk waiting. I was not prepared for her speech. "Well, ladies, as you know, I am the *curriculum coordinator*"—again I saw italics when she said her title—"and there seems to be a misunderstanding among you. We will have to have a working relationship. After all, that is part of my job. Now, I has a fine relationship with the other teachers in fourth, fifth, and sixth grade. It is just you who don't want me to help you. You must be prejudice against me because I'm black. Well, I has eleven years of teaching experience before I became *curriculum coordinator* and I is well qualified, so you will just have to learn to work with a black person. Now then, the color of my skin shouldn't make any difference to you. I am qualified and I would like to work with you. There ain't one of you who are so good that you don't need my help, although you white folk might think so. Just because you is white, you have no right to think you is superior because let me tell you, you ain't. Now remember, I am the *curriculum coordinator* and it is my responsibility to observe in your classrooms and to help you improve your teaching techniques, and from what I see, you is certainly not very effective. Are there any questions?"

There were no questions. The others had heard similar speeches.

"Now, some of you is doing your behavioral objectives wrong. Please remember there is information in the library for you to follow. These here objectives are very important and must be written correctly. It is necessary that a black school like P.S. 123 look good in these reports. I have noticed some of you doing a very poor job and you are teaching different areas in your classroom. This next six weeks, I want you to plan together so that each class will be studying the exact same things at the same time."

I wondered how it was possible to meet the needs of each student if every teacher had to teach the same things and decided to ask. "Mrs. Miller, most of my children need drill in simple addition and subtraction and letter or simple word recognition in reading. Would the other teachers have to drill their students if they don't need it, or would I teach areas that my students would not be able to do?" Several teachers nodded.

"Well, Mrs. Evans," she said sarcastically, "you must get together. You must teach the same things." When she realized that I was about to say something more, she raised her voice and yelled, "I am the *curriculum coordinator*. I know what is best. You has to plan together. You must teach your classes the same things. Is that understood?"

I planned to invite her into my classroom that next week, but she gathered her papers and stomped to the door. "Well now, excuse me. I has so much to do. You know I am a very important person. See you all next week. If you has any questions, just write them down and put them in my box. You get together in your planning, hear?"

CHAPTER 5

You Are Not Welcome
at P.S. 123

MAGGIE WAS WAITING FOR ME out in the car. When we reached the apartment I shared with my husband, Paul, I invited her in for a cup of coffee. I sensed that she was upset by the meeting too, and I wanted to talk to her about P.S. 123.

As we sat in our comfortable little apartment, sipping hot black coffee and listening to the quiet, we seemed to revive. Maggie had chalk dust on the back of her arm and her short curly hair was rumpled. She looked tired as she rocked back and forth in the old orange chair. Pushing a strand of long blond hair out of my face, I leaned my back against the cold white wall: the quiet, the hot coffee, and a friend—a delightful combination!

I had not realized how bitter she was about P.S. 123. "If you think this afternoon was bad, you should have heard her in the beginning of the year."

"Why?"

"She never stopped talking about blacks and prejudice and how it affected her and hurt her and how we white folk took out our prejudice on the children. God, today's speech was mild when I think of some."

"I'm glad I didn't hear her first speeches. This one was brutal."

Maggie took her shoes off and stretched. "Well, you wouldn't believe what it was like in the fall. There were so many schedule changes I never knew if I had music or P.E. or when I had it or what time to go to lunch, and they kept changing the time to start school, so I never knew if I would be late or early. It was just wild." Rocking faster, she continued, "The schedule kept changing. No one was told. That made it twice as bad and you know what it's like asking Mrs. Black, the secretary. Half an hour later, she might answer you." We both giggled.

"You know, I would be just fine if I didn't have to attend any of those meetings. If they'd just leave me alone to teach, but every time I sit through one of those meetings, I get so mad I could go home and pound pillows! I just want to scream when Mr. Carter or the curriculum coordinator start blaming all the school's troubles on the white teachers' prejudice."

"Yes," I said. "Prejudice must be responsible for broken windows, no books, no supplies, lack of discipline, special education kids in regular classes, bad plumbing, and bugs!"

Maggie nodded her head vigorously. "All caused by those white teachers' prejudice."

"Isn't that ridiculous? I just want to teach them as much as they can learn in the next few months." It was a relief to realize that she felt as I did.

"What do you do about disciplining students?"

Maggie groaned. "Well, you know, don't you, that it doesn't do any good to send them to the office? Sometimes Mr. Carter doesn't even see them. They are put in the cafetorium and not supervised. They run around and play or leave and roam up and down the halls." She rocked emphatically. "One day when I sent Jimmy to the office for disrupting the entire class, he reappeared at my door handing out bulletins. My, he looked pleased with himself, after cutting up in class. There he was, rewarded for his bad behavior."

"Doesn't he ever paddle any children?"

"Oh no, he won't paddle them. I was in his office one morning when a mother pleaded with him to paddle her boy. She said she didn't have the strength to, and you know what? He refused. Yes, indeed. Can you believe that? And that boy's behavior has gotten worse and worse." Her eyes seemed to grow bigger and rounder as she told the story.

"I never taught in a school where teachers were allowed to hit children," I said. "If it were necessary, the principal always did the paddling."

"He told us in one of the first faculty meetings that he didn't believe in hitting kids. Mr. Carter told us the story of this principal who reported a student for playing hooky and the boy came back that afternoon with a shotgun and killed the principal. Well, he said that he wasn't going to end up dead just to discipline a kid!"

"What a dreadful story!"

"He really said that. Just ask Debby or Hilda. They couldn't believe it either."

"Do you think it happened?"

"I think that Mr. Carter is just scared of the parents and the older brothers. You can never tell what might happen in that school. I think he's afraid to do anything to those kids."

I got up and refilled our coffee cups. "What do you think about Mr. Carter's talk on loving the students? I believe that my students need my respect more than my love and I need their respect to teach effectively."

"Oh, I agree. After he talked about loving, I read several books on the disadvantaged child, and those authorities write the disadvantaged child needs self-esteem."

"Respect. Did the books mention loving the students?"

"No. In fact, one authority thinks it is detrimental!"

"Tell me more about P.S. 123 last fall."

"Did you hear about the first assembly?" When I shook my head, she continued. "The entire school went to this assembly at the beginning of the year, and the kids just booed and hooted Mr. Carter right off the stage. You know, they aren't one bit afraid of him. They think he's a big joke."

"How sad. I wish they had real respect for him. They need a man to respect and it would make our jobs so much easier."

"It was Mrs. Dickson who made them shut up. She yelled at them that he was their principal and how dare they act that way, and if they didn't respect him, who would they respect—and the whole time he just stood there and didn't say anything."

"How embarrassing," I gasped.

"Then the kids finally stopped. So, he spoke to them and welcomed them to P.S. 123 and told them that they were superior to anyone else. Just as good as the whites were—no, better! And that they didn't have to take a back seat for anybody, because they were smart, and don't let anyone tell them different. After he stopped speaking, I thought some of those sixth grade boys were going to rip the cafetorium apart. They were so unruly and they left the place like a herd of animals."

"Why does he keep on talking about race?"

"Don't you know? This is the first year he's been principal and it's the first year P.S. 123 has been integrated. Most of these teachers are new in the school. Even the whole office staff is new. P.S. 123 used to be a neighborhood black school, just first through sixth grade."

I thought about Maggie's comments and realized that she answered a lot of questions. This helped explain the lack of friendliness among teachers, the tension in the hallways, and the countless racial remarks.

"Why don't you stay for dinner? Paul will be home soon, and there is plenty."

Maggie looked embarrassed and reluctantly agreed. "I hate to cook," she said. "A home-cooked meal sounds great!" I put the meat and macaroni-and-cheese casserole together quickly, and we continued talking while I tossed the salad.

"Did you hear about the parent-teacher meeting? No? That was quite the scene. To begin with, Mr. Carter put Mrs. Potter in charge of the meeting. You know, she was to greet the parents and make a speech and everything."

"Who is she?"

"She is a sixth grade teacher, and this is only her second year of teaching. Can you believe it? Not too many parents showed up, but he ended up greeting them anyway because Mrs. Potter was sick and didn't even come. The whole meeting was like being in church. They stood around the piano and sang hymns. Oh yes, they did!" she said as she saw the look of disbelief on my face. "Hymns! And when they didn't sing, they prayed. It was the most amazing school meeting I ever attended."

"You mean no officers were elected? No school business was discussed?"

"And there hasn't been another since then. I guess that was all for the year. You just can't imagine, there they were singing and praying, and swaying around and saying, 'Amen, brother.' It looked like a revival meeting. Don't get me wrong. I'm a Bible Belt Baptist and I believe prayer works, but God expects us to do our jobs and at that school there is a lot that needs doing."

Just at that moment, Paul walked through the door, looking handsome in his Marine Corps Service "Bravo" uniform. He had met Maggie before and was pleased to see her again. After he changed into shorts and a t-shirt, I asked her to repeat some of the choicest stories for him while I put the food on the table.

As we ate, she told us about the parents' night at school. "This was for the parents to meet the teachers and see the classrooms. Some teachers didn't have any parents show up at all. Just a few came to see me, and naturally they weren't the parents I wanted to meet most."

"If we could find some mothers who would come into the classroom and help, there are so many things they could do," I added. "Wouldn't their children be proud?"

"You know, most of the mothers work or their health is poor or they have babies at home."

"I'd like to ask them anyway," I argued. "I wonder if Mr. Carter would approve?"

"I doubt it. He doesn't want anyone snooping around his school, and you'll see for yourself that he's afraid of parents."

Maggie abruptly changed the subject. "Did you know that two other teachers have left besides Mary Ann Jenkins? Yes, one at the beginning of the year and one over the Christmas holidays. I don't know her name, but she was real scared of her students. She had a fifth grade class. Every time I saw her, she looked terrified. I know some of the boys brought knives because I saw them. They sassed her and knocked over desks. One even started a fire in the closet. They were always fighting and—"

"But surely Mr. Carter helped her?"

"He didn't even suspend them. All he ever said was it was her fault that she couldn't handle them."

"Oh no. I am glad I have younger students."

"Me too. Some of those fifth graders already have police records!" Maggie continued, "Another time, a teacher tried to take a knife away from one of her students and she got her hand cut. But he did suspend the boy who bit Hilda."

I shook my head. The problems seemed overwhelming. For a while we talked about other things, but inevitably the conversation returned to P.S. 123.

"You take your children outside, don't you? He never allowed any of the teachers to take their classes out last fall. We stayed inside the whole time and worked. I honestly don't know how I lived through it. It was so hot in September and October."

"Well, during my job interview, he said that I could take them outside. But that isn't what he said at the faculty meeting!"

"Wow, you are lucky."

"By the way, did you know that the county policy book does not forbid recess? I don't know why Mr. Carter said that."

"It doesn't? Then that's all I need to know! My class is going out tomorrow."

Perhaps one of the most revealing things she said that evening was that Mr. Carter had a child in a private church-affiliated school. I don't know why that distressed me more than any of the other things she related, but it did. I remembered his indifference toward Edward's illness and my search for books that the children could read. I thought about his child having the best that a private church school could offer.

As Maggie was leaving, I asked, "What do you plan to do about report cards?

"What do you mean?"

"He mentioned that no child was to be given a grade lower than a C. But is that based on average third grade work or on whatever level the child is on? Most of mine are doing first or second grade work."

"Yeah. Mine too. I give grades lower than C. You have to when the child has not done anything!"

"I would rather write a comment stating progress than give Ds or Fs, or as Mr. Carter suggests, all Cs." I sighed. "Wouldn't it be great not to grade at all?"

"*Umm,*" she replied. "I really don't think Mr. Carter would approve a written report card. It just isn't very conventional."

She left shortly after dinner, promising to pick me up in her car earlier that next morning, since we had a meeting with the county science coordinator at 8:30.

The rain pelted against my face as I dashed from the car onto the sidewalk. The broken drainpipe poured water into a huge lake by the steps. I waded through and hurried to open my classroom door. Inside, the room looked dreary and dark even with all the lights on. There was a large puddle on the floor from the leak in the roof and water dripped onto the shelf. I moved all the storybooks to a drier place, checked all the desks to make sure each had the morning word games, and then walked down the hall to Mrs. Madison's room for the meeting.

Mr. Edwards, the science coordinator, was a young man, very energetic and pleasant. He faced a group of sleepy teachers and enthusiastically asked how the ABC Science Program was going. Most of the teachers ignored his question. I suddenly realized that no one had used the program, especially since my shelves were filled with all the different colored boxes, each containing a different level of work. I had looked in several boxes and noticed that most of the boxes were empty or had broken equipment.

Mr. Edwards was very excited about his program. He urged the teachers to use it. In fact, several of the teachers were taking the education science course necessary for teaching the ABC program.

I had taken the course and agreed with the fundamental ideas. Children would learn scientific procedures or processes through individual experimentation, rather than memorizing facts or just reading about science in a book. Since it involved experimentation rather than reading, children who could not read well would not be held back. An excellent idea, however, the program consumed much class time. Working at an individual pace, a class could be on several experiments at one time with all taking different, individually administered tests at different times. It involved endless paperwork, charts, graphs, and tests. Even ignoring those drawbacks, I could not imagine using the program when few of my students could read the instructions, follow directions, and work independently.

From his speech, I learned that the entire school was supposed to use the ABC program and that textbooks would not be available next year. How could a school that could not afford books to teach a child reading, or supplies such as paper, pencils, chalk, toilet paper, art paper, screening room curtains, and so on, have the money to support this program? The kits alone were quite expensive, and each one contained materials that were disposable after one experiment, but then had to be replaced. Mr. Edwards admitted that the county did not have the funds to replace the missing articles and that each classroom teacher was expected to buy them herself.

"I hope that next year, the materials will be supplied by the county," he added.

Since I had the ABC boxes in my room, he followed me back to check several of them. I think more supplies were missing or broken than he anticipated. "Well, now, Mrs. Evans, since you have the boxes in your room, why don't you check them for missing items and then give me the list?"

"Mr. Edwards, I might not know what is missing. I am sure that you could do a more thorough job. Isn't there a master list of all the items needed for each experiment?"

"Oh, I don't know. I guess I'll have to check that." He wrote in his little notebook. Noticing the moon map on the wall and the pictures of NASA flights, he asked, "Are you teaching about space? These are excellent photographs of the space flight and astronauts. How did you get these?"

"I was given them when I worked for NASA as a research writer on a summer intern program."

"Really, my my! Well then, you must really like science. What do you think of the ABC program?"

"Mr. Edwards, I believe that children need to learn reading before they need an expensive science program."

"Yes, of course," he sputtered. When I briefly described my reading book problems, he appeared quite surprised. "Why that's just dreadful. You will have the reading books you need tomorrow. I will see to it personally." Again he took out his black notebook and wrote inside. "Now then, do try the ABC Science Program with these children. You will enjoy it, I'm sure." He backed toward the door, saying, "I must be going. It's almost time for school to begin."

He left as the children straggled in from the rain. Most were soaked. Their shoes squished as they walked and their hair was plastered to their heads. Coughing and sniffling, they sat in the cold room and waited to dry. Several bussed-in students were absent. The next day, I received their notes. Sharon's mother wrote, "Der mis evan, Sharon no ran cloths to ware. She get Wet thank you." Sandy's mother wrote, "Sandy shoe wet from yestiday. He ain't got none today."

With fewer children, the classroom seemed empty. Several of the boys—Nicholas, Danny, Jeffrey, Sandy—were absent. I hoped they were not sick. Since we could not go outside in the rain, we played silent speedball with the red yarn ball I made over vacation. They brightened considerably while playing the game and enforced the rules rather well.

"You is out!" shouted Kelvin.

"I ain't," sulked Dexter.

"I wants to be leader, too. How come only boys get to be?" yelled Felicia.

"You is all out now 'cause you talked," laughed Nanci.

Later Patricia said, "Gee, Mrs. Evans. That's the first time I ever played a fun game inside. Can we do it again tomorrow?"

That afternoon, I planned to show them another film on cold lands that I had borrowed from the public library. When we tiptoed up the stairs to the film room, another class was already there. I thought perhaps they were running late and walked into the library to check the sign-up sheet. Much to my complete disgust, my name had been erased and Mrs. LeBlanc was written over it. The next time I signed up, I used thick black magic marker.

Since we could not see a film that day, I spent the time talking with them about the cold lands we visited and finding them on the map again.

"I knows where Alaska is."

"Me too."

"Find Iceland, Larry."

"That's too easy," he complained. "Give me a hard one."

"Who can find Switzerland or Norway? North or South Poles? Very good. Put the pointer back please, Jimmy. Now, who wants to talk about a favorite cold land?"

"Me!" yelled Billy and then he raised his hand. "I like Alaska best 'cause I want to see a totem pole."

Sandy wanted to go to the North Pole. "I gonna shoot me a polar bear."

"I want to see reindeer," said Nanci, "so I go to Lapland."

L'Angela raised her hand and shyly said, "Mrs. Evans, tell us another story."

"I'd love to. This is a story about Switzerland. It is cold in the Swiss Alps in the wintertime." I wrote the words on the blackboard. "Alps are mountains, very tall mountains. Now, how do you suppose you could get to the top of the mountain?"

"Be a mountain climber," said Eric.

"Yes. Many families, grandmas and grandpas and even little children, climb mountains."

"The dog too?"

"Yes, Danny, even the dog goes along."

I continued with the story. "In the summer, parts of the Alps are covered with grass and pretty flowers but the tops or peaks of the mountains are covered with snow, even in July. You can see the cows grazing when you walk by the chalets or houses.

"Now, if you don't want to hike, you can ride up the mountain in a cable car." I showed them pictures of the cable car.

"It look like a box," said Edward.

"Like a flying box," giggled L'Angela.

I showed them the cables and how the machines pulled the cable car up the mountain and explained how it felt to ride in one. The children always enjoyed stories. Then they looked through the postcards and travel brochures to find pictures.

"I wish I could really go there," said Nanci.

"Yeah. Me, too. I ain't never seen the mountains even," said Patricia.

"Children, it is important to dream big! When you work hard, you can make dreams come true."

"You mean daydreams come true?" asked Sylvia.

"Once I wanted to hit a home run, 'cause I ain't never before, and I thought about it lots and practiced—and I done it!" shouted Cecil.

That afternoon was the first that week I did not have a meeting to attend or children to keep in. Maggie was keeping some boys in after school. So I spent the time making new ditto work sheets and running them off on the machine. The paper cutter I planned to use was broken. It remained broken for the rest of the school year.

Then I moved several desks. Tynetta had brought a note to school saying that she could not see the board, so I put her in the front row. Her mother had also written, "My Tynetta, she have week kidneys so the dr say she gots to go when she wants, okay?"

In other classrooms, I always let children leave the room

whenever they wished, but that system did not work with this class. The boys leaving unsupervised spent much too long in the bathroom. I could not continually go after them, so I sent them to the bathroom in pairs, timing their return. That worked well with the boys, except for Nicholas, who had to go alone because none of the boys wanted to partner with him. But the girls used the bathroom connected to the classroom. If Tynetta wished to use the bathroom before lunchtime, all she needed to do was ask. I hoped she had not been uncomfortable those days before I received her mother's note.

Several mornings later, Mrs. Johnson, the reading supervisor, appeared. She was a tiny woman, white haired, pink cheeked, and soft-spoken. "My, this is a cheerful, pleasant classroom! And a well-behaved class!" She brought with her several boxes of books: pre-primer, primer, first, and second grade books, as well as a pile of magazines. "You may use all these as long as you'd like." I thanked her again and again. She smiled courteously and left as quietly as she came.

"Guess what is in the box?"

"A turtle?"

"No," shouted Billy. "Books! Reading books!"

The children were so excited about their new books that we decided to have reading right away.

"This is the first brand-new book I ever held," stuttered Felicia.

I realized as we took them out of the boxes that they were not county books but Mrs. Johnson's private property. What a kind and gracious lady! Reading went well that day because the children were enthralled with their new books on various reading levels that matched their abilities. Each read a story to me. Then each read a story alone and answered some questions. They also worked a phonics ditto. I spent the remainder of the time with the non-readers, working with letter recognition.

They cut out pictures from the magazines that began with the letter they recognized.

"This here is a house for H, okay?" asked Sandy. It was a pleasant morning. The children were all working hard.

In addition to our reading lessons, we started to write stories together. By using their vocabulary and writing the story on the board, they learned to read words they spoke. One of the first stories they wrote was about an elephant.

"Once upon a time, there was an elephant. His name was Peter. He was a bad elephant. He pulled up trees. He broke buildings. He smashed cars. He could eat lots. Once he ate a million hot dogs. He worked hard. He was tired at the end of the day. He brushed his teeth. He put on polka-dot pajamas. He went to bed."

Each child would suggest the next sentence in the story until no one had anything more to add. The children were delighted with their story and excited that the elephant could do whatever they wanted him to do. They never grew tired of the bad elephant.

"I wished I had him for a pet," said Jack.

"Nah, he eat too much," said Larry.

"Yeah, but he'd squash my little brother." Jack grinned.

Many other stories were made up, usually about brave heroes, beautiful girls with long straight hair, flying children, lots of food, and always happy endings.

Occasionally I would pair the children and have them read to each other. This system was very helpful and made the "teacher" and "student" feel important. The majority of the morning was spent with reading and related skills.

That week, quite by accident, I saw the school nurse walking through the cafetorium. I left my lunch, followed her quickly to the clinic, and found her ready to leave. Her blue uniform was starched stiff, her black hair curled tightly around her white cap. "What do you want?" she barked.

"Have you time to see Edward?"

"No. I don't. Can't you see I'm fixing to leave?"

"Would you please stay just a few more minutes? I have written you several notes about him."

"Well, I ain't seen none."

I stood my ground in the doorway, blocking her exit. She glared at me and then finally agreed to look at him. After a cursory examination, she pronounced, "Well, he sick. He got teta, a fever, and need to go to the clinic. Now, move out of the way, I'm leaving and I ain't going stay a minute longer." She put her coat on and walked out the door. "You know, I can't take him to the doctor. His mother or sister has to do that. Be sure to tell them the doctor is free."

Again, I wrote a note that afternoon for Edward to take home. I told him what it said and helped him read it to me. I spoke with his sister after school. She was in third grade also, and I told her about Edward. She promised, "Yes, ma'am. I tell my ma." Edward was in school that next day—sleeping, complaining of headaches, noise, and stomach aches. My note went unanswered.

A week later, I saw the nurse again. She was chatting with Mr. Carter in the outer office. Their conversation was a personal one. I waited to speak with her and when she turned, I said, "Hello, do you remember examining Edward? Well, nothing has been done and he is still sick."

Her pleasant expression vanished. "I done told you that I can't take him to the doctor and his mother can't read and they don't have no phone. Why don't you take him yourself, since you is so concerned?" She repeated that suggestion to Mr. Carter and he volunteered to let me take Edward to the doctor. I had less authority to take Edward to the doctor than the nurse had! I suggested several solutions to the problem, including the nurse visiting his home.

Finally, Mr. Carter said, "Well now, is what he got contagious?"

The nurse nodded yes.

"Then he can't come to school till he's better."

"I suppose I got to tell his mother," grumped the nurse. It had taken more than one month to help Edward. He was absent for a week. When he returned, he no longer complained of headaches. Now he had a bad cold and the sores on his head caused by the teta infection were painted with a purple medicine. Considering the length of time it took to help Edward, I was thankful it was not a more serious illness.

Edward was absent the week that the furnace died. At 60 degrees, the room was so cold that I joked about being in the Alps. The children shivered in their thin sweaters and cotton shirts or dresses. It was hard to write with numb fingers and worse with mittens. By mid-afternoon, those who had worn their coats were huddled up inside them. Even a trip into the playground sunshine failed to warm them. I told them all to wear warm clothes the next day, as I did not know when the furnace would be fixed.

The room was no warmer the next day, and the children did not bring sweaters. Perhaps they did not have any to bring. Most of the children had colds. Those with fevers slept much of the day. They could not go home since no one was there, and the school clinic was full. Coughing, sniffling, and sneezing punctuated the classroom work.

That night, Missouri, the janitor, assured me that the classroom would be warmer. On Wednesday, it was warmer than it had been all week. That was the day that Mr. Carter finally decided to close the school because it was too cold for the children and they might get sick. As I waited for my class, I heard the news from one of the children running down the hall. "Hey,

Evans, ain't no school today." The town crier hustled importantly around the corner.

Mrs. Black cautiously admitted that it was true. The bussers who had just arrived were sent home and the neighborhood children, with much hooting and hollering, ran out into the playground. The teachers, however, many sick themselves, were not allowed to leave. I spent that day sitting in a quiet, warm, and empty classroom. I felt as though the children, like small birds, had flown away, leaving me in a rectangular cage that was latched firmly with a solid gray metal door.

Many of the children stayed to play on the playground. Occasionally, I watched them from the window. "Hey, there's Mrs. Evans. Hey, look at me!" Felicia waved.

I spent the afternoon thinking about report cards and the grades that I planned to give. Mr. Carter refused to let me write comments. "Now, you remember, no grade lower than C," he warned as I left his office. A. B. C. D. E. F. E grade was new to me. An E meant the child was failing but tried a little and showed some interest, at least more interest than a child receiving an F. The arbitrary letters bothered me when I first started to teach, but never were they as inadequate as they were for these children. If D meant below average, then the majority of my students could be classified as D. But if F meant not working at a third grade level, then half of the students would be F. When I discussed my dilemma with the other third grade teachers, I found that there was no problem at all. "Just give Cs," they advised. Only Maggie planned to give Ds or Fs.

I decided to check my students' class folders that were kept in the office and could not be removed for any reason. Much to my dismay, I found that half of the students had no folders at all. The others all had grades of B or A along with comments like, "He is a nice boy." Or simply, "Pleasant child."

When I mentioned to Mrs. Black that many of my students

didn't have school records, she said, "Well, if you ain't got none, you'd better make some up."

On the way back to my room, I decided to write "working below grade level" on most of my students' reports cards and then grade them as to their performance in pre-primer, primer, first, or second grade. Still, some would be D students and others such as Nicholas who had not done any classwork would receive an F. I just could not give grades of A or B if they weren't earned. Many parents disagreed with my decision.

The first parents to appear at my classroom door were Tynetta's. I was putting the morning work papers out on the desks. The door and windows were opened in a futile attempt to move the hot, stagnant air. The classroom was too well heated that day. When I turned from the blackboard, Tynetta was standing beside me, and walking toward me was an obese woman, a handkerchief and purse in one hand; the other held her coat closed. Tynetta's father was a small, thin man dressed in work clothes. He never spoke during the entire confrontation. Instead, he retired to the doorway and leaned against it.

"Mrs. Franklin, there won't be much time to talk with you as the bell is about to ring for my class to come in. Would you like to make an appointment with the secretary for any day after school?"

Mrs. Franklin sat down in my desk chair and began to wail. "I's sick. I's real sick." She snuffled into her handkerchief. "I's got to go to the hospital today and the doctor says I might die." She wailed again. Her husband shifted his feet. Tynetta did not move. Both husband and daughter stared first at me, then at Mrs. Franklin. "I gots to see you right now about my Tynetta and I can't come back no other time."

"All right, Mrs. Franklin. I will certainly try to help you as much as possible."

Tynetta stood alongside her mother, absorbing the entire conversation. Then her mother pulled the report card out of her large purse and waved it at me. "How you give my Tynetta such bad grades?" Then she pulled out some of Tynetta's papers, the work papers we corrected together in class. "All these here papers," she waved them at me, "these here are all real good. How come you give my girl an E in reading? Why she read real good! At home she read fifth grade books." She gasped for breath, wiped her face with her handkerchief, and started to yell at me, "Ain't no other teacher give Tynetta such bad grades. How long you been teaching? You ain't no teacher. You don't know nothing. I think you just don't like us blacks. You know she read good but you don't give no good grades to us blacks."

I was totally shocked by this rant. I knew why I had given her that grade. I had struggled with an E or an F and finally settled on the E because Tynetta did occasionally try. I found it hard to believe that Tynetta could read fifth grade books at home.

"Mrs. Franklin, Tynetta's papers are class papers. These papers are worked individually and then corrected together. I asked the children to draw lines through their mistakes and write the correct answers."

"All these here papers are A."

"Yes, after being corrected they would be. Tynetta added the A at the top of the papers herself. Do you have any of her individual papers? Papers she has done herself that I have corrected and graded?" Mrs. Franklin answered me by waving the papers she held and stamping her feet.

"Mrs. Franklin, Tynetta is reading in a first grade book. She has difficulty learning new words and reads slowly. Her comprehension is also on a first grade level." She eyed me suspiciously.

Finally she said, "I ain't getting nowhere with you. Never could get nowhere with no white honky. I gonna see Mr. Carter. Then I gonna go to the school board. Ain't no whitie gonna give this here grade to my Tynetta. She can read good." And she picked up the papers and the report card. With her husband and daughter trailing behind, she hustled down to the office.

A few minutes later, Nadette, the office aide, appeared at my door. "Mr. Carter want to see you in his office right away."

All three of them sat in front of Mr. Carter's desk. They stared at me when I walked in. Mr. Carter asked, "What is your explanation for Tynetta's grades?"

I gave him the same reasons I gave to her mother. "Would you like Tynetta to read for you?"

No one wanted to hear her read. At last, Mr. Carter said, "You may leave."

A few minutes later, but before the bell rang for the morning classes to begin, Mr. Carter walked into my room and said, "You better be real careful with the grades you give out. Now these folk think anything below a C is prejudice. I ain't so sure but what they say is right. And I warned you about giving low grades. You better remember this next time. I finally got her calmed down. Why, she was going to the school board. There ain't no need for all that fuss. I just told her you made a mistake and Tynetta will get As and Bs next time." He glared at me, stomped to the door, opened it and slammed it behind him.

I was horrified to think that grades were given on the basis of skin color. That entire morning, I mentally reviewed the grades that I gave and believed each was justified. Ironically, the highest grades were earned by two black students, Eric and Nanci. It appalled me that Mr. Carter believed Mrs. Franklin's story. Why had no one wanted to hear Tynetta read? And then promising Mrs. Franklin As and Bs next time!

As I recovered from the morning's confrontation, I looked

up from my desk to see a small, shy young woman standing in the doorway. She whispered, "I am Jimmy's mother and I would like to speak to you about how could I help Jimmy? I know that he can do better than this."

"Could you set an appointment with the secretary in the office and—"

"Oh, I already have. Mrs. Black told me to just go right in." The children inspected her with interest and Jimmy worked industriously at his desk.

Standing at the doorway, I quietly said, "Jimmy daydreams a lot and rarely finishes his papers. Even the ones I have sent home are not brought back finished. He is capable and has improved since December, but it would help if you would go over his assignments at home."

She nodded. "I will speak to him about daydreaming. I thought he was fooling around. You send home his work. I will see it gets done."

She was pleasant and concerned, but parents should not have to visit during school hours. It is not fair to students or the teacher and parents do not always learn all that they need to know in a few brief minutes. I knew that parents were not supposed to visit during school hours and wondered why Mrs. Black continued to send them to me.

On my break, I decided to talk to Mrs. Black. "Is it possible to catch the parents before they come to my room? They have to walk past the office." She stared at me and then turned away. Her back seemed to say that she was too busy with important work to answer me. "Mrs. Black, I certainly would appreciate it if you would give the parents' appointments to meet with me after school." Again she did not reply.

By the time the class got to music that day, I felt that I had taught an entire week. I sat in the teachers' lounge, grateful for the break. Putting my feet on the table, I sank down into the old sofa and closed my eyes. I clearly heard the music from Mrs. Williams's room. She yelled at several of my students. The children were trying to read the words from the music books. I knew the song was too difficult for them to sing, much less to enjoy. Soon her screams of frustration began to drown out the melody. "No! No! No! You there, boy! What's the matter with you? You stupid? That it, huh? You just a stupid black ape?" I heard a few children laugh and tried to imagine to which child she was talking. I heard the crack of her ruler and the sounds of a hollering child being dragged across the room. Her door opened and the child was pushed out into the hall. "I don't want no black ape in my room. Go back to the zoo where you belong, boy!" Then her door shut and the song began again.

Maggie walked in with a stack of papers and two books. We looked at each other and together said, "You're not going to believe this."

Maggie said, "One mother barged into my room and screamed at me. I couldn't understand a thing she was saying and I didn't know what to do, so I just screamed right back! I don't know who she was or why she was so upset. Her last words were, 'I'm going to the school board about you.' Can you imagine? Well, from now on I think I'll keep my door locked."

"My day started with Tynetta's parents."

"Oh, I'll bet that was a wild scene!"

When I left the teachers' lounge that day, Jeffrey was waiting for me out in the hall. He was a difficult child to talk to—hostile and cold. I was not able to change his attitude very much. He was crying and looked perfectly miserable. "What is the matter?" Jeffrey did not answer. "Why are you standing out in the hall, when you should be singing?"

"She throwed me out," he snarled.

"Why?"

He looked at me desperately and said, "She called me stupid, that mother fucker black whore," and tears welled up in his eyes and slid down his cheeks.

"Why did she say that, Jeffrey?"

"I couldn't read the words in the book and I was singing the wrong words loud and she said I was stupid 'cause I can't read," he sobbed.

"Jeffrey, just because she called you stupid doesn't mean you are, unless you believe her. Do you believe her?"

At first there was no answer, just a few more stifled sobs. Then he said, "No, I ain't stupid. No, I ain't!"

He wiped his face on his grimy sleeve. I sent him to get a drink from the water fountain. He was quieter and less hostile that day than ever before. Perhaps I had loosened one small brick at the base of the wall that surrounded Jeffrey.

The rest of the day was somewhat less dramatic. Dexter started several fights. Sandra cried and rocked back and forth at her desk. Nanci forgot her lunch. Edward slept. Cecil threw a tantrum. Nicholas and Jimmy pestered several classmates mercilessly. Money was missing from Jack's desk. Poor Jack's face was red from crying. Behind the sobs, I could understand, "My mom's going to kill me!" Ida Mae Lee, the special reading teacher, did not take her students until fifteen minutes were left in the period. Danny forgot to go to speech therapy, and the teacher came for him. It was rumored that Sandy had a knife. I was told by Nadette, the aide, that I could not have any art supplies for Valentine's Day. At 3:00, I was brusquely informed that I must attend a teachers' meeting.

Before I could pick up my register and coat, another mother walked into my room. "Mrs. Evans?" She was well spoken and well dressed. Walking over to my desk, she took one of the children's chairs and sat down. "I am Mrs. Jones, Eric's mother."

"Yes, I am very pleased to meet you."

"I want to talk to you about Eric's report card." That surprised me. Eric worked hard, read on a third-grade level, and was a conscientious student. His report card was almost all As.

"I am interested in this C in conduct," she said. "I won't tolerate misbehavior on his part. I tell all my children that God might not have given them any brains, but if they listen good and work hard they might learn something. That's their part of the bargain, you know, to behave. Could you tell me what Eric is doing to get a C?"

"Yes, Mrs. Jones. Whenever Eric is corrected or asked to rework a problem, he sulks and pouts. He does not take advice without talking back. He has lost playtime because of this problem, but he is improving."

She nodded her head. "I thought so," she said. "That will stop right away. I am sorry that you did not tell me sooner."

"Eric is a good student and a very good reader. I am sure that his behavior will improve since Eric and I have had several discussions."

"Good, you let me know if he starts acting up. You know, I am a librarian. I help him read at home. I am glad he is doing well."

Just then, Nicholas, who was staying to do some work, walked over. "Nicholas, I will help you in a minute, but now I am talking with Mrs. Jones."

"Oh, gee, I want to go home." He kicked the desk leg, sat down loudly, and shoved his books off the top of his desk onto the floor.

"My goodness, what dreadful behavior," exclaimed Mrs. Jones. "I would not let any student act like that in my library. I would cane him good, I tell you. You don't have to put up with that." Standing, she gathered her purse and coat, thanked me for my time, and left.

I looked at the top of Nicholas's head. The rest of his body was squeezed against the wall. He solemnly promised me to do the work at home and gleefully fled down the hall. I was 10 minutes late for the teachers' meeting.

Mr. Carter stopped talking, all the teachers stared at me, and naturally, the only seat left was in the front of the room. I climbed over Miss Bernardo's pile of books that she took home nightly and sat down. The entire faculty continued to stare at me. I looked at Mr. Carter and said, "I am sorry to be late. Mrs. Jones, Eric's mother, was in my room when the teachers' meeting was announced. She wanted to see me for a few minutes."

"Well, Mrs. Black has not scheduled that meeting."

"No sir, although I asked her to, she hasn't scheduled any of my meetings."

Mr. Carter turned his attention back to the group and again he called the roll of those teachers who had not done their behavioral objectives. Several of the teachers objected.

"I has too done my objectives," declared Ozell Lewis.

Mr. Lewis and Mr. Carter usually got into at least one heated argument each meeting. Ozell stood up and said, "You ain't got no right to say I ain't done my objectives."

"You calling me a liar? You watch what you say, hear?"

"Don't you threaten me. You ain't much. I could take you easy."

But Mr. Carter didn't respond, so Ozell sat down again.

"These here objectives got to be in every week, Ozell. You just no good and lazy. I wants them in. Now your name been on my list before."

"Why should I write up new objectives when I is still doing the same things in P.E.? Huh? You answer me that."

"You got to hand one in every week, Ozell. Ain't no use

arguing. That there is a state law." Ozell dissolved into grumbles and snorts, lit a cigarette, and glowered at Mr. Carter.

With that argument out of the way, Mr. Carter said, "Girls, pay attention. I wants these green forms filled out for the free lunchers. Those that receive federal lunch funds, the 98-01 forms gots to be handed in every month." None of the teachers had ever done this before, so in February, they began to make out sheets for the students. To add to the confusion, free lunch was not to appear on that sheet, but on another one. Only federally funded lunches appeared on the 98-01 green sheet.

"Now some of you teachers ain't handed in your registers. I is tired of nurse maiding you. You gets these in tomorrow! Hear?" Much to my chagrin, I was one of the teachers on his list. I did not even know that registers were handed in every month! That night I struggled with the number of bussers absent and the number of walkers present and the cumulative total.

With that final announcement, Mr. Carter stood up, nodded to Mrs. Dickson, and left the room. Mrs. Dickson picked up her notepad, nodded at all of us, and quickly followed him, tugging on her girdle as she left.

CHAPTER 6

The Month of Hearts

A S I TRIED TO TEACH A PHONICS LESSON that next day, workers on the playground made pounding noises, which did not compare to the noise directly above us: shouting, thumping, scraping, and muffled screams. The class was relatively attentive, however, considering these distractions. After more than thirty minutes of this noise and knowing that if I left the classroom there would be chaos, I sent Jeffrey to Mrs. Dickson with a note:

Dear Mrs. Dickson,

Isn't the noise from the playground distracting? There seems to be a bit of noise above us too. Would you be so kind as to help keep the upstairs noise down? I would really appreciate it. Thanks a lot.

Lisa Evans

That was a big mistake!

Jeffrey looked bewildered when he returned, as if he had blundered into a lion's den and brought home the lion. Mrs. Dickson stormed into my room right behind him. "Who the hell do you think you is? You goddamn white bitch!" She waved the note in my face. "If you got off your big fat ass once in a while, you'd know that the noise is from outside. How dare you write me this damn note."

"Yes, I am aware of the outside noise, but I am talking about the noise above us."

"Well, that certainly ain't my class, Mrs. Evans," she sneered. "That must be Mrs. Potter's class."

"But Mrs. Potter's class isn't above me. Yours is!"

"Well, that don't make no never mind. You can hear her all over the school." She waved the note at me again. "I'm going to keep this here as evidence that you had the nerve to send me this note. I think I'll just show it to Mr. Carter."

"I'm certainly sorry if I upset you. Thank you for explaining the situation to me." As she stomped toward the door, I said, "Do have a pleasant day." She was completely outraged by that and slammed the door so hard that the windows shook and the ceiling lights swayed. My anger at her reaction quickly disappeared. Her look of complete hatred was unnerving.

When I mentioned the incident to Maggie during our break, she was sympathetic. "You know, everyone has had a run-in with her, but I don't see what she can do to you. I really wouldn't worry about it. Did the noise stop?"

"It is a little better than it was."

Although Maggie was reassuring, I did worry! I couldn't get her look of hatred out of my mind. I feared that I had made a formidable enemy.

Even the long-awaited books did not solve the reading problems. I knew the children were on too many different reading levels. It took much too long to hear each child read. After the novelty of the new books wore off, the real problems remained. With seven or eight reading levels, some children did not get enough individual attention. This concerned me, as it was imperative that each child learn as much reading as possible each day. If they didn't, how would they ever catch up?

I decided to ask all the third grade teachers to my room that afternoon. I had a plan that would make reading much easier for everyone. We would even have more supplies to work with if my ideas were accepted, and this was a perfect time to start since it was the beginning of a new grading period.

The sun was warm on my back as I waited for the teachers after school. The room had been swept and the walls looked cheerful with posters, children's stories, and their projects. Hilda, Debbie, and Fay came in together. Fay found an ashtray and sat down. "Let me tell you about that little bastard," said Fay. "Why, he is completely uncontrollable."

Mrs. Madison walked into the room leaning heavily on her cane. She looked tired. Maggie was sitting on the table, correcting papers. At last, Mrs. LeBlanc appeared in the doorway. "I hope this isn't a long meeting. I have so much to do. I just can't stay more than ten minutes. What's this for anyway?" she whined.

We got down to business. They all quickly agreed that they had a wide range of abilities in reading and admitted that they were not satisfied with any method that they tried. "Do you think you might have seven different reading levels?" I asked.

"Hell," said Fay. "I have thirty kids and thirty different reading levels." I knew exactly what she meant.

My idea was a simple one. Each teacher would have a class of students all on the same level or as close to each other in reading ability as possible. We would trade students. I thought that the children would be able to walk to another class without much difficulty, especially if each teacher stood outside her door waiting for them. That way each teacher would have one reading level to plan for and the children would benefit by having concentrated, individual attention. "That sounds great," said Maggie. The other teachers nodded their heads.

"Let's try it," said Hilda.

"What about dividing the seven levels into high third, regular third grade, high and low second grade, high and low first grade, and primer?" I asked. "Most of the students belong in the last four categories, but I think that it is also important to challenge those who can read with work more difficult than much of their regular classwork." They all agreed to that, too.

"Well then, let's draw for levels." I wrote each level on a piece of paper, folded it, and put it into a cup. I passed it around to the others and took the last paper out of the cup. I pulled high third grade! Each teacher seemed satisfied with her choice except Mrs. LeBlanc.

"Oh, I don't know. I don't think this is such a good idea. It will be too hard, and I will have so many students. Anyway, I would teach reading to my own class, too. I don't want to participate."

"What level did you draw, Mrs. LeBlanc?"

"Low first grade, and you know what problems they are."

"Would you like to switch with me?" offered Debby.

"No. No. I guess I just won't do it," she said.

Although the others were exasperated with Millie LeBlanc, they finally persuaded her to try the system and she conceded. "Okay. Okay. I'll try it with you. You're right about one thing. It can't be worse than what I've got." We all agreed to begin the following Monday. The teachers were excited about changing the reading plan. We decided that any discipline problems would be sent back to the student's own teacher and be dealt with there.

I immediately offered to lend all the materials and books I had on the various reading levels. The others agreed to pool their resources, too. The teachers left that afternoon more cheerful than usual. Perhaps we all had hope.

Maggie had drawn third grade and Mrs. Madison, high second grade. We exchanged materials and sorted the readers for the other teachers. I was hopeful that this reading program would solve some of my class problems. Besides more reading, the children would have a chance to move to another room where they would have a change of scenery and a new teacher. It did not occur to me then that we should have asked the advice of the reading supervisor or of Mrs. Miller, the curriculum coordinator.

At the end of school that day, Maggie and I walked down the hall together with Mrs. LeBlanc. She grumbled and complained all the way to the office. "Well, this just won't work. I know it will be a real mess! I don't want any part of it. It isn't fair that you made me."

"Why Millie, you agreed to this plan," said Maggie.

"I can change my mind, can't I?" she huffed. Perhaps realizing the futility of her complaints, she began to mumble and walked out the door ahead of us.

"I wonder how long she will try the program."

"I don't know," sighed Maggie. "Did you know that she has the smallest third grade, only twenty students, and mostly white children?"

"You must be kidding." Maggie shook her head. "But I have twenty-six children and you have more."

"Right."

"How did that happen?"

Maggie laughed. "Every time a student left, she just continued marking him on her attendance sheets. The office thinks she has thirty students and so places any new children with other teachers."

When I told my class about the new reading program the next day, they were very excited. "Hey, how come we ain't started today?" demanded Jimmy.

"We will start on Monday. Now, I know that you will walk quietly to the other rooms and will be better behaved than all the other children. Why, all the teachers will know who is in this room because you are so polite and work so hard." The children beamed.

"I guess that mean I got to be good?" sighed Cecil.

I knew that any complaints of noise or children running loose in the halls would end the reading program quickly.

I had another surprise for the class and promised to tell them about it as soon as everyone, even Nicholas, had finished some of the morning work. They worked diligently. Nicholas put his name on the paper and copied an entire page from the spelling book. It was neatly written but none of the questions were answered and several of his new spelling words were misspelled. "Nicholas, why did you copy the page? All you had to do was answer the questions."

"It easier to copy, Mrs. Evans. Them questions too hard." With help, he learned five of the fifteen spelling words, a major accomplishment.

All the children had learned to write script and only such letters as "q" or "f" gave them much trouble. I checked each child's papers and collected the penmanship. Nanci put all the class papers on the bulletin board. The children were so proud of their work.

"First time I ever has a paper up," said Sandy.

"Yeah, me too."

"How come you put up everyone's?" asked Sylvia.

"Because everyone did his or her best, Sylvia."

It was time for their surprise. "I know," said Felicia. "Extra playtime!"

"Yah!" shouted Danny and then squirmed uncomfortably and blushed when I looked at him. We tiptoed outside to a bleak playground. The rope swing was useless, dangling high above the children's heads, and one jungle gym had collapsed leaving long, rusty metal pipes sticking out of the ground. I would not let the class play near it. Those new basketball backboards lying on their side against the fence were beginning to rust, but when I asked in the office about having them installed, I received one of those stares.

We exercised, or rather, the children did. I stood with a bulging red cape and watched. "Come on Dexter, I'll bet you can go faster than that!" When they finished, I asked, "How many like to jump rope?" All the girls raised their hands and several boys, too. "And how many like to play baseball?" Most of the boys shouted.

"But we ain't got no ropes."

"We can't play ball without no ball and bat."

The children all started to talk at once. My surprise for them was jump ropes, a wooden bat, and a softball. Their eyes were wide and round. "Wow!"

"Man, you is the best teacher I ever has!" yelled Billy.

"Teams!" shouted Cecil.

"I carry the stuff. I'm P.E. this week," said Eric.

Cecil and Jimmy were captains, and the teams were chosen. They ran down to the middle of the playground, set up bases, and began their baseball game. They were excited and pleased with the bat and ball and were very careful with the equipment. They hollered at Dexter for letting the brand new, clean white ball roll into the mud. "Hey, you watch that ball. You get it out of the mud, boy! Go get it."

"Shit!" said Sandy. "I can't hit that mother fucker." The silence around him was immediate. They all looked at me.

"Swing the bat level, Sandy," I said. The boys looked at me again and gasped in relief.

The girls had begun turning the jump rope and singing jump rope chants. I turned one rope for a while. Marjorie said, "Your turn to jump, Mrs. Evans."

"Yeah," echoed Nanci and Patricia.

"Come on, Mrs. Evans!" And so, encouraged by the girls, I took my turn jumping as they turned the rope.

Before we went in, all the equipment was collected, and Eric was the envy of his classmates since he carried the bat, ball, and ropes and put them all into the closet. Everyone wanted to be P.E. leader that next week, so they could carry the new equipment.

I knew they would enjoy the ropes, bat, and ball, but I also hoped that taking care of them would teach responsibility. The sight of Felicia's beautiful corduroy coat, now buttonless, belt-less, dirty, and torn was a constant reminder of a lesson that must be learned.

Several other teachers who noticed us out on the playground asked where I had gotten the P.E. equipment. When I told them I bought it for the children, they looked at me with surprise and ended the conversation. I knew that all of the teachers were aware that I took the class outside every day, but I still had not been approached by Mr. Carter.

Days later, however, a new schedule was posted outside the office for P.E. Every teacher was allowed fifteen minutes outside, which is just long enough to take the class outside and line them up to bring them back in. It was the first time that playground time had been scheduled officially that year by Mr. Carter. My time was scheduled for 9:30, during reading, so, because none of the teachers was using the schedule—I was still the only one going outside—I offered to trade with Mrs. Potter, who had the 11:00 slot. "Just go on out," she said. "We won't use it."

I was amazed. It was vitally important to the welfare of the children and to the discipline in my class to spend time outside.

Besides, playtime before lunch helped the children's behavior in the cafetorium and they seemed to eat most of their lunch. Now that the boys played baseball, there were fewer arguments except those provoked by Nicholas, Dexter, or Jeffrey. Unfortunately, they still had difficulty playing or cooperating with their classmates.

The visiting math teacher appeared for the first time that afternoon. She happened to arrive during a math lesson. I do not think she agreed with my teaching addition and subtraction so late in the year, but we drilled and worked one written problem daily at the same time that I taught new concepts, including measurements, time, and shapes. I was determined that the class would be able to add and subtract by June. We also worked with money and would eventually set up a store with the children taking turns as the shopkeeper. Since using the book was too difficult (sets, planes, geometric figures, complicated written problems, and detailed directions), I usually made up their drill sheets. Mrs. Matthews was appalled that I was not using the book more. "Why, these sheets aren't difficult at all," she said.

"I would like them to learn basic math before June."

"But what about sets and geometry?" she asked.

"Mrs. Matthews, I am sure several of my children would benefit from your instruction. Would you stay and work with them?" She agreed to stay.

I asked Patricia, who now recognized her numbers, and Dexter, who still could not subtract, to work with her. I told her their difficulties. She nodded and walked over to my students.

Mrs. Matthews was an attractive, well-dressed woman, 40 or so. Her brown hair had been recently set. Her wide blue eyes were heavily made up. She took the children to the front board and gave each a set of counting sticks and a problem that was much too hard for them to solve. When Patricia put chalky fingers on Mrs. Matthews's suit sleeve, the woman immediately pushed her hand away and brushed off her sleeve. Neither answered the problems correctly and still got the wrong answer when Mrs. Matthews explained it again. After ten more minutes of this, Dexter had become belligerent and Patricia was making up her answers.

Finally, Mrs. Matthews took their counting sticks and sent them to their seats. She patted her hair to make certain that it was still in place and walked carefully down the aisle to my group in the back. "I simply cannot work with them. They cannot learn." Her hand fluttered in and out of her purse. She wiped her hands on a handkerchief and straightened her jacket lapels. "That boy is hopeless, simply hopeless."

I nodded at her. "Just what do you suggest that I do?"

"I think that girl is unable to learn. Why, she doesn't even know her basic addition and subtraction."

"Do you have any suggestions?"

"No. Nothing at all. Maybe a few basics." With that, she picked up her supplies and hurried out the door. I knew she was relieved to leave. I was annoyed that she had given up so easily.

As I checked the arithmetic papers, I found that Cecil had done every single one incorrectly. The answers were so wrong that I knew he made them up. I felt certain that he could add and subtract these problems because he had answered similar ones yesterday. "Cecil, you will have to answer 10 problems before leaving today." He ignored my warning.

As Cecil watched his classmates leave at 3:15, he realized that I did want those problems finished. He threw a violent temper tantrum, and when he stopped, I said, "Cecil, you have just 10 problems. Why don't you finish them? I will be glad to help you."

His answer was to beat his head on the desktop and shout, "I ain't going do no fucking math." After 20 minutes and many more curses, he handed me a tear-sodden paper. All 10 were done perfectly.

"Cecil, what an excellent job! You have a perfect paper. I am very proud of your effort." I started to put an A on the top of his paper, but he grabbed the paper out of my hands.

"Don't you give me no A, Mrs. Evans," he growled. "I wants F. I likes F. They means I stupid. Then I don't has to work none."

What an amazing attitude for a nine-year-old boy. He stuffed the paper in his back pocket and squirmed when I said, "Only someone very smart could do all those problems perfectly. Have a pleasant afternoon." His outburst surprised me and made me realize again how very much there was to learn about these children.

I also noticed that many of the children could do a process perfectly one day and completely wrong the next. They could not apply an old process to new concepts, either. They seemed to learn each process separately. I did not know if they did them wrong on purpose—although I suspected Cecil's recent performance was on purpose—if they were too tired to work the problems and so made up the answers, or if they really forgot in a day's time how to do the problems.

That night, I thought of a method that I hoped would help Cecil do his best work every day. I gave him one problem at a time. When he finished, he brought it to me. If it were correct, I praised him, and if he made a mistake, we corrected it together. This extra attention and incentive seemed to give him the reassurance he needed. I used this method with several other students, as well.

February was the month of hearts. I pinned up several on the bulletin boards. The students drew Valentine's Day hearts on their calendars during arithmetic. I had planned a Valentine art project, making different animals from heart shapes, but the lack of supplies ended that idea until Maggie told me about the art teacher. "Sure, just sign up and she will come to your room." Luckily, the sign-up sheet was not filled and Mrs. Washington came the Tuesday before Valentine's Day.

I was delighted that the children would have Valentines after all. "Class, the visiting art teacher will be here today. You will be able to make Valentines." The class was silent. Edward put his head on the desk. Marjorie pouted. They all looked unhappy. I remembered their reaction to making Christmas cards and wondered why the class disliked art.

Soon a large black woman appeared in the doorway, pushing a grocery cart full of construction paper, glue, and scissors. Mrs. Washington loudly inquired, "Is you Mrs. Evans? Does you want your class to make Valentine animals?" I smiled at her and invited her in. Her cherry red sweater fit her tightly and her hair was piled in shiny black curls on the top of her head. I did not have time to tell the children to put their books away before she yelled at them, "Hurry up and clear off your desks! I can only stay an hour. You there, boy, did you hear me? I said put your books away, NOW!" Eric looked startled and upset.

"Okay, now we is going to make some hearts and this is how to do it. Pay attention. If you make a mistake, you can't have no more paper. Hurry up. HURRY UP! Pass out those supplies. Why you so slow, boy?" Jeffrey looked at her with undisguised hostility. I began to have misgivings about the art teacher since I had finally gotten Jeffrey to peer out from his wall, even with an occasional rare smile. His face was closed tight when he sat down. I felt so sorry for him.

"Now you fold the paper like this here." She waved the red paper at the class. "Don't do it while I am talking, you do it when I tell you to. Dear Jesus, you hear me, boy?"

"But I know how to make a heart," protested Eric.

"Well, that don't make no never mind. You stay with me, boy, and do as I say or I'll take the paper away," she sneered at him. Several of the students who did not like Eric laughed.

"Now you pick up your scissors and cut it just like this. You, hey you, dummy! Look up here! Why do you think I'm standing up here? When you're finished, hold up your heart." I could have predicted the ones who would have two halves instead of one heart: Danny, Sandy, Nicholas, Shirley. She was furious. "You stupid idiots. Why don't you listen? I showed you how to do it and then you go and ruin good paper!" She yanked the paper and scissors out of Shirley's hands and flapped the paper in her face.

"Now you all look here. Just look what this stupid black girl's done. Don't that beat all? And with me up here telling you how to do it, you go and do it wrong." Tears appeared in Shirley's eyes. Even louder than before and with less patience, she showed them how to cut another heart. Danny and Nicholas did it wrong again.

"Shit," said Sandy. "I ain't going to make no fucking heart." He crumpled all his paper in his fist and put his head down on the desk. Then she stormed over to Nicholas and beat him on the head with her scissors, calling him a number of names ranging from "dumb black" to "moron." She cut a heart for him. He held that heart for the rest of her stay and made no attempt to cut another one.

The loudness of her voice and the insulting words infuriated me. I could not believe she was allowed to act this way. I started to the door. "Hey, you, Mrs. *ahh*, where is you going? You're not going to leave me alone in here, is you?"

"I am going to the library to pick up several books. I'll be back shortly."

"Well," she said, "I should hope so." I wondered what she thought those completely unhappy and thoroughly intimidated third graders could possibly do to her if I were not there.

As I walked down the hall, I heard her bellowing as she discovered Sandy's wadded up paper. "How dare you, boy. How DARE you ruin a perfectly good piece of paper. Answer me!" I wondered if she was shaking him. I thought of going back to be sure he was all right, but Mrs. Black motioned me into the office.

"Oh, Mrs. Evans, the supplies you asked for, well, you can't have them. There just ain't enough chalk, pencils, magic markers, or paper for the teachers. Also, there ain't no scissors or construction paper of any color." And then she smiled at me. I suddenly wondered why Mrs. Madison always had more than enough supplies, and why Mrs. Dickson always had plenty of art paper for the bulletin boards. I was immediately ashamed of such suspicious thoughts, but upon returning from the library, I watched Mrs. Dickson walk up the steps from the office carrying paper, art supplies, and a fistful of chalk. Later, when I looked in at Mrs. Black, she at least had the decency to turn her back toward me. Perhaps I should have confronted her. Instead, I walked back to the classroom.

The children were quiet, but Mrs. Washington could be heard. "Now look at that! What kind of animal is that? Here, you fix that. Hey you! That's too much glue. You're wasting all that glue. Stop playing with those scissors, boy."

I walked down the aisle to look at the Valentine animals. Most of them were the sorriest creations I have ever seen. Felicia sat at her desk sucking a glue-covered thumb and twisting a pigtail. Her animal was not finished. "Well," Mrs. Washington bellowed at me, "It's about time you got back here. I thought you said you'd only be gone a minute. I must say, your class made the ugliest Valentines I has ever seen. A complete waste of paper and my time!

"Oh, I am already late. Hurry up! Clean off your desks. You there, pick up the glue bottles. And you, the scissors." I was grateful that no glue was spilled. She watched as the children threw away the red paper scraps, grabbing at children whose scraps were too big to throw away and shaking Nicholas when he walked up to the wastebasket because he had not handed in the scissors. "So you trying to steal them, are you? You nigger! Give them to me. What else can you expect?" And then to me or perhaps in her frustration to the world at large, she announced, "And he can't even cut out a heart without cutting it in two, dear Jesus!" We watched in silence as she packed up her cart and lumbered out the door. I thought of the children who were waiting for her arrival and shuddered.

"Children, so your Valentines won't get crushed in your desks, please put your name on the back and let the paper-passers collect them."

Eric raised his hand. "Do we got to keep it?"

"No, Eric. Why?"

"I want to throw it away."

I wondered how Mrs. Washington would feel if she had seen every one of my students stand up, walk to the wastebasket, and with dignity, throw away those Valentine animals.

To improve their mood, we went out to the playground right away. As I watched the baseball game and the jump ropes spinning through the air, I thought about Mrs. Washington's unprofessional behavior. I never signed up for art again. I could not believe that any teacher would act that way. It was apparent that the children despised her, and I didn't blame them.

They were restless and difficult the rest of the day. Cecil had several temper tantrums. Dexter and Nicholas and Jeffrey had two fights. Jeffrey threw his books on the floor in arithmetic, and Felicia refused to stay in her seat. She kept walking down the aisles bothering classmates. Every child spoke back when corrected, "I ain't doing nothing." "Shit, you can't make me." "Hell no, I ain't picking that up." But when I insisted, they slowly complied.

I never mentioned their use of curse words. Perhaps because I didn't mention them, I heard them less and less. Temper tantrums, fights, and moods were common behavior in my classroom. It is impossible to ignore a temper tantrum in a small room filled with an audience of children. Fights broke out continually but they were short-lived. Flaying arms and legs caused several bruised shins. Fights, pouts, and dark moods passed over the children, brought on by the weather, a lost pencil, being called a name, not enough sleep, or too little to eat— or almost anything else.

Unfortunately, moods are rather contagious. It is a very strange feeling to teach arithmetic to a group of children when half of them have their arms folded, their lower lips protruding, and their eyes closed. I could not decide whether to treat these moods seriously with quiet hushed tones or to try to humor them or to continue to ignore them until they passed. I found that sympathy was useless, but humor helped.

Cecil's temper tantrums erupted without warning and he was afflicted with pouting bouts. That day he looked so comical. "Cecil, look in my mirror. You won't recognize yourself." Curiosity overcame him. He opened his eyes and started to chuckle. "Hey man, that's some sight!" The entire class laughed with him.

Teachers often discussed behavior problems. Most disciplinary methods that were followed, Mr. Carter forbade. In faculty meetings, he would say, "There ain't be no paddling, no putting children out in the halls, no putting children in the bathrooms connected to the classrooms." I found that the fastest way to end a discipline problem was to remove the child from the group. The entire class was not disturbed. The child calmed down faster. And I was given a few minutes without the distraction. A quiet talk with the child usually ended the problem for a while. My room was too near the office to put kids in the hall, however, and standing one of the boys in the bathroom was ineffective. The only time I put Nicholas in the bathroom, Tynetta immediately had to use it!

I knew that some teachers put misbehaving children in the storage closet. That idea horrified me. And there was a lot of paddling. With that monstrous yardstick, I was well equipped to paddle them, but the idea of hitting children was foreign to me. I did, when the situation warranted, wave the yardstick around and definitely, the sound of it hitting a desk or wastebasket was frightening.

In the past, I had relied on reasoning with them and if that failed, a quick trip to the principal. Unfortunately, here the trip only removed the irritant for a few minutes. They rarely received lectures. Instead, they sat in the cafetorium unsupervised, and from there, roamed the halls, banging on doors, or went home. Sometimes Mrs. Black favored a child with a few harsh words. Usually they were simply returned to the classrooms.

It was difficult to reason with my students, primarily because it took me a while to figure out the events in school that were important to them and to set up suitable rewards and punishments. It seemed that the majority did not care about good grades or good notes to their mothers. Nor did they mind being kept after school, the method I was using currently. Each time they misbehaved or talked back if corrected, I added five minutes to their stay at 3:15.

They were my guests. Now, I had to think of activities that would make them not want to repeat another stay with me. Of course, I talked with each one individually and they always believed that they could do better, but rarely knew what type of punishment they deserved. Sandy said once, "Mrs. Evans, hurry up and whop me so's I won't be late for my baseball game, okay?"

With a six-hour-and-forty-five-minute day, just having to stay should have been loathsome enough. It wasn't! They did not mind staying with me, and the longer they stayed, the more prestige they had with their classmates the next day. I discussed with each one, usually the same students, what they should do while there. "Sleep?" "Copy spelling words?" "Do math?" "Do homework?" "Read the rules?" were some of the suggestions. Or "I ain't had to write 'I be good.' for a long time?" Daily, I asked them if they learned anything from staying with me. A few realized that if their behavior improved in class, they would not have to stay after school. I pointed that out again and again.

I was more fortunate than Maggie in keeping students after school. She was the only other teacher that used this method. Several of her students' mothers complained. One stormed into her room and screamed that Maggie caused her to have a nervous breakdown because she kept her boy after school. Another mother reported Maggie to the school board. None of my students' moms appeared to notice that their children got home late.

With the same offenders each day after school, it became apparent that another method was necessary to help these students learn self-discipline. I'd heard of teachers making children eat paper, glue, chalk, or soap, or wear signs around their necks, or stand in the corner or closet, to put their noses in a circle on the wall—or even some teachers who taped the students' mouths closed. Others were not allowed to eat lunch. These methods were offensive, and I didn't see how they would help any misbehaving student.

That week ended with an exchange of Valentines. The memory of the abusive art lesson was still fresh in my mind. Only a few of the students brought Valentines and then only to their best friends, rather than to the entire class.

I made a Valentine for each student with sayings that they could read and pictures that reminded me of them. "Look, I got a baseball player on mine," said Cecil.

"What it say?"

"Batter be mine, Valentine!" laughed Cecil. "Ain't that funny?"

"Mrs. Evans, I never had no teacher make me a Valentine. How come you did?" demanded Sandy.

"Oh Sandy, I give Valentines to people I like, and I happen to like all of you."

"Yeah?" growled Jeffrey and then he smiled and his eyes sparkled.

His smile was my Valentine!

CHAPTER 7

There's a Judas Among Us for Sure

THE CHILDREN LINED UP in the hall that morning. Many of them were late on Mondays. Few had lunch money or pencils. It was as if Mondays crept up on them unexpectedly. Bewildered and silent, the girls' hair was still in Sunday's curls, and the boys still wore white Sunday shirts. I greeted them with a cheery "Good morning." Then, noticing Cecil munching on a large dill pickle, I asked, "Cecil, what are you doing?"

"Eating a pickle, Mrs. Evans." It was obvious from the tone of his reply that he thought my question was silly. "I'se hungry," he volunteered to clarify the situation.

Cecil nodded solemnly when I asked, "Is that your breakfast?"

"Yes ma'am," he munched. After Cecil finished his pickle, he joined the others in the morning opening ceremony: reciting a Bible verse, saying a prayer, and the Pledge of Allegiance, and singing "America the Beautiful."

That same morning, Edward complained of a stomachache. "Did you eat breakfast?" He shook his head, no. "What about dinner last night?"

He shook his head again. "No, ain't nothing to eat!" He couldn't remember the last meal he ate. I immediately sent him to the cafetorium with a note, "Please give this boy a carton of milk and some bread. He has not eaten since yesterday." Edward returned too quickly to have eaten anything. "They won't give me none," he said. He buried his tear-streaked face in his hands. I could not believe that the cafetorium women would refuse to feed a hungry boy.

Before I could walk down to the cafetorium, Jack walked up to me quietly and said, "Mrs. Evans, my ma packed me an extra sandwich. Edward can eat it if he wants." Wiping his tear-stained face on his sleeve, Edward accepted the sandwich with dignity and ate it quickly. I knew that there were several others who had not eaten breakfast, and I wondered if it were possible to feed the children some type of breakfast, perhaps a carton of milk and a slice of bread. I decided to ask Mr. Carter if this could be done. I wondered how many naps or fights were caused by hunger.

Later that week, I announced several changes. "There are several important things to talk about this morning. The first is that the pencil-lending business is bankrupt." I wrote the word "bankrupt" on the board. "Does anyone know what that means?"

"Ain't got no money," said Larry.

"Yes, but since I don't lend money, what doesn't the business have?"

"No pencils?" asked Eric.

"That's right! Starting this week, you will have to bring your own pencils. How will you find a pencil to bring, Sandra?"

"Take one from the drawer."

"Felicia?"

"Take money from my ma's purse and go buy me one. I don't like no short chewed pencil. I goin' buy me one new every day."

"I ain't got no pencil money," said Barbara.

"Do you have candy money?"

"Yes ma'am, my ma always give me candy money."

"Why not buy a two-cent pencil with some of your candy money?"

"Aw, ain't get much candy then."

"Class, what is your job right now? Your dad might be a car mechanic. That is his job. What is yours?"

"Go to school," said Sylvia.

"Learn to read," said Curtis, my new student.

"Yes. Very good!" I wrote the word "student" on the board. "You all have a most important job: to be students. You will learn skills in these next few years that most jobs need—reading, arithmetic, writing, responsibility. No one will want to hire you if you forget to bring your tools to work. Can you imagine trying to fix a car engine without tools?"

"Shit, ain't no way you could fix nothing!" said Sandy.

"Well now, your tools are pencils and books."

"Paper too," said Kelvin.

"Also, I do not want any more students walking in late." I looked sternly at Barbara and Nanci. They both giggled.

"What would happen if your mother or father went to work late every day?"

"Nothing," said Jimmy. "He work for a friend."

"You gets in trouble."

"What kind of trouble, Marjorie?"

"You gets yelled at."

"Sometimes, if you're late lots, the boss man fire you!" shouted Jack.

"Yeah man, you is right," said Sandy.

"You wants us to come to school on time 'cause this here's our job?" asked Nanci.

"Yes, that's right."

"That ain't no fun!" pouted Nanci.

For the remaining months, the children brought their own supplies. No longer did fifteen children appear without pencils, and the majority of them tried to be at school on time. I was pleased with the improvement.

My next announcement took them by surprise. "Today, you begin your new reading program."

"I don't know where I go," whispered L'Angela.

"Me neither," lisped Danny.

The children lined up in their different groups. "Remember, everyone will know you are from this room because you are so well behaved. Walk quietly down the hall and listen to your new teacher." The children squirmed in line eager to leave the room.

Soon twelve children in the top reading group waited outside my door. I told them to come in and take seats in the front of the room. Each desk had several reading papers on it. Since Eric and Nanci stayed in the classroom, they were responsible for passing out reading papers, putting up charts, and setting up any equipment we used. They seemed to enjoy these jobs enormously.

Pleased that the new reading program had actually begun, I planned all the different projects that we would do: dictionary usage, writing stories and poems, reading library books as well as third-grade readers, and of course, reading skills. Fortunately, we had third-grade books. I also wanted to use the tape recorder and planned to have several plays. Twelve motivated children would make any activity possible.

After greeting the children and learning their names, I told them about some of the projects they would work on. They were pleased about writing stories and excited about being in a play, but poetry did not win much support. I told them to spend any free time working on projects or reading library books of their choosing. A file box held index cards to keep track of the books read.

This plan delighted Julius, a tousled-haired boy who devoured books, rather than simply reading them. That morning, the group worked on a vocabulary sheet, read one textbook story, and went to the library individually for their first "free time" reading book. As the group worked, each child read to me. Richard, a shy, thin boy with enormous brown eyes, stuttered over the words. Wanda and Theresa had some difficulty with the third grade reader, but the others made few mistakes.

The hour went by very quickly. "It is time to put your books away."

"Aw," said Julius, "Already? That was stimulating."

"I don't want to leave," said Veronica. But they lined up without pushing or shoving. "Goodbye, Mrs. Evans, see you tomorrow." Then they left as quietly as they arrived. It was a novelty to be with children who did not need basic instructions. That was the first time I realized that I taught, actually taught, an entire hour without pouts, temper tantrums, reminding children about behavior, or prodding a student to work. I had to agree with Julius, "How stimulating!"

As my class returned, they read the board for instructions and spelling books appeared. Edward moved the word chart for his group to see. "Class, before you begin, let's talk about this morning. How did you like reading? And changing classrooms? And a new teacher?"

"How come we has to come back so soon?" pouted Felicia. "I was having fun."

"Me too."

"The hour did go by very quickly, didn't it?" I agreed.

"That ain't enough time."

"I like my new teacher," said L'Angela. "She nice."

"I like you best," shouted Jimmy loyally.

"What did you do today?"

"Read a whole story," announced Larry.

"You didn't read no whole story, boy," fussed Marjorie.

"Did so."

"We colored," said Tynetta, "then I worked a puzzle 'cause my work was done."

I sent a note to the third-grade teachers with Tynetta, stating how well the system had worked in my classroom and complimenting each teacher on her well-behaved, hard-working children.

Maggie's class was out on the playground when my students appeared. The boys played baseball with her class and some of the girls chatted in the shade, while others jumped rope.

"I am real pleased with the morning reading. My group behaved well except for two boys from Mrs. LeBlanc's room. They decided to run up and down the aisles. One said Mrs. LeBlanc doesn't care what they do. Can you imagine? I told them, 'Not in my room.'"

"I guess Mrs. LeBlanc is very dissatisfied, but I think the other teachers are happy. My morning was good too."

"Felicia, pick up your coat and put it on the railing."

"Listen," Maggie whispered, "do I have a problem."

"With whom?"

"A little girl, Rosa. I gave her a very low reading grade and her father is furious. Last year, Rosa got As and Bs, but I tested her, and the score was lower than I anticipated. Of course, I kept writing notes to her mother, and when her mother came to school, she insisted on taking a third grade reader home to work with her child. I told her that the reader was too hard, but she refused to take anything else. Now," Maggie said, "I know the parents are going to the school board because their child can't read and they didn't even know there was a problem. Her dad is furious about all those As and Bs Rosa's been getting."

I agreed with her father's point of view. "Wish he could talk to Tynetta's mother."

"Wouldn't that be something!"

"I have a new student, Curtis, very quiet and well-behaved." I pointed a black-haired boy out to her. He was enthralled with the baseball game and had joined the team that was winning. "That makes twenty-seven. You know five have left since September."

"I have had quite a few children enroll and then leave. They don't stay long."

"I wonder why the families move so often. Where have the children gone? Could this be one reason they are so far behind in their learning?"

Maggie shrugged and lined up her class.

As I stood watching the children, I gazed through the wire fence across the dirt road to the small wooden frame houses of The Projects. The majority of my class lived there. The newspaper had recently printed a series of articles on these federal welfare houses because the inspectors found them to be in deplorable condition. The articles stated that rats skittered across the floors, the plumbing was faulty, the electricity sporadic, roofs leaked, and windows were broken.

I looked at the long row of one-room houses that had been built as temporary housing during World War II and realized that adults and children were crammed into those one-room shelters. I remembered Kelvin saying, "Yes, ma'am, this was a real wild weekend. We all got drunk, me too! And then my cousin Zeb got in a fight with Duke, and he got knifed bad. I seen the whole thing. I wished I could be like Zeb. He put on a swell fight."

I waited for the boys to gather all the P.E. equipment and looked at P.S. 123. It was not in much better condition than The Projects—cracked windows, leaky roof, sketchy plumbing, rusted P.E. equipment, scarce or unusable teaching supplies, busted clocks and a dysfunctional P.A. system. These children were receiving a third-rate education.

There was only one man who tried to improve the building conditions at P.S. 123. Missouri, the janitor, arrived before seven in the morning and was still working when I left each afternoon. He was a tall, gaunt man. The bones of his ribs stuck out from his ripped t-shirt and his cheekbones protruded abruptly, leaving his brown eyes sunken. His dark skin had wrinkled and yellowed with age, and a cigarette seem permanently attached to the corner of his mouth. He was industrious and very kind. When a leaky sink or toilet was mentioned, it was fixed before the next day. Even though the school had no extra light bulbs and no money to order more, he would replace classroom bulbs with ones from storage rooms or closets. He returned the softball to my heartbroken students when it landed on the roof and helped us fight an impossible battle against an invasion of red ants.

The children made his work easier by picking up papers from the floor and putting them in the wastebasket each afternoon. I often told them how fortunate we were to have him take such good care of the school building.

When I thanked him, he would look at me, squint his eyes from the cigarette smoke, and say, "This here's my job. That's all." But I think he was pleased. "You know," he said, "I can tell what goes on in a classroom just by sweeping up." He nodded. "Your room always real clean, no papers on the floor and things put away. Some of these here classrooms are just a mess. You wouldn't believe the trash all over. Some of these kids are bad ones, and those teachers can't make them mind no how."

He guessed it was worse in the high schools. He continued to sweep the floor, stopping occasionally to light a cigarette. "Don't you work too hard now," he said as he pushed a day's dirt out into the hall.

That next morning, I saw several more third-grade teachers and asked them how they liked the reading program and what the children thought. "I don't give a damn what the monkeys think. I like it," said Fay.

Hilda and Debby nodded. "It's real good. My children enjoyed it," added Hilda. "I didn't have any discipline problems."

Mrs. Madison came out of her room as we walked down the hall. "Oh yes, I like it very much!"

I saw Mrs. LeBlanc after talking with the others. She did not have one positive word to say. "I don't like it at all. There are too many children, only two less than I teach all day long. And I just can't teach them all. Besides, I don't like such a slow group," she whined. I reminded her about having a teacher's aide help her class for that hour. I know she didn't hear me. "And those others are so bad. My own class is good, but they're just wild in reading." As a farewell salute, Millie LeBlanc said, "You know, I heard that the reading supervisor and the curriculum coordinator are not pleased with this new program. After all, they weren't consulted. I'll bet they put an end to this!" She gave me a thin smile and, looking pleased, walked slowly down the hall.

In reading class that morning, we worked on homonyms. I brought a branch stuck into a flowerpot to make a pear/pair tree. They all hung pear-shaped cutouts with pairs of homonyms on the branches. They also continued reading a story in their books. Toward the end of the hour, we made up several characters and a setting for a class story. The two girls who read more slowly than the others read with me and worked on vocabulary. Julius, by working quickly, began writing his story. "You know, Mrs. Evans," he said confidently, "I am writing the great American novel."

As soon as my own class was seated and working, two handymen barged through the door without knocking. They carried a box of tools and a stepladder. Clanking and banging down the aisle, they set up the ladder in the front of the room. As an afterthought, one of the fellows looked over at me and said, "Hope we ain't disturbing you, lady." I smiled. Collectively we put our pencils down and watched attentively as they took the P.A. system off the wall. "We got orders to fix this here." I never heard the P.A. system used in any of the classrooms and did not know mine was broken. I wished they would replace the broken window panes or patch the leaky roof.

"That was just like a commercial on TV," said Eric. The class enjoyed his joke and reluctantly went back to work.

Each day, one short assignment was written on the board that I did not read to them. Today it said, "Write five words that start with the letter A." I wanted them to realize how important it was to learn to read and to follow directions.

I asked them to show me an example of a word that was unfamiliar to them, by using phrases such as, "Find a window pane or the rung of a chair." I labeled these new words and reviewed them often. I brought in mysterious items for them and asked, "What is this? How does this taste? How does this smell?" Sometimes I hid the mystery item in a brown bag and asked them to identify it by touch. I wondered if it were possible to teach them all that I wanted to by June.

As I returned from lunch, I noticed a sign in the office window: "Faculty Meeting 3:15." I wondered why they didn't have a scheduled day and time, as in other schools, but at least this meeting was announced before I was already late. That afternoon was tiring. Nicholas threw all his work on the floor and refused to finish it. Again, I wrote his mother a note similar to all the other ones: "Please help Nicholas finish his classwork. He was unwilling to do it again today. It is important that Nicholas learn to add and subtract. These are his five new spelling words."

I pinned it to the back of his shirt. It did not help to send work home with him. Notes that I sent home to his mother were never returned, nor had she answered the note I attached to his report card. Meanwhile, Felicia, who had tormented the reading teacher and was sent back to the room early, pouted and sucked her thumb. And Cecil fought with Jeffrey over a tooth-scarred pencil.

"That's mine."

"It ain't."

"I gonna punch you out," shouted Cecil, and he climbed onto his chair waving his fist. Danny sat at his desk and felt for muscles on his thin arms. He bent his arm up like Popeye but no matter how much he strained, he did not find a bulging muscle. Jimmy drew circles on his math paper until I encouraged him to finish and Dexter brooded because he made several mistakes in subtraction that I asked him to correct. Sandra did not feel well and tearfully told me, "Mrs. Evans, I'm going home. I going call my grandma."

"Why, Sandra?"

"I have a fever and a stomachache. Feel how hot my head is."

"Do you want to stay for the afternoon story?" When I said that, she began to cry. Her grandmother came right away.

"Here is Sandra's work. She may feel like doing it at home."

"Yes, she always perks up at home. Her fever goes away and she plays real nice."

"Isn't that interesting."

"Oh yes, she don't stay sick long."

As they left that afternoon, I realized that the day was like many others. I wondered if the children would improve or if they would continue to behave poorly till June. I wanted to keep Cecil after school because he misbehaved all day and scolding him made no impression.

"Cecil, I won't keep you after school today because I have a meeting. Your morning behavior must be better tomorrow or you will lose ten minutes of playtime." He scowled at me ferociously, kicked at his chair, and then darted out of the room. I did not like the idea of taking away playtime, but it did not improve his behavior to keep him after school.

I was not in the mood for a faculty meeting that day. Taking notepad and pencil and my raincoat, I locked the door of the classroom. Felicia had ripped my name off the door, tore the sign into tiny bits, and scattered the pieces all over the hall. I followed the white paper pieces to Mrs. Madison's room.

Mr. Carter was sitting on Mrs. Madison's stool when I went in. He held several papers and looked upset. I sat down in a front desk and waited. Miss Bernardo struggled in with fifteen or more textbooks, plopped down into the chair, and sighed. Most of the teachers looked weary, with chalk dust on fingers or elbows, smudges on chins, and mussed hair. We waited silently. After fifteen minutes when the last teacher straggled in, the meeting began. Mr. Carter cleared his throat, stood up, and said: "This is a special faculty meeting called about a real important matter. Someone has written a letter about me and P.S. 123 and sent it to the newspaper."

Gasps from the teachers—I was not surprised. The letter had taken more than three weeks to appear.

"I won't have such sneaky goings on and it has to be one of you who done it. It couldn't be a parent 'cause the letter know too much. The newspaper man called me to ask if these here things were true. Said he received this here letter and was checking up on it." The room was silent. He continued, "This here letter complained about the leaking roof and the broken windows. Now there ain't nothing can be done about that. And the clocks that don't run. You know that I said they'd be set when we get on some kind of schedule. And this person," he sneered when he said that, "also mentioned a photocopier that ain't being used."

"Why, I use it every day," drawled one of the fifth-grade teachers.

"No, this here one is the one in the teachers' room upstairs."

"What one is that?" asked the same teacher.

"So it has to be a teacher who wrote this here letter. No parent would've knowed about that."

"Ahh," the teachers rustled in their seats and whispered.

"It's the one we talked about that day, right Mrs. Evans?"

"Yes," I said.

He leaned over and watched me closely. "Now, if one of you girls here know how to work that thing, you can show me 'cause I don't know how." He looked at me again, but I said nothing.

"This here traitor, yes, traitor, mentioned the noise in the cafetorium. Well now, that ain't my fault neither. That is the fault of the cafetorium committee who's in charge of the cafetorium. Complaints of too much noise and running around and such—that is your fault. That has to stop. So, you girls better think of something to do about it, hear?" He got off the stool and paced back and forth. "We got us a Judas in our midst. Yes, that's it! One of you girls is getting us all in trouble. You know that any problems in the school are all your fault. Not mine. Well, you just look around. There's a Judas among us for sure."

Uncomfortably, the faculty stared at each other and looked back at Mr. Carter. "You know teachers aren't liked in this here community. Ain't you heard of them radical groups? They might snatch you right out of the classroom if they don't like what you is doing. You got to be real careful what you say and do. They might come after you, specially this here Judas. Why, if they knew about this, they get her for sure.

"Now, one of your own kind is trying to get you in trouble. I wants to know who it is and I has ways of finding out. But I'm telling you this, jobs are hard to get, and you needs my recommendation to get another job. I has a letter from that teacher who quit at Christmas. She want one. I'll show her, quitting like that, I'll write her one that keeps her from getting another teaching job. You remember that! I can have your job any time I wants, but you don't say nothing about me and I don't say nothing about you." He grimaced angrily, shouted the last few sentences, and pounded on the desktop.

"If you got any complaints, you bring them to me. You know I always gets things done. You don't go to the school board." He glared at Mrs. Potter. "And you don't go to the newspapers. Keep it in the family. I hope this here Judas has learned her lesson, and don't forget, you're the ones to suffer. This here letter ain't going to do nothing but bring trouble." With that he turned and left the room. I knew that he would try to find the "Judas" as he promised. I believed that he was a vengeful man.

As we left P.S. 123 that day, Maggie said, "Who could have written that letter?"

"I—"

"I am really surprised that anyone cared enough to write it," Maggie interrupted. "Most teachers here don't give a damn. Wonder why she didn't comment on the discipline problems?

Seems like she just went on about the clocks and the leaky roof."

"I agree. But maybe they were discussed."

"What do you mean?"

"Well, according to the way Mr. Carter put it, the reporter asked the questions. He had the letter and read it to him."

"Gee, yeah. Do you think the newspaper will print it?" Maggie shook her head as she asked the question.

"Why not?" I asked.

"Mr. Carter probably answered all his questions. You heard him in the meeting. None of this is his fault. Nothing he could do about it. And P.S. 123 is a black school run by a white school board in a white community."

"So?" I knew if my letter had reached the *Washington Star* or the *Washington Post* about a school in Montgomery County, Maryland, it would be on the front page with repercussions reverberating throughout local government.

"I just don't think a white paper would print it. Besides, one school board official works at the newspaper. It would make the school board look ineffective."

A feeling of futility swept over me. I knew writing or meeting with the school board hadn't changed anything. Mrs. Potter tried that. Now I wondered if my letter would accomplish anything.

To my surprise, a few changes appeared the next day. The first thing I noticed was the hall clocks. Each was set correctly. Another P.E. schedule was in my mailbox. 10:15 to 10:30 was my new time. Even the cafetorium was altered somewhat, as the tables were arranged in rows with eight children at a table instead of four. Each section was marked for the class. As I ate my lunch that day with Hilda and Fay, Mr. Carter walked in. It was the first time I ever saw him there during lunch hour. He looked uncomfortable, turning his head back and forth, his hands thrust deep into his pockets. He wandered around the tables, shooed some boys out of the doorway—they returned as soon as he moved away—and then he walked toward us. He looked at us and said, "Girls, from now on you got to eat with your students. Not at a separate table."

"Mr. Carter, my class is not misbehaving. They know I am watching them."

"It don't matter. Everyone gots to eat with their students. You too, Mrs. Evans. You set an example for them," and he walked away.

I enjoyed having time to talk to the other teachers, to eat my lunch without the children interrupting. Hilda said, "Do you know most professions have a lunch hour?"

"Yes, teaching hasn't reached the twentieth century. Do you believe we have to eat with those damn monsters?" demanded Fay. "I'm just going to quit."

After lunch that day, I told the class, "I will be eating lunch with you tomorrow."

"You gonna sit at my table?" asked Felicia.

"No, she going sit at my table. Ain't you, Mrs. Evans?" demanded Cecil.

"I will sit at a different table every day. Now then, do you remember the rules for the cafetorium game?"

"Aw, the girls always win," pouted Kelvin.

"That 'cause you is bad," said Nanci.

"Nanci, be kind. Tomorrow there will be no talking at all. There has been too much noise in the cafetorium recently and even though you are better behaved than most classes, some of you forget about our rules and shout. When you have finished eating, you will sit quietly."

Cecil rolled his eyes at me. "Mrs. Evans, what if we wants to trade food or something?"

"You can do it quietly." After a few days of no-talk dining, I planned to let them practice speaking quietly again.

As the weather warmed up, I wanted to eat outside with the class under the lone playground tree and read a story to them after lunch. Unfortunately, that idea did not win Mr. Carter's necessary approval. "No, Mrs. Evans, you just can't do that."

"Why?"

"Well now, I don't know why but you can't, and that there is my final decision."

That afternoon in our talk session, I said, "Pretend that you have a car that needs to be fixed."

"What color is it, Mrs. Evans?"

I laughed. "It's your imaginary car. Shut your eyes and think of any car you want to own and remember that it won't run." When they looked ready, I said, "Who would you take your car to—a friend who wasn't very good at fixing cars, was really lazy, and would not have the car fixed by the weekend? Or a good mechanic who would fix your car quickly?" This was one talk session that taught me more than the class learned. I wanted them to think about having a reputation for doing a good job and about the importance of repairing possessions. The entire class vowed adamantly that they would take their car to their friend. I asked them how they would feel if their friend broke the car so that it could never be used.

"Damn," said Sandy, "I'd get myself good and drunk."

Cecil agreed. "Just 'cause he ain't no mechanic, he still my friend."

Eric looked troubled by this logic, but I think he was unwilling to venture an opinion.

CHAPTER 8

The Beginning of Wisdom

WEDNESDAY INCLUDED three of Cecil's temper tantrums. The last time, I took that large yardstick and slammed it down on his desk. He was startled enough to stop yelling and kicking. Nicholas did not do any of the schoolwork and spent much of his time either trying to climb up the wall while seated in his desk chair or sitting backwards in his chair and rolling his pencil along the floor. Again, I wrote a note, asking his mother to come in for a conference; it was the end of February and I still had not seen her! Felicia and Marjorie had a hair-pulling fight in the bathroom. Luckily, I rescued Felicia before she was pushed head-first into the toilet. They never went to the bathroom at the same time again after that incident. Jeffrey sulked the entire day. He had arrived in that unreachable mood and remained oblivious to his surroundings.

Despite the tantrums and sulking, some of the children were improving in their classwork, and gaining more self-confidence and self-control. Dexter was able to do first-grade subtraction such as 4 − 2 = 2. Eric no longer whined when he was corrected and now was reading fourth grade books. Sharon and L'Angela were completing all their classwork. Larry and Billy were making fewer careless mistakes. I could not tell if these changes were due to my efforts or theirs. I hoped they would all be able to read at grade level and do third-grade arithmetic by June. But less than four months remained.

I was concerned with several of my students' behavior. I had not been able to curb the frequency of their outbursts, nor had I found effective rewards or punishments. Cecil, Dexter, Kelvin, Jeffrey, Nicholas, Felicia, and Marjorie had not noticeably improved. Jimmy, Danny, Barbara, and Nanci continually irritated their classmates, and a third group of children—Sandy, Sandra, Edward, and Jack—were unhappy with themselves and with school in general. The remainder of my class was made up of students who were usually well behaved and tried to do the classwork. I continually thought of new ways to meet these behavioral problems and to encourage learning, but there were days when I went home discouraged with the teaching situation and distressed by the ongoing problems at P.S. 123.

When I spoke to Mr. Carter about milk and bread for several of my students in the morning, he was not pleased with the idea. "Well now, we just can't afford to do that. What if all the other teachers decided to do it? No, I just can't allow you to do that." He openly disliked me and seemed to enjoy thwarting any or all of my requests. Did he suspect I had written the letter to the newspaper?

I mentioned Edward feeling sick from hunger and asked if federal funds could cover this extra food. He looked skeptical and finally said, "I guess those children might have some milk if they can't work—because they is so hungry—but don't you send too many."

When I told one of the workers that several of the boys from my class would come to the cafetorium in the morning, she was obviously annoyed and glared at me. "Send them in here. Make all that mess. More work for us," she muttered.

I said, "You know Edward was very hungry when I sent him to you the other morning. And he returned to me in tears."

"Well, that too bad!" she said and turned her bulky body away from me.

That next day, I sent several boys with Edward for milk. Since they wore a milk moustache when they returned, I knew they had some breakfast. I think they were more attentive that morning.

I followed the new playtime schedule and took them out at 10:15, which was only fifteen minutes after they had returned from reading and certainly very poorly timed for us. It went very badly. The children were unable to concentrate that hour and a half before lunch, having already been outside. They were used to finishing all their work, playing, and then eating. Now there was no incentive to get their work done, since they had already been outside. No one was out on the playground when we usually went out, so I considered asking Mr. Carter if I could change. Since he had told us all that there was no playtime, I was concerned about him withdrawing all playtime. I decided to switch again with the teacher who had our regular time.

P.E. and music were changed to 1:45. I was pleased with this time, as it broke the afternoon work hours in half. Eating with the class at lunch was tiring, and several ended up eating on chairs against the wall with their trays on their laps. Jack and Nicholas would spend many lunches there. Of course, it was difficult for me to speak to the children while I was eating. But watching Felicia suck on her food and then wipe her fingers on one of her pigtails, or Cecil eating Jell-o with his fingers, or Dexter pouring an inch of salt over his food, definitely dampened my appetite. I realized that I was with the children continuously each day from 8:30 to 3:15, with a 20 minute break at 1:45. My teaching day was longer than ever before.

The uproar in the cafetorium was somewhat under control.

Unfortunately, the classes responsible for the most noise before made just as much noise with their teachers sitting with them. Fay Morris's and Millie LeBlanc's classes were the worst. Fay Morris's students still ran around the tables, threw food, and started fights. One of Mrs. LeBlanc's boys almost ran over Angela while he chased a friend around a table. I recognized Steve since I taught him reading. He was well mannered and hard working. When I grabbed him by the shoulders, he struggled and then looked up. He was quite surprised to find not Mrs. LeBlanc, but me. He looked embarrassed. "Sorry, Mrs. Evans," he muttered. After twenty minutes in the cafetorium, I was relieved to return to the classroom.

I read them all a story. Next I asked the children to write a class story. It was about a cow named Mrs. Evans. "Once there was a cow named Mrs. Evans." The entire class giggled. "She always wore a green hat in the sun and big sunglasses." The story was interesting. The cow could fly, she lost her green hat, and she had a boyfriend—in approximately that order.

Apparently, the letter to the newspaper made some impression on Ozell Lewis, the P.E. instructor. That afternoon during scheduled P.E., the children exercised and played several indoor games instead of sitting at their desks. But not much of an impression—it was a beautiful day, and I wondered why he did not go outside?

I felt exhausted during my 20-minute break. Although I planned to find several books in the library for the reading group, I decided to do that after school. So I propped my feet up on the table in the teachers' lounge and closed my eyes. The hum of the Coke machine was oddly soothing.

Mrs. Madison shared the time with my class. Her students were in music. I wondered if her arthritic condition were worse. Just walking down the hall with her class and then getting a Coke had left her breathless, with beads of sweat on her forehead. She was always pleasant. She never mentioned classwork and looked uncomfortable when I said, "I wonder if these changes were due to that letter."

"Oh, I don't know," she said and changed the topic to the weather.

For the next few days, Mr. Carter patrolled the cafetorium at lunchtime. He did not stay long, but he did put in an appearance. There was slightly less noise. Several of my students learned to use spoons and napkins, but Felicia still sucked on her food and refused to use those implements. Three tables won the cafetorium game that week and were very proud of their colorful tablecloths and enjoyed their extra desserts.

As I continued to eat with the children, I noticed that they always ate the starchy foods on their trays first. Each lunch had white bread, noodles, corn or spaghetti, potatoes, sometimes a small piece of meat, milk, and dessert of Jell-o, fruit, or ice cream. The vegetables were rarely eaten and always overcooked, and at least half of my students did not eat the meat. Edward never ate the Jell-o. Sandra and Sylvia always bought the lunches and drank the milk but did not eat the rest. Dexter never ate the meat or vegetables, but finished off any extra rice, potatoes, or noodles. I allowed trading toward the end of the lunch period when it became apparent that some students did not intend to finish their meals.

When I asked Sandra and Sylvia why they didn't eat their lunch, they chorused, "I don't like it."

"Perhaps you should ask your mothers to pack you each a lunch."

"She don't want to bother," said Sylvia.

Watching these poor eating habits, I decided that at least one bite should be eaten of each food on the tray. In this way, Edward found out he liked Jell-o as much as ice cream. He had never had it before. With this new rule, most of them ate a bite or two of the meat and vegetables.

To encourage the class to try everything on their tray, I made up a story about a little boy named Samuel, who was lost and very hungry. He wandered along until he found a small house in the woods. The kind old people who lived there invited him to stay for dinner. Samuel had never seen the food that was on his plate. It was purple and blue and gray and it smelled strange. His stomach rumbled.

I went into great detail about how hungry Samuel was and how strange the food looked. "Well, class, what should he do?"

"Hold his nose and eat it," suggested Jimmy.

"Yeah, he better eat that food!"

Whenever I noticed that something had not been tasted, I reminded them about Samuel. Their reaction was immediate. I wished they'd grasp phonics or subtraction as quickly.

After the letter to the newspaper, more small improvements emerged. The clocks did keep the correct time, and faculty meetings were announced. For a while, parents did not appear during school hours, and children had organized P.E. with Ozell Lewis. Unfortunately, the letter only accomplished minor things. The major problems remained. Discipline troubles increased. It was common to hear stories of knife fights, tantrums, or thefts, or to hear children say, "Don't you fuck with me. I go get me a shotgun!" or "No whitie goin' make me do nothing. I do like I want."

Tension due to racial prejudice increased in many classrooms. Teachers stared suspiciously at each other and remained silent. They were painfully aware that someone was a Judas. No one asked me if I wrote the letter.

The lack of supplies and the depressing condition of the school building also lowered teacher morale. Many of these situations would have improved with help from Mr. Carter. However, it became difficult to find him. He no longer appeared in the cafetorium, nor did he conduct Monday faculty meetings. Each time I entered the office, his door was closed but the light and radio were on and, according to Mrs. Black, "He too busy to talk to you," or, "He out now but he be back," or, "He somewhere in the building, but I don't know where," and then she would lean against the counter and stare at me.

On Wednesday, I escorted Cecil to the office. A series of outbursts had wearied me, and when he continued to talk back, I knew it was time to remove him from class. Mrs. Black eyed Cecil and then me. I said, "He is misbehaving, Mrs. Black, and I would like Mr. Carter to talk with him."

"Well, he can't right now. He ain't in right now."

"That's just fine." I helped Cecil sit down. "He will be glad to wait." Cecil glowered at me, and I thought how pleasant it would be to spend a few minutes without him in the classroom.

"Well, he can't do that."

"Why not?"

"Well, Mr. Carter ain't here."

"Yes, I know. You told me that."

"He ain't going to be here, neither," she blurted. She didn't look pleased with the idea of Cecil keeping her company. I looked at her. "He out of town and won't be here all week," she finally said.

"I see. Cecil, you may return to the room as soon as you feel that you have improved your self-control," I told him and then hurried out of the office.

As I walked down the hall, I heard Mrs. Black say, "Hey, you can't leave him here."

Apparently Mr. Carter left without telling any of the teachers and without placing someone else in charge. Mrs. Black was trying very hard to conceal the fact that he was gone, but I wondered why his absence was so mysterious.

When I saw Hilda, Debby, and Maggie during the day, I told them the news. They were as surprised as I was. I realized that one of them would tell Fay Morris, and then the whole school would know.

An emergency meeting was called by Mrs. Miller, the curriculum coordinator, that afternoon to tell any of the teachers who Fay might have inadvertently missed. "Mr. Carter is away and will be gone this week." Mrs. Miller appeared pleased with her new position of authority. She patted her hair and smiled. "Don't send children to the office. You will have to handle your own discipline problems. If you can't handle your own discipline problems, then you shouldn't be no classroom teacher. Understand?" Since that was the only reason for calling the meeting, it ended early.

Maggie talked to Mrs. Miller after the meeting to tell her about the great success we were having with "her" reading program. "You know this is an important experiment and it was your idea. You told us to 'get together.' Why, I'll bet you get credit for being first with this new reading development in the county!" Maggie and I had discussed this approach after I suggested telling Mrs. Miller she was responsible. I stood at the door and watched. Mrs. Miller looked very pleased.

"My, yes," she said. "I want all you teachers to write down everything so I can present my new reading program to the school board. You see they get that done, hear?"

Maggie nodded.

This was a difficult week. Cecil was uncontrollable. His eruptions had increased. He lost all his playtime and made a joke of it. But it made little difference if he lost playtime, stayed after school, or sat in the back of the room. With Mr. Carter gone, I tried putting his desk outside the open door in the hall, but moving him into the hall made no difference, either.

"How come Cecil getting away with being bad?" asked L'Angela. Several boys joined Cecil with their versions of sulking, fighting, and pouting, and five of them did not have playtime that morning, which sobered all but Cecil. He continued to pout, would not talk about his behavior, and spent his time thinking up new tricks for entertaining his classmates that afternoon. After throwing food at lunch and then grabbing Jimmy's hamburger, Cecil ended up sitting against the cafetorium wall.

I think his classmates thought he was a hero. They "*ahh-ed*" and "*ohh-ed*" each time he did something that was not allowed. That afternoon Cecil had two more temper tantrums—one over a pencil stub and the other over an arithmetic paper. "You may do that paper at home, Cecil." He was so surprised that he threw all his work and books on the floor. "Would you like to wash off your face in the boys' room?" I said, hoping that the break would calm him down. Then I walked to the back of the room and continued with a small group of children drilling arithmetic facts. They used the old yardstick to point to the right answers. Sandy handed it back to me when Cecil ran up the aisle, shoved Nanci, knocked her books on the floor, and rushed to the door. "Cecil, pick up Nanci's books before you leave." He kicked the door, opened it, and, from the outside, slammed it as hard as he could.

I followed him outside the classroom, caught him by the arm, and, still holding the yardstick, I broke it with one swing over his bottom. He was as surprised as I was. Only after he returned to the classroom and his seat did he yell. "I gonna tell my ma. You ain't got no right to paddle me."

"That's enough, Cecil." He sobbed and put his head down on the desk. That yardstick was stern proof to the students that I was serious. I put the two pieces on the chalk tray and walked back to the math group. The class was silent for the remainder of the afternoon.

"Cecil, pick up the papers and books around your desk, please." He did so without looking at me and sat without further incident until 3:15. The others lined up and walked out the door, looking back at Cecil as they went. "Cecil," he stuck his head in his desk. "Cecil, look at me." I could see images of other teachers hitting their students with rulers and paddles and remembered how I disapproved of their actions. Cecil's face was still tear-streaked when he looked at me.

"Cecil, you cannot continue to misbehave." He glowered and stuck out his lower lip. "Remember how you promised in January to be the best there is?"

"Yeah, in baseball," he mumbled.

"Not just baseball, Cecil, in behavior and in lessons. You must do your very best."

"You took my playtime, so I ain't team captain today."

"No, Cecil, you took away your own playtime. Do you remember why?"

"Ain't doing nothing."

"What about your fight with Jeffrey?"

"He started it. He took my pencil."

"Grabbing Jimmy's food?"

"He don't want none."

"Yelling and running in the halls? Pushing the girls? Fighting with Nanci? Not doing your work?" I sighed. "Cecil, think about your behavior and tell me if you honestly were being the best you could be."

"I ain't doing nothing!"

"Cecil!"

He sighed too. I think he was tired.

"I guess I'll be better, but do I have playtime tomorrow?" he asked sorrowfully.

"Yes, you do, but you must earn your playtime. I will take five minutes off each time you are not doing your best. That means six reminders in one day, and you won't have any play-time left. You know, Cecil, your classmates like you very much. They like to have you play with them." He picked up his coat and walked slowly toward the door. "Good afternoon, Cecil."

He turned and looked at me. "Mrs. Evans?"

"Yes, Cecil."

"You sure hit good for a girl."

I did not know whether to laugh or weep. I was not pleased with my actions that afternoon and was horrified that I paddled a child. How could I abandon reason, even if his behavior were uncontrollable? I was no different than all those teachers I so smugly criticized! I wondered how this would affect Cecil's behavior. I even briefly thought about those "radical groups" that Mr. Carter always warned us about.

Maggie knew from the paleness of my face that something had happened that afternoon. "Say, what's wrong?"

I blurted, "I paddled Cecil."

She laughed with relief. "Oh, I thought it was something serious. Don't worry about it. His behavior is atrocious. Besides, maybe it did him some good." She tried to reassure me, but I knew I should have handled the situation differently.

That next morning after the children returned from reading, we had a discussion on "What makes me mad."

"My little brother," said Jack. "He constantly follow me."

"I got to take care of the baby and never play," said Barbara.

"Losing my spending money," said Marjorie.

"Ripping my new kite," said Larry.

"Being called names," said Nanci. "How about you, Mrs. Evans?"

"Students who lack self-control and disturb the class make me angry—especially when they talk back." They all looked at Cecil. He grinned widely. The rest of the class grinned too.

While they were doing their morning spelling, sentence writing, and penmanship, I realized that they were quieter than they had been all week. Cecil had both a pencil and paper. "Do I got playtime?"

"Yes, Cecil. You are doing very well." He looked pleased. I hoped that Cecil's behavior would improve after this confrontation. I never planned to use that form of punishment again.

I was thankful that it was Friday. Fay Morris saw me waiting in the hall for Nicholas to return from the bathroom and said, "TGIF. You know, 'Thank God It's Friday.'" She led her class upstairs to the film room. I wondered how she could stand all the noise the children made, but she mentioned once that they were quieter in the halls. I began to suspect that she wore earplugs. That afternoon after the students were gone, I finished checking all their papers. Cecil had completed all his assignments except spelling. I made several work dittos to use that next week and then, clearing my desk, I met Maggie in the hall.

"No work?" she asked upon seeing my empty arms.

"No, I need a complete rest. No schoolwork this weekend."

"How was Cecil?"

"Believe it or not, he was the best behaved he has ever been!"

She nodded. "I'll bet that was something he could understand."

As we rounded the corner, Mrs. Dickson was leaving the office. "Good night, girls," she said and smiled. I wished her a pleasant weekend, but Maggie didn't say anything at all. We pushed against the heavy double doors. Spring was in the air that afternoon. Maggie shuddered. I looked at her and knew she was still thinking about Mrs. Dickson.

"She reminds me of a snake. I just never know when she will bite." After that note incident, she terrified me.

As I walked past Mrs. Dickson's station wagon to Maggie's car, I noticed her new bumper sticker: "The Fear of God Is the Beginning of Wisdom." Remembering the way Mrs. Dickson pounced on me, I looked at the bumper sticker thoughtfully. She seemed to be giving fair warning.

The heavy white curtains were drawn, the dim room quiet. The floor was hard and cool. My head was on the rug, my legs touching the wall. I closed my eyes wearily. The complete silence was comforting, restoring. The room whirled in my mind and changed into the room at P.S. 123. I never seemed to be able to leave that school. It followed me everywhere, even chasing me in my dreams.

I tried to list objectively the accomplishments of the last two months: shy L'Angela would run up and talk to me and to her classmates. Dexter no longer disrupted the class. Jeffrey smiled and appeared more relaxed, but he still did not play well with his classmates, although he did have a friend now. Edward had milk for breakfast and fewer headaches. The reading program was a success in spite of Mrs. LeBlanc. Other plusses: my students did not have to suffer through any more art classes and they played outside every day—and even had some equipment.

My legs began to tingle. I stretched but did not open my eyes. I tried vainly to think of anything else and could not. I wondered at my impatience. Most of the students were doing their work. Fortunately, reducing playground minutes was more effective than keeping them after school because Mr. Carter put an end to that practice. I sighed as I remembered that, according to county rules, third grade students couldn't be kept more than 15 minutes after school, and that was after two months of my keeping them up to 30 minutes. Maggie's complaining mothers had won.

I fidgeted and tried to keep my mind from Mr. Carter. I felt his hostility when he sneered, "I can have your job." His mouth formed the words, "Your prejudice is the reason for all of these here problems. We gots us a Judas!"

I heard the sound of the old yardstick breaking and later, Cecil yelling. Uncomfortable, I pushed that image away too and drifted awhile. I fell asleep and dreamed. The office walls slanted peculiarly. From the back of a long line of teachers, I watched Mrs. Black hand out supplies: mountains of paper, stacks of chalk, cartons of toilet paper and paper towels, boxes and boxes of art supplies. The line moved forward, but I never got closer to the counter. I watched the other teachers stagger out of the office with more supplies than they could possibly use in a year's time. At last, I was the only one left, but there were no more supplies and Mrs. Black turned away, her broad back covered with blue cotton flowers.

I woke stiff, changed my position, and closed my eyes again. Random faces and sounds engulfed me, as they had before—the lingering hatred in Jeffrey's eyes, deep and hard; Larry's round face dotted with freckles staring at the film; L'Angela's braids and bows bouncing as she jumped rope longer than anyone else; Nicholas snarling, biting, and kicking the desk; Barbara proud of a new dress, her face scrubbed clean; Nanci the spinner of tales, late again. "Call Nanci, Mrs. Evans, she bothering me." Then there were Eric and Billy racing across the school yard, tumbling and falling into a ball of arms and legs; "God damn, oops sorry, Evans," said Sandy; Dexter's happy face when he finished ten subtraction problems correctly.

I pushed away the distress of seeing teachers scream and hit students and my paddling Cecil, the sneering looks of the teachers' aide Nadette, and the glares of Mrs. Dickson. I refused to acknowledge the hissed words, "Judas, Judas, Judas." But then the phrase, as if taped, "Welcome. Welcome to P.S. 123" wound on a circuit through my thoughts. I was not welcome. I was there to teach these children. Nothing else mattered.

CHAPTER 9

March, 1970

B EFORE SCHOOL STARTED THAT MORNING, I asked Mr. Carter for a recommendation. My husband's flight training was ending. He would be transferred to his next duty station in August, and I wanted to apply early. He agreed to write one for me.

That day, the March wind blew huge puffy clouds across a bright blue sky, the sunshine was warmer, trash swirled around the playground, and Billy's kite was a success.

I thought about leaving P.S. 123 as I watched my class. Cecil was very attentive and helpful. He wanted my approval and even told several of the boys who began pushing in line, "Hey, cool it, man! You knows you ain't supposed to do that." That day, Nicholas did not do his work, which was not unusual, but he did not pester his classmates—that was unusual. Several of the students were absent. I knew they were sick.

For the first time since arriving at this school, my teaching day was relaxed and pleasant. I fervently prayed there would be more days like this ahead. It had taken longer to win their trust and cooperation than I expected.

That afternoon, a faculty meeting was announced over the loudspeaker in those rooms with a P.A. system. The workmen never returned mine. "Mr. Carter used it for the first time and damn near scared me silly," said Fay. "It was so garbled that I had to ask Debby what he said."

Maggie alerted me to the meeting.

I arrived early since there were no students to talk to about behavior. I sat in the back. Ozell Lewis lumbered in and settled beside me. He looked so uncomfortable squeezed into a third-grade desk. Maggie came in and sat behind me. "I brought a stack of papers to check. That's the only way I can keep from being upset. I decided not to listen anymore. So you will have to tell me if anything important is discussed." I smiled and nodded. I had already decided not to let anything that was said disturb me. As usual, the meeting began late. Mr. Carter did not mention being absent last week, nor did he expect anyone to ask about it. No one did. He looked dapper today, wearing a white turtleneck instead of a shirt and tie.

We waded through his discussion of missing behavioral objectives and the reading of the teachers' names, plus a short but typical argument with Ozell. Then Mr. Carter demanded the 98-01 federal forms for free lunch, which none of the teachers had done.

"These here green sheets are important. I gots to have them from every teacher from September. You hear? Ain't none of you done this. I am tired of your lack of responsibility. You get these here federal forms in by Monday."

"Mr. Carter, I don't know who is 98-01 and who isn't," gulped Miss Bernardo.

"You what?" shouted Mr. Carter.

"I, well, I . . ." She violently twisted a sheet of paper she held in her hands.

"How many of you know who qualify for federal lunch and who don't?" No one raised her hand. He looked bewildered.

"Mr. Carter," queried another teacher, "what about the free lunchers? Do they go on this sheet too?"

"No, no!" He sounded exasperated. "Let me explain this here 98-01 federal form again." If he had discussed the form sometime in the months before I arrived, I could not tell it from the looks on the faces of the teachers.

The following week, a list of 98-01 students was sent to each teacher. To my surprise, several of my students who brought their lunch money regularly were on the list: Billy, Jeffrey, and Cecil. They did not know that their lunch was paid by federal funds. Edward's sister was a 98-01 student, but Edward was not. The same peculiar situation existed between Felicia and her brother, Cedric. Also, there were several students who could not afford lunch, but were not 98-01 students. They did receive free lunch, although I did not know who paid for it. I wondered how to have a child listed for free federal lunches. The green forms were difficult to find and rarely available in the office.

"I will need five, please."

"Five? You gets one."

"This must be done from September to now."

"I don't know about that. Mr. Carter says you get one." So in the month of March, forms were filled out for children who qualified for 98-01 free lunches. The 98-01 federal forms were not available the following months, so no further records were kept that year.

At the next faculty meeting, Mr. Carter continued with his agenda. He stuck his hands in his pockets and jingled some coins. "Now, about these here discipline problems. Don't send them to me. You got to learn to handle your own problems yourself. I ain't going to take the time from my busy schedule to see these here students. After all, the principal has many important duties."

I looked at Hilda's tired face and thought of her difficulty with a large thirteen-year-old student in her third-grade class who tried to stab a classmate with his knife. She had sent for Mr. Carter to come right away, and he sent back a message saying that he was too busy. Mrs. Black had finally come down to help her.

She told us, "You know what Mr. Carter was doing? He was sitting behind his desk working on some papers when I finally dragged Leroy in there. I could not believe it. Then he talked to him a few minutes, told him to be good, and sent him back to my class. What about calling the police?"

I was grateful that I did not teach Leroy. The child had been tested in September for special education, but no effort was made to have him placed in a special class even though the necessary forms were filed. And so, he remained in Hilda's class until April when his parents moved.

Then I thought about Mrs. Potter, a petite redhead whose students threw desks at her, cursed, and threatened classmates with knives. Mr. Carter's voice cut into my thoughts, "After all, I can't have my time taken up by problems you should handle, you understand?"

Having addressed that point, Mr. Carter sat down on the stool and announced: "Now, a man from the University of Mississippi, Dr. Holstein, is going to visit us and he wants to speak with you teachers."

I nudged Maggie. "Listen to this," I whispered.

"He might even visit your classroom. He is an authority in disadvantaged education and a special friend of mine, so I invited him to come, and I wants you to cooperate with him, you understand? I don't want none of you to be impolite." Just then, Mrs. Potter got up and left. Her husband came for her at

4:00 and she never kept him waiting. We all watched her leave and I wished I could leave with her, but the meeting did not continue much longer.

On the way home, I said, "Well, what do you think about that man, Dr. Holstein?"

"I don't know, but I wonder why he is coming. Do you think the school board sent him?"

Maggie lowered her voice and said conspiratorially, "Say, I wonder if that man is a spy and will report to the school board, or if he is planted by Mr. Carter to try to learn exactly what the teachers are thinking?" She giggled nervously.

"That sounds a bit melodramatic, doesn't it?" I asked.

Two days later, Dr. Holstein arrived with Dr. Kemp, the Assistant Superintendent of Schools. Mrs. Dickson appeared at my door. "Mrs. Evans, I will stay with your class while you talk to Dr. Holstein. He is upstairs in Mrs. Miller's office."

"Oh, the children are to be in music in five minutes. If you like, I will come then."

"Well, you have to talk to him, you know," and she slammed the door.

He was sitting with his back against the window. The light made it difficult to see him but he was a slight black man, with thinning hair and a deep voice. Long, slender fingers played with a pen. Hilda and Ann Potter were already sitting there. I wondered why this particular group had been selected. "Come in. Come in. You are Mrs. . . . ?"

"Evans," I said.

"Yes, well now, what do you think about teaching at P.S. 123?"

Both Hilda and Ann Potter chimed, "Oh, it is just fine. No real problems. Everything is fine." They nodded and smiled. He looked at me.

"Dr. Holstein, who is this information going to?"

"Well, well. This is a confidential discussion. No one will know who said what. The county is concerned. All the teachers are being talked to and it is important to solve P.S. 123's problems. You must tell me everything possible." He seemed very sincere. Then he asked me, "Mrs. Evans, how do you like being a teacher here?"

Hilda and Ann gasped when I answered bluntly, "I don't teach. The moments of real teaching are rare."

His pleasant expression changed to one of dismay, as I told him the problems I encountered on a daily basis. Without hesitation, I went through the entire list of my concerns, beginning with the inadequacies of the school building—including the leaky roof, boarded windows, and poor plumbing and heating system—and continuing into the lack of supplies and equipment, ranging from P.E. equipment to reading books, pencils, paper, art supplies, and toilet paper. He started to ask a question but, as I pressed doggedly on, sat back in his chair and nodded at me to continue.

I mentioned the apparent favoritism in doling out supplies, the fact that Mr. Lewis rarely taught P.E. and never took the students outside, that only recently were all the children allowed outside for fifteen minutes of playtime, and that teachers wasted valuable preparation time in the morning guarding doors. I mentioned that I worked with the children from 8:30 until 1:40 without a break, that discipline was handled entirely by teachers with no help from Mr. Carter, that some children who deserved federally funded lunches didn't have them, that the school nurse was unavailable, and that the cafetorium was often in an uproar. Then I paused.

He tapped the tips of his fingers together, wrote some notes, and nodded at me again to continue. I mentioned that some of the teachers were verbally or even physically abusive to the students, that Mr. Carter was absent for an entire week without notice or putting anyone in charge, that it was difficult to have children tested for special education and equally difficult for tested children to be placed into special education classes, and that the library did not contain books the majority of third grade students could read.

I decided to mention the constant tension and pressure the teachers encountered and the emphasis on white prejudice as the reason for the school's problems. I also mentioned several incidents that illustrated the teachers' low morale.

Dr. Holstein look stunned. "Yes, my, my, well that is why I am here—to help with these problems."

Hilda and Ann looked frightened. Were they wiser to be cautious?

Then he asked how I taught reading. I explained our new system and the methods I personally used. He was impressed, and said several times, "You must be an excellent teacher. Now then, with all these problems, why haven't you gone to the school board?"

Finally, Ann spoke up. She admitted that she had, but without any success. And then she added, "Someone wrote a letter to the newspaper."

"Have you considered getting a group of teachers together and going to the school board?"

"Dr. Holstein, the majority of the teachers don't want to complain. They were threatened with losing their jobs. Others have a few years left until retirement and are patiently waiting for the end," I said quietly.

"Yes, of course. Thank you for being so candid. Ladies, this has been very helpful."

The rest of the afternoon, I reviewed the discussion in my mind and wondered if I should have spoken so plainly, but I just couldn't accept the sugary, "Why everything is just fine, Dr. Holstein," when I knew that very little at P.S. 123 was just fine.

That afternoon, I sat through one of the most distressing faculty meetings of the year. Mr. Carter introduced Mr. Holstein; our distinguished visitor spoke for a few minutes to the entire faculty. "I am sorry that I did not have a chance to speak with all of you. I do not plan to make a detailed comment now, but I have noticed and been made aware of several serious problems. Rather than discussing them now, I will write them out in a lengthy report, and I certainly hope that you will follow my suggestions." Mr. Holstein nodded at us and sat down. I wondered how many teachers he interviewed. Uneasily, I realized that Mr. Carter knew.

Next, we listened to a most humiliating talk by Dr. Kemp. I assumed that, as the assistant superintendent, he knew a great deal about education.

He strutted back and forth in front of us and began to gesture with every sentence. "It is obvious that P.S. 123 has some serious problems, but these are caused by the large number of young, inexperienced teachers. That is, those who have taught one or two years. Certainly, the rooms and the halls are much too noisy. Why, just walking into the building, the noise is overwhelming."

With a sweeping gesture toward the halls and then to us, he said, "Now girls"—his voice low and patronizing—"you need help in discipline. Students must not run in the halls, you know, or down the stairs. Why, they might get hurt. Don't you agree?" He smiled winningly. "Well, that is very simple to solve. Ask the student to walk back up the stairs or walk back down the hall. That is all, girls." His voice oozed with condescension. "Just tell them to do it over. I am sure it won't happen again."

He paused and looked at us. "Now, any other discipline problems should be handled with understanding. If you follow these suggestions, you shouldn't have any further problems." He rubbed his hands together briskly and walked back to the front of the room.

Mrs. Potter's student threw a desk at her because she asked him to get ready for lunch. Hilda's student bit her arm and tried to knife a classmate because he wanted to be first in line. Cecil threw violent temper tantrums for no obvious reason, but Dr. Kemp just solved our problems. Use understanding, the learned man said!

I would have enjoyed watching him teach Mrs. LeBlanc's or Miss Morris's or Mrs. Potter's classes. For that matter, I was told by a substitute teacher that my class was unbearable and the worst she had ever taught. "How can you stand this every day?" she had asked. Dr. Kemp could try his hand with Cecil!

I thought of Dr. Kemp's clean, quiet, pine-paneled, air-conditioned office, his mahogany desk and thick rug. What did he know about P.S. 123 or its children? I turned to look at the other teachers. Maggie had forgotten not to listen and looked furious. The other teachers wore blank expressions. We sat politely listening to a man who had never taught elementary school. I wondered how he would handle Jeffrey's smoldering hatred, Nicholas's apparent inability to learn, or Marjorie's constant mood swings. I knew he would be unnerved with Sandy's curses, Barbara's lack of basic hygiene, Nanci's brashness, and Danny's vacant stares.

He concluded his visit by saying, "Certainly, Mr. Carter is doing an excellent job. We are very pleased with his performance." He patted him on the back. "And Dr. Holstein's visit has been most beneficial. Now remember, girls, you must learn to cope with your students' behavior. Be firm but understanding!" he said and nodded good day. I never saw him again.

It was apparent to me that teachers in this county were thought to be inept and dim-witted, that it was necessary to speak slowly to them and to use second grade vocabulary words to ensure comprehension. After all, we were just classroom teachers, and females besides.

That next week Mr. Carter was absent, but this time, a faculty meeting was called Monday afternoon to tell the teachers. Mrs. Dickson was put in charge. She was very pleased with the temporary promotion. I was not surprised by this choice. "Now then, ladies, discipline problems are to be handled in the classroom. Do not send them to the office or put them outside your door."

That week our acting principal spent most of her time drinking coffee and talking with Mrs. Black and Nadette. Her class was ignored and, as a result, they were extremely noisy. Thumps, banging, and screams punctuated the air above me. Having learned my lesson earlier, I did not write her another note.

The week moved slowly toward Friday. The days were typical. Cecil had several tantrums on Wednesday but appeared contrite when he had only five minutes of playtime on Thursday. Many were absent that week. I was told by Mrs. Black that "the germ is floating around." I tried to avoid Mrs. Dickson and did not see the other teachers except at lunch. I taught the children a new unit on space and handed in my teacher's register on time.

Mrs. Dickson was there when I put the register in the office. She picked it up, leafed through it, and said, "Just a minute here, Mrs. Evans. Take this back. Your book is done all wrong. How come you can't do it right? Why, it's so simple," she smirked.

I took it back without saying anything to her. I checked it over later, determined that it was done correctly and returned it to the office unchanged.

It rained all day Friday, which turned the playground into a brown, gooey swamp. We played indoors. They enjoyed the record of African music. I found wooden sticks and an old drum for them to use, and those without instruments danced. Many of the children could dance well. They enjoyed themselves so much that I resolved to play music for them more often.

It was the end of the second week when Dr. Holstein's letter arrived. The faculty meeting was announced at noon, and the meeting began without delay at 3:10. Mr. Carter said, "First off, I will read this here letter from that Dr. Holstein who visited us. I haven't read it yet myself. Then I will comment on what he say."

The letter began, "P.S. 123 has many serious problems aggravated by Mr. Carter's lack of leadership. He does not fill the role of principal." Mr. Carter visibly blanched, stumbled over some of the next sentences, and then continued reading the list of problems I mentioned to Dr. Holstein. Not one of my comments was missing! He found the reading program inadequate, as well as the supplies and books. He urged a reading program centered on audio-visual equipment, films, and tape recorders.

He wondered why the children were not taken out for P.E. and found that program inadequate. He stated that there should be more playtime scheduled for the children, since the disadvantaged child has a shorter attention span and needs frequent breaks. He mentioned the disorder in the halls, cafetorium, and classrooms and urged Mr. Carter to take a stronger hand in disciplinary measures. He believed that the school building was inadequate and thought the school board should initiate immediate repairs. As to the lack of supplies, Dr. Holstein thought that situation could be remedied without difficulty. He encouraged the school to set up a Saturday playground program because the children needed extra activities of this type. He then ended on an optimistic note, with hope for improvement in the future.

Mr. Carter folded the letter and stuck it into his pocket. He cleared his throat. "It was Dr. Kemp's instructions to read this here letter to the faculty. So, now you heard what he say. I got to tell you what to do. Some of you don't like to take orders, but now you have to. He say I was to be more of a leader. I'm going to do something even if it's wrong. We can't have no lack of organization in any way here."

He immediately attacked Ozell for his P.E. program and Ozell yelled right back, "I do so teach. How the hell can the kids do tumbling outside? We don't have mats inside neither. I is tired of everyone telling me to do something different. I is following the county plan for P.E."

Mr. Carter was firm. "You have to take them outside."

Ozell continued to whine. "It is too cold, or too wet, or—"

"You have to take them outside and that is final!" Ozell deflated and sulked in the corner, smoking furiously.

"Now, he was real hard on me, too, saying I ain't leading. You girls will just have to do as I say from now on, and I won't tolerate any of you disobeying me. If you must send those misbehaving students to the office, send them with their books. They will be supervised in the cafetorium by a teacher aide. From now on, there will be penalties for not getting your reports in on time." He cleared his throat. "The cafetorium noise must stop right away! I will personally review everything, and if I don't like it, you will have to change it. Yes indeed. There will be some changes around here. There will be no more playtime, except scheduled. You remember the county forbid playtime." I winced. "I am against helter-skelter playing. Besides, these here children need all possible time in the classroom."

I wondered what Dr. Holstein would think if he knew that his well-intentioned letter would change nothing at P.S. 123 and make many things worse. Mr. Carter did not sound like a leader. He sounded like a dictator. His diatribe ended at 4:50.

When the meeting was over, I walked up to Mr. Carter and waited for him to finish speaking with Mrs. Dickson. They both noticed me and Mr. Carter seemed annoyed. "What do you want?"

I was embarrassed by their obvious intimacy and starting talking quickly. "I'm willing to work at the Saturday playground that Dr. Holstein mentioned. Perhaps we could have a record player, a baseball game, maybe arts and crafts if we could get supplies, and a story hour. Each activity could go on at the same time, which would allow the children to choose the way they want to spend their morning. I am sure that my husband would be willing to work with the students, and I know several other friends the children would enjoy."

They both stared at me. "I don't know, Mrs. Evans, this here is only an idea." Abruptly he turned away and continued talking to Mrs. Dickson. I watched him pat her appreciatively. They laughed together.

As Maggie and I left the school that day, I said, "You know, the majority of Dr. Holstein's letter is a list of my complaints."

"You didn't leave anything out, did you?"

I laughed ruefully. "I guess not." I knew we were both thinking about teaching and wondering how our days could be made any more miserable by Mr. Carter. "He will make changes," I said.

"Yes, but I wonder what changes he will make," muttered Maggie.

"You know, I volunteered to work on Saturday."

She did not look surprised. "I will also. It would be so great for these children to have a place to go on Saturdays."

"Yes, all sorts of things could be happening at once—sports contests, lemonade and cookies as a treat when it gets warmer, and we could have plays and charge ten cents admission. We could use the money for supplies."

The Saturday playground received no support from Mr. Carter. "I have to get the school board's permission on this. You know, we'd be responsible for these here kids. I just can't say, but it don't sound like a good idea to me." Saturday playground never became a reality.

Recognizing that problems in the school would not be resolved, I concentrated on my class. The reading group's first stories were complete. They were so proud. I typed them, put them into a book form, and gave each child a copy. They read them eagerly, asked questions about the stories, and complimented each other. The students read them to their own classes and showed their illustrations. I was pleased with their enthusiasm and gave Mr. Carter a copy.

"What's this?"

"A copy of some class stories. I thought you might like to see what they have accomplished."

"Huh, oh, okay." He took the book and walked away.

Eric wrote:

I sell motorcycles. I am twenty-two year old I have twelve motorcycles left in case you want to buy one. I will save you one. I have long hair black shoes brown coat. I live in Seattle. My house on 25 Alice Street has eighty-two bathrooms and one hundred bedrooms. It cost $12,000 in 1980. I sold a motorcycle to a girl. She is pretty and has twelve boyfriends and ten girlfriends and sometime she live in Egypt and the Congo and in four more places. They is Brazil, and Washington DC Milwaukee and St Louis and Los Angeles and Buffalo and if you want to see me I will be in Washington DC for all motorcycle lovers.

Nanci wrote:

Two boys ran until they came to a place that they could hid from a boy. The place was a space station. They got into some seats and sat down. Then the boy that was going to beat them up came in the space station. The boy saw them and sat down behind them. The boys looked in the seat in back of them. They saw him and ran home. They came back out. They had their balls and bats and bowling balls and bags and golf balls and golf sticks. The boy was still behind them. The boy caught up with them and took their bowling balls and bowling bags and golf balls and sticks and their balls and bats. The boys cried. The boy with the glasses was nineteen years old. The boy without the glasses was nineteen also. They didn't have much fun that day. They were fat and skinny. The boy that was chasing them was eighteen so he was scared. They lived in outer space. The boys lived on 42 Space Street. The boy that was chasing them lived at 99 Space Moon Lock Street. The boy without glasses was name Moon. The boy that was chasing them was name Mars.

The students used magic markers for coloring their illustrations. All the students wanted to start on a new story right away. Some would write a story each week. Besides writing stories, the reading group finished its third-grade readers and began a fourth-grade reader. The two girls who were not as skilled had caught up to the group by reading with me individually and working at home. We planned a play for the reading class and began to work on that. Any free time was spent finding a reading book in the library. Julius read two or more books each week. One day, he stopped in front of my desk and said, "I enjoy the challenge of your class."

That afternoon, I reminded Mr. Carter about the recommendation that I asked for two weeks earlier. "Mr. Carter, please come into my room at any time to evaluate me. I certainly appreciate your writing a recommendation for me."

He appeared preoccupied and nodded. "Yeah." When I reminded him again the next week, and the week after that, he responded, "Mrs. Evans, you only been at P.S. 123 a short time and I just don't think I can write one for you."

"Three months isn't a sufficient length of time?"

"No, it isn't. Usually a teacher teach six or seven months before I write one."

"I will need a letter of recommendation before June since most school systems have their September staff selected before the summer vacation starts."

"Yeah, okay." Finally he agreed to write one that week. I waited each day that week for him to enter the classroom and observe or to stand in the hall and watch the class, or come out to the playground, but I never saw him.

Ida Mae Lee, the reading teacher whose classroom was linked to mine by the bathroom, motioned to me from her doorway. It was a gray Wednesday and I wondered if the children would arrive before it began to rain. She was pointing out the window at a group of boys. "Look at them, would you? Why, they are trying to beat each other to a pulp!" She banged on the window. "You there, stop that!" The boys got up, grinned, and strolled away. It looked like a movie production to me.

"Don't that beat all? These niggers are just jungle animals. Put clothes on them but it don't make no difference. Just a bunch of monkeys! You should see the way they come dancing in here. Wild as you please. They don't want to read no how. These young ones don't have no polite ways about them. Now their parents used to. My husband and I ran a store once. Their parents were real humble-like. These ones?" She sniffed to show her disdain. "If you ask me, the devil and the Communists are behind all of it! That's right, you mark my words." She shook her finger an inch from my nose.

Her tirades and racial slurs always upset me. I nodded at her. "I have some work to do. Have a nice day, Mrs. Lee."

"Ha," she said, "with these niggers? You got to be kidding."

As I walked through the tiny bathroom separating her room from mine, I noticed pencil writing all over the walls of the girls' bathroom. Besides houses and flowers, the printing was easy to read: "Marjorie eat boy pusy juse. Marjorie like boy pusy. Marjorie fuck good. Marjorie eat her brother. Black is bootiful."

I was stunned by the words. I read them over again. It seemed incredible that they were on a third-grade girls' bathroom wall. I wondered who had written this. Marjorie was spelled correctly. Nanci could spell Marjorie's name and, of course, Marjorie could, too.

The graffiti had to be erased. I walked down to the cafetorium and borrowed a can of cleanser from one of the staff. After greeting my students that morning, I called all the girls to the back of the room. "Girls, I saw the bathroom walls this morning. Writing on the walls is not allowed." Marjorie and Nanci looked uneasy. "It is not important that I know who wrote on the walls, but since you all use the bathroom, you will all help to keep it clean. I am sure you will enjoy a clean bathroom." There was no way that twelve girls could fit in the bathroom and clean, so I divided the group alphabetically and sent the first group in, armed with paper towels and cleanser to work for five minutes. It took two shifts for the walls to sparkle. They scrubbed so hard some of the paint came off.

I could hear Marjorie muttering, "Well, I didn't do none of it."

"Me neither," hissed Nanci.

"So, who put all those flowers on the wall?" Marjorie asked in turn. The group with Marjorie muttered louder. Luckily, Felicia did not get into a fight with Marjorie, but their voices were so loud that I closed the door leading to the classroom. The boys sat at their desks pretending to work as they listened.

Larry came up to my desk, grinning. "First time I ever seen a group of girls get punished."

"They are not being punished, Larry. They're cleaning."

"Yeah," replied Larry. "That's what I said!"

The girls were relieved that I did not try to find out who did it. Nanci and Marjorie were great classroom favorites. The walls remained unadorned except for some class paper drawings for the rest of the school year. That, however, was not the end of this incident. A few days later, Mr. Carter stopped me in the hall and asked, "Mrs. Evans, is it true that you is making your students scrub the classroom walls? Tynetta's mother, *ahh*, Mrs. Franklin, she call the school board to complain and they relay the message to me. You know she was right upset, but I suppose you can explain?" I was amused and when I told him about the graffiti on the bathroom wall and all the girls scrubbing, he actually smiled.

Later that day I spoke to Tynetta about the bathroom-scrubbing incident. "Were you angry with me for making you scrub the wall, Tynetta?"

"I didn't do nothing," she replied sullenly.

"Not even a flower?"

"Only a tiny one and I had to scrub the whole wall."

"All by yourself, Tynetta?"

"Yes, ma'am."

"None of the other girls helped you?"

She didn't answer. I felt sorry for Mrs. Franklin. No wonder she called the school board. I hoped she would call me and complain the next time. At least I could tell her the truth, but I doubted that she would believe me.

That next morning, I discovered an envelope on my desk containing a torn half-sheet of paper with one typed paragraph. This was my recommendation. It had taken more than a month to receive and stated:

To Who it may Concern:

Mrs. Lisa Evans has been a third-grade teacher at PS 123 about twelve weeks. The limited time employed here do not enable me to give a valid picture of her overall performance however, I feel she has the making of a fine teacher. She is very determine and works very hard with the children.

I wondered what a prospective employer would think of these comments, but considering the encounters I had with Mr. Carter, I was grateful to get it.

"Maggie, I have my recommendation."

"Really, that's great!" After reading it, she looked up. "Is this all?"

"Yes."

"Why, that's ridiculous. Anyone could see after one week that you are doing a fantastic job."

"You know what is most distressing?" She shook her head. "He has never observed me teach." Maggie groaned.

It was even more ironic to realize that two months later, without ever visiting my room, Mr. Carter was able to fill out a complex county form that evaluated my teaching ability, knowledge of subject matter, appearance, and ability to get along with fellow teachers on an abstract scale ranging from 1 to 5.

The remainder of March went by slowly. The gray, dreary days blended into weeks. Several incidents broke through the numbness of tension and routine, and two fads surfaced. Huge black combs appeared overnight, protruding from hip pockets or lodged in tightly curled hair. Their owners, intrigued with their new possessions, used them frequently. "Hey man, where your comb? You ain't cool without no comb."

Patiently, I convinced them that ownership did not need to interfere with their classwork. "Kelvin, put your comb away." As it was, several of these combs found their way into my desk drawer to be returned at the end of the day.

Along with these combs, a strange back ailment afflicted the girls, beginning with Marjorie. She began to walk with her legs spread apart and her hips pushed back, much like a retreating stork. "Marjorie, did you hurt your back?"

"No ma'am. I is fine."

It amused me to watch all the girls practice their new posture and forget it when jumping rope or chasing a ball. When I spoke with Nanci about her posture, since hers was the most exaggerated, she said, "Cool, huh, Mrs. Evans? What you think?" and bobbed away with a borrowed black comb hanging from her pigtail.

The second report card brought no complaining parents, and my notes of concern went unanswered. Danny's mother did not come in for a conference. Danny was behind in all his subjects, and I hoped that she would help him with reading. Nicholas's mother did not respond. Nicholas just sat in class. He had not improved in any learning areas and, unfortunately, his behavior was much worse. Moving his desk as far from his classmates as possible helped a little. He was unwilling to do the simplest work papers, and often hid his head in his desk. Working with me alone or with several other children did not help.

I wrote a note to Dexter's parents about his improvement in subtraction and asked them to help him at home but received no reply. Notes to the parents of Kelvin, Jack, and Cecil about behavior problems went unnoticed. Felicia and Sandy signed their report cards for their parents and had to take them home a second time. They were not upset when I noticed. I think they expected it.

I also learned of a problem Jimmy was facing each day after school and the real reason for the bruises on his face. "Jimmy, were you in a fight?"

"No, ma'am."

"Why are you bruised?"

"I don't know."

"Jimmy, is something wrong?"

"They says if I tell they beat me." He started to sob.

"But they already have."

"Yes, ma'am." He sobbed harder.

"Who is 'they,' Jimmy?"

"Some older boys stop me and ask for candy and if I don't have none, they beat me up. Yesterday, I give them some but they says it ain't enough so they beat me."

Since he could not walk all the way home with a group of third graders, and his mother would not be able to meet him, I suggested he stay with me after school until he thought the gang had gone home. This also gave him an opportunity to finish his classwork. He stayed behind for those last two weeks in March, but later resorted to running all the way home. This situation improved as the weather grew warmer and the junior-high-school boys found other prey.

When Mr. Carter was told of the problem, he responded, "Those junior high boys are pretty rough. Ain't much we can do."

The intolerance and cruelty that existed among my students

no longer surprised me. Their willingness to torment, laugh at, beat up, steal from, and lie to each other was not unusual. Scuffles were frequent, anger intense. We discussed being good friends and helping others, but it made only a momentary impression.

Those last weeks of March, I encouraged more students to finish their work by building a fishing pond, complete with a pole and magnetic hook. Snoopy sat alongside the pool and fished. In the pond were extra class jobs or fun papers for them to work, but they could only fish after their daily assignments were corrected. Then they filled out a fishing license and fished. I did not realize how delighted my students would be with this. Even Nicholas and Danny took their turns at fishing. I stumbled onto one activity that the whole class enjoyed! We wrote "whopper" stories, with everyone telling about the biggest fish they ever caught. Nanci's fish was a block long! The children never tired of the fishing pond, and even brought other students in to see it. "Don't touch nothing. You ain't got a license," admonished Edward to a friend.

Another addition to our class day was toothbrushing practice during the hygiene lesson. The health clinic gave each child a new toothbrush and toothpaste. Using a huge fake tooth and toothbrush, I showed them the recommended way to brush. To complete the lesson, they all practiced with their own new toothbrushes.

"I ain't never had a toothbrush before," said Angela.

"Me neither," added Kelvin.

"At least, not one of my very own. I always share with my sister," said Patricia shyly. Several of the boys clowned and brushed huge imaginary mouths or their noses and tongues. I told them how important it was to brush as often as possible, even without toothpaste.

Sharon giggled. "This here toothbrush tickles my teeth." I wondered how many of them would continue brushing at home, but whenever I asked during a health lesson, they all solemnly assured me that they never forgot.

The last faculty meeting of the month was as vitriolic as ever. Mr. Carter lit his pipe, blew smoke into the air, and said, "You been stealing coffee cups from the cafetorium. They ain't gonna have none left. From now on, you can't go into the kitchen for nothing." Since the refrigerator was in the kitchen, I wondered where we were supposed to put our bag lunches.

With a vindictive but fleeting monologue about teachers who could not handle their own behavior problems, he introduced Miss Thomas, the special services representative for the county. She was a well-dressed young black woman who had grown up in The Projects and understood the problems of our students. I thought her job was to discuss the children's school problems with the parents. "You teachers are always making me into the bad guy," was her opening statement. "I am the one who always has to give the bad news to the parents, and I am sick and tired of it. From now on, you can contact the parents and speak with them yourself." The bitterness in her voice was apparent. "You must think I can work miracles or something. These parents are difficult. They see me coming and know right away that their kid was bad. From now on, you contact me if you think a child is truant, but classroom problems, you solve yourself!"

It disappointed me that this woman saw herself in the role of the "bad guy" when she was supposed to communicate with the parents. Certainly, they would be more willing to accept her advice than mine. Sadly, the classroom teacher could not expect help from special services.

My feelings of despair with education and the position of an elementary school teacher increased as I endured the faculty meeting sitting in Mrs. Madison's immaculate room. Surrounded by racial prejudice, negative advice, unnecessary paperwork, no supplies, petty harassments, unhelpful administrators, considered incompetent or dim-witted by county supervisors, and yet expected to teach a class of ill or hungry children who lacked self-discipline and the desire to learn. This was the unenviable job of a teacher at P.S. 123. I stared out the dirty window into a world promising springtime. Disconsolately, I wondered if anything would change here, and if the squabbling adults would allow these children the chance they deserved.

I did not hear the meeting dismissed. Maggie said, "Going to stay here all night?"

I stood up. "What about Miss Thomas, the bad guy? I just can't believe she said that."

CHAPTER 10

Black on White

THE TENSION THAT FILLED THE HALLWAYS of P.S. 123 in December 1969 increased the following April. Feelings of depression, fear of reprisal, despair with students, and frustration with the administration were common among teachers. Each day brought more problems that were insidiously labeled "the teacher's fault." I felt the tension press against my forehead. Many of the teachers complained of exhaustion at the end of each day, and absences among teachers increased.

Certainly, racial prejudice played its role in the problems at P.S. 123. Fortunately, though, my students did not appear to fight or tease their classmates because of skin color. More fundamental irritants such as, "That my pencil, boy" or, "She got my quarter" or, "I'm supposed to be first in line" and "You ain't the P.E. helper, I is!" occupied their thoughts. On the other hand, I saw other students fight over a skin-deep question and wondered why their teachers did not interrupt the dispute.

The parents were a different matter. I had already heard Tynetta's mother: "You can't never get nowhere with no whitie," and of course Tynetta's reading grade was a prime example of blaming problems on racial prejudice.

Another parent, Sandra's dad, wrote a note to me when his daughter's extra paper was stolen. It said in part, "I ain't going buy no more paper for no nigger to steal," and continued, "Don't you sit my girl by no nigger." When I asked Sandra if she possibly had lost these supplies, she tearfully said, "No, ma'am!"

"Sandra, I am sorry, but I don't have any paper to give you. Perhaps you could borrow some from your friend, Sylvia?" I did not mention changing Sandra's seat, so she asked me to do so.

"Well, Sandra, I will think about the very best place to move your seat, and after school, we will talk about it and then move your desk." This appeared to satisfy her.

I never placed my students according to skin color and had no intention of starting now. To sit Sandra as her father wished, I would have to group all six of my white students together in one corner. I decided to sit Sandra by Sylvia, her only friend, and then cautioned them both that too much talking would end the arrangement. The girls were delighted.

But this only began Sandra's problems. The attitude of her parents—who could not afford to send Sandra to a private white school when P.S. 123 was integrated—eventually made it impossible for her to complete the school year.

Unfortunately, this tension was not limited to parents or children, for the teachers were affected. One older black sixth grade teacher, Mrs. James, told me solemnly in the teachers' lounge, "I is very fair. I keep track of everything in this notebook."

"Everything?"

"Yes. If a black boy sharpen his pencil, next a white boy sharpen his, and I write it down, so I remember."

"What else do you keep track of?"

"Oh, things like bathroom visits, class duties, reading groups," she said in a matter-of-fact tone of voice.

Confused I asked, "But Mrs. James, what if a white boy doesn't need to sharpen his pencil or go to the bathroom?"

She just looked at me blankly. "Ain't never happened," she said.

The reverse of Mrs. James's attitude occurred, too. The reading teacher's disdainful comment, "A nigger is a nigger is a nigger," the art and music teachers' unpleasant, even hostile attitudes, and the general indifference of some teachers impeded the children's progress.

There were, of course, problems among the teachers. Some could not accept white teachers working with black students or acknowledge the effort we put into our work. The staff was divided, fed by vicious gossip. This constant belittling added to the tension and pressure. The leader, or at least most feared teacher, was Mrs. Dickson. She had the most influence with Mr. Carter and seemed to be the most vindictive. I never taught at a school where teachers were so unprofessional. Teaching was apparently one of the least important events of their day.

The alienation of teachers was most unfortunate. If the teachers had been able to form a supportive network, we could have muted Mr. Carter's assaults. It was obvious to me that Maggie and I were the only two teachers willing to speak up against daily injustices. There would be no support from the others—some wished to live out their days to retirement as quietly as possible, some feared the loss of their jobs or a transfer to a less desirable position, some blindly supported Mr. Carter, and the rest, I believe the vast majority, simply did not care.

With the appearance of a white teacher's aide, Mrs. Smith, an unpleasant situation erupted that the teachers aggravated. Besides possessing a surly disposition, Nadette, the office aide, was slow and frequently incompetent. It was not atypical to be given 15 dittos, instead of 27, two weeks after a request was made. Mrs. Smith, however, was delightful. Not only was the work done the same day, but each morning she asked for more! We all welcomed this patient, hard-working woman.

Unfortunately, a fierce rivalry between the two teachers' aides surfaced, with the secretary, Mrs. Black, siding with her friend, Nadette. So intense did the pressure become in the office, that I found Mrs. Smith crying in the teachers' lounge. Not only unpleasant comments, but subtle sabotage of her careful work proved too much. "They asked me why I work so hard, and I told them that was my job. I want to help you teachers. Then Nadette laughed at me and said, 'I ain't never hustling for no white teachers,' and now Mrs. Black won't give me work to do or they hide what I've done." Her talk with Mr. Carter did not improve the situation.

After listening to Mrs. Smith's complaints, I asked, "What do you plan to do?"

"Nothing, I guess. I might lose my job, and we need the money bad." She sniffled into a tissue, wiped her eyes, and left the teachers' lounge.

Even the lack of supplies was aggravated by Mrs. Black, a pompous dictator who reigned over a tiny kingdom of mundane items such as chalk, pencils, paper, erasers, art supplies, toilet paper, and paper towels. Since she held the key to the supply closet, any supplies I received greatly depended upon her generosity. Teachers were never allowed to visit the supply closet, even if accompanied by Mrs. Black.

It was particularly distressing to write a list of required supplies and then receive no more than two or three items. I had to list the number of sheets of paper I wanted, but at least I did not have to count the number of paper towel sheets. Inevitably, the list would be returned with the comment, "This here is all there is, Mrs. Evans." So I would pick up five pieces of white chalk, one-half packet of paper towels, which would be used up in several days, five sheets of yellow paper (how could 27 children have art with five small sheets of paper?), and a half-ream of ditto paper that was enough for four assignments. There were no magic markers, no classroom work paper, no white or gray art paper, no scissors, no rulers, no glue, no staples, no rubber bands, and no paper clips.

And yet as I walked down the hall and peered into other classrooms, I saw that some teachers had many of the items that Mrs. Black assured me the school did not have. Her favoritism annoyed me because my students were not receiving their meager share.

The attitude of Mr. Carter toward the white teachers was apparent. He often blamed the problems of P.S. 123 on the white teachers' prejudice. The lack of books, the classroom noise, the poor cafetorium discipline, the inadequate school building, the disobedient children were all caused by "You white teachers. You just hate us blacks." An entire faculty meeting was devoted to this subject. "The children know that you don't love them. Matter of fact, you hate them. They see you ain't fair and that you don't like the black teachers. You will just have to learn to love us blacks. They see you favoring your white students, giving them high grades and never punishing them. They know who you like best. It's all your fault if you have problems. You cause them all. Now you white teachers is making fun of the black children's speech by demanding good English. You don't do that no more, hear? You let those black kids talk like they want. You ain't superior. You don't know any more than any black. You whites just think you do. I want you white teachers to come down to the students' level. I don't want you to correct their mistakes no more. You trying to make them feel inferior! You trying to make them feel bad!"

The day after this speech, three of the third-grade teachers were eating together after the cafetorium tables were rearranged. Mr. Carter walked by the cafetorium and looked in.

Seeing them, he said, "There's too many whites at this here table. I'm going to sit down here and integrate it." He was not smiling and none of them considered it a joke. He stayed no more than five minutes. "Well, I guess that was long enough," he said. His overriding concern with racial discrimination increased during the school year. It never occurred to him that many of the teachers were only interested in the welfare of their students, not their skin color.

CHAPTER 11

Springtime

T HE TREES WERE WEARING lacy green leaves across the street from the fenced-in playground. Stalwart blades of grass lined the tree trunks. Fluffy white clouds hung motionless in a bright spring sky, and the warm sun dried the muddy brown clay. Spring crept over the drab schoolyard, bringing a sparkle of hope.

I watched the children play. Coats were discarded as it grew warmer. The baseball game was going well except for occasional disputes or arguments between team captains. The girls jumped rope skillfully. Nicholas, Jeffrey, and Dexter stood with me and watched their classmates. They had lost the majority of their playtime for that day, but Nicholas behaved so poorly that he was erasing the next day's playtime too. Grumbling and muttering, they waited for the hands of the clock to creep toward lunchtime.

It was the first of April. The children were restless as they waited in line for lunch. It was hot in the hallways. Opening the doors allowed a friendly breeze to whisper through. Standing by the doorway to the cafetorium, I looked out into the neighbor's yard. The gray clapboard house leaned to the right. The screen door was torn; the porch and steps sagged. The yard was littered with rusty box springs, broken bottles, parts from an old car, a discarded refrigerator, and a faded chair that was slowly losing its stuffing. An old man sat on a bottomless chair, tilted back against the wall. His body looked worn, and his eyes were closed. Blue gray smoke curled upward from the butt of a cigarette clamped between his fingers. As I waited, I thought of that old man, of lost dreams, and wondered about the future of my students.

My thoughts were interrupted by Mrs. Dickson's agitated voice. "Mrs. Evans, you have an emergency phone call in the office!"

I gasped and ran toward the office. My husband, a Marine Corps lieutenant, was flying that morning. I feared his plane had crashed. Several weeks before, one of the training flights had crashed in the swamp. No one ever called me at work, so there must be another accident! The Vietnam War, for which my husband and those with him were preparing, was half a world away, but they faced daily and deadly risks even as they trained. I prayed for him and those on his flight as I dashed down the hall. I rounded the corner to the office and there stood Mrs. Dickson and 20 of her students. They all whooped and hollered. Mrs. Dickson's voice boomed, "April Fool!" They laughed and laughed, slapping each other on the back, and pounding the floor with their feet.

At first, I did not realize that they were yelling "April Fool" at me. Slowly, the fear of disaster faded away and with relief, came irritation. I nodded at them and, turning, walked back to the cafetorium. Later, Mrs. Dickson came up to the table and said, "We fooled you real good!" and laughed some more. I resented her harassing me. On checking with others, I learned her April Fool's jokes were limited to white teachers.

After lunch, I stopped by the office to ask for the federal lunch program sheet—there were none—and to check my teacher's mailbox. One white paper waited. It was a blank, official self-evaluation sheet that would become part of my permanent teacher's file. There were several sections for me to judge my own work: Professional Competence in the Area of Responsibility, Professional Growth and Attitudes, and Personal Characteristics. Specific questions ranged from, "Do I demonstrate depth of knowledge of subject matter?" to "Do I motivate pupils to work to capacity without undue tension?" and "Do I demonstrate an awareness of the purposes of education in a changing society?" It also included other questions such as, "Do I demonstrate a wholesome sense of humor?" and "Do I use good judgment and tact?" Instead of answering "yes" or "no," percentages were used and the total score was to appear at the bottom of the page. Without hesitating, I put the paper into my bottom desk drawer, hoping that the unorganized office would never notice that mine was not returned.

The spring sun beamed into the film room. The air inside was stifling. Opening all the windows and the door did not help. Naturally, the furnace was still on, and the radiators were hotter than they were all winter. Sharon led the songs, while I found the films I ordered. One was not rewound and the other was in the wrong container. The film projector was a new one. I threaded the machine and plugged it in, but nothing happened. Jack turned the lights back on, Sharon began another song, and I checked the machine again. Not only was the projector bulb missing, but this time the film feeder was not working.

Mrs. Wilson, the librarian, was also in charge of the film room. Sharon began "Row, Row, Row Your Boat" and I walked across to Mrs. Wilson's room. Damp brown hair stuck to her round pink face. Sweat glistened in the folds of her neck. "The film projector—" I started.

"Oh yes," she cheerfully agreed. "The projector is broken."

"Mrs. Wilson, why didn't you send word to me since you

knew by reading your schedule that I would be here at 2:00?"

"Oh well, I'm so busy," she stopped and sputtered. "Anyway, now you know."

One of the films I ordered would be returned by the time the projector was repaired. The children greeted my news with groans and grimaces. So, instead of seeing a film, we discussed springtime.

"How many signs of spring have you noticed?" I asked after we returned to our classroom.

"What do you mean, Mrs. Evans?"

"Does it look different outside than it did a few weeks ago?"

"It warmer," said Cecil.

"Very good!" I began to write a list on the blackboard. "Cecil says it is warmer and Sandy found some green leaves."

When they couldn't think of any other signs, we decided to walk out on the playground and look for springtime. L'Angela saw a robin and Eric saw some flowers across the street. After our search, we finished the class springtime list, and made a vocabulary chart of spring words. The children used these words later to write a spring poem.

"On the way home, look for signs of spring we missed today."

The next morning, Sandy and Kelvin hustled in before the bell rang.

"Hi, Mrs. Evans. Is tadpoles a sign of spring?"

"Yes, indeed!"

"See, I told you. Look, we bring some. We found them yesterday."

"Oh, that's wonderful. You will have to tell your classmates about them."

They were very excited and Kelvin said, "Gee, I ain't never seen all that stuff before. Do it happen every year?"

"Maybe you ain't never looked," suggested Sandy.

The rest of the class straggled in. Rain in the morning meant that the bussers would be absent since they did not have any raincoats or extra shoes, and their mothers would not let them wait for the bus in the rain. The classroom smelled damp. Jeffrey took his shirt off and wrung it out over the sink. The rest of the paper towels were used to wipe wet faces and hair. They crowded around the tadpole jar.

"Now these here are tadpoles and they is a sign of spring," announced Kelvin and Sandy proudly.

I noticed the new bulletin board in the hallway when the classes changed for reading. In the center of the red paper was a large mirror, and at the top, the question, "Do you like what you see? How can you improve?" Walking past, the boys gawked at themselves and made silly faces. The girls played with their hair.

My reading group was smaller than usual. We began with dictionary skills and then worked on the play for Friday. Veronica wrote it. Cindy was the old lady. "How do I look, Mrs. Evans?" Nanci was a baby. She sat on the floor and sucked her thumb. Eric was the older brother and Julius was a dog that crept around howling and barking. Several other children worked on simple props, and another group made a background mural. It was a simple story that would take ten minutes to perform, but the children were enjoying it immensely.

"I don't got enough to say," complained Cindy.

"Add some more lines," I suggested.

"You mean, I can? Gosh," she said, "what should I say?"

I smiled at her predicament. She was a naturally talkative child.

Julius warned, "You know it is always beneficial to practice!" I thought about him as I watched the rehearsal. He was an intriguing student, now reading fifth and sixth grade library books, excelling in every area, and equipped with an unusual vocabulary.

"Do you know why I wanted to be a dog?"

"No, Julius."

"Because it takes the most imagination."

Mrs. Johnson, the reading supervisor, was checking Mrs. Miller's new reading program that day and entered quietly. The children were too engrossed in their work to be disturbed by her. Her blue eyes twinkled as she watched them work on their play. She brushed a white curl out of her eyes and settled more comfortably in her chair. It was not until the reading group was ready to leave that she rose and walked over to me. "I like your classroom very much," she smiled at me warmly. "It is so bright and cheerful. You work so well with children. You are an excellent teacher."

Compliments were so rare at P.S. 123 that I beamed.

"I enjoyed my morning here," she said, and left as unobtrusively as she arrived.

Maggie said later, "Mrs. Johnson was really complimentary about my class. When I asked her if there were anything she could suggest, she said, 'No, you are doing everything you possibly can.' That's so nice to know!"

I wondered if Mr. Carter realized the work teachers were willing to do for a few compliments. His belligerent attitude and constant threats defeated most of the teachers.

With spring and the over-heated classroom, the students were restless. Some complained of the heat, but others, like Felicia, wanted me to close the windows because she was cold. She sat with a sweater wrapped around her, the arms of the sweater tied under her chin. Cecil's temper tantrums reappeared. Dexter bullied Sandra in the halls. Nicholas made funny noises that rose from the depths of his desk. Assignments lagged and interest waned. It appeared to be a rampant outbreak of spring fever.

One remedy to lessen their malaise was more frequent breaks. I decided to shorten the play period before lunch and go back outside in the afternoon. When we discussed this, the students were delighted. I also told them that there would be a baseball pro to help them with their game tomorrow at 11:00. I discussed their batting and pitching problems with him, and he offered to help.

"Who is this man?" asked Larry.

I smiled and said, "Lt. Evans." The class accepted his name without comment. This good news rejuvenated the class, and so I continued with my planned lesson. We talked about money. Next to food, this was a favorite subject. "How much is a lot of money?"

"A billion trillion," answered Nanci.

"There ain't no such thing," scoffed Cecil.

"Is too!" shrieked Nanci.

I interrupted with a question, "If someone gave you one million dollars, would that be enough?" Nanci couldn't decide. I wrote the sum on the blackboard and then wrote down how many pennies that would be. They were amazed. "All right, if you had this money, would you save it?"

"Hell no!" Sandy shouted, and then looking embarrassed, hid his face in his book.

"Would you save a little of it in case you need it later?" Patricia would and so would Eric. "Would you give some of it away to a friend who needed it?"

"Just a little," said Tynetta. They were as excited about this discussion as if someone planned to give them the money that afternoon.

"*Ahh*," Billy said. "You want us to say how we'd spend it, right?"

"Right. You can write a story or make a list but be sure to put the most important thing first. Kelvin?"

"You mean, what I'd buy first?"

I nodded.

"Anything I want?"

"Yes, anything at all."

I found that they all wanted the possessions of an upper-class society. Sandra wanted 400 fur coats and some diamonds. Eric wanted a castle with 1,000 bedrooms and 900 bathrooms with a refrigerator in every room stuffed with food. Patricia wanted a trip to see her grandmother who lived up north. Curtis wanted a room filled with bags of money. The boys wanted cars, boats, and motorcycles. The girls wanted clothes and jewelry. Everyone wanted food, color televisions, and new houses.

After all the lists were finished, I told them that there were only a few people in the world who had a million dollars or more. When Eric wanted to know who, I named a few. Although they did not recognize the names, they were excited. The reason I started this discussion was to have them realize that a dream could become a reality. I told them the American success story—some people with no money and not enough food worked hard and realized their dreams.

After our discussion, I gave each a bag with paper money and cardboard coins to count. We exchanged bags several times. All of the children had difficulty counting the money and making change.

Some of my students were still thinking about the discussion when they left that afternoon. Barbara walked up to me after the others left. "Mrs. Evans, that don't work."

"What doesn't, Barbara?"

"No, ma'am, it don't. I ask for milk for my baby sister and a quarter for me but I don't get none."

"Who did you ask?"

"God!" said Barbara. "Our preacher say, 'God hear us and give us what we wants,' but he don't hear me." I looked at her matted dirty hair, sweat-stained face, and toes poking out of her torn sneakers. Very sorrowfully she shook her head and said again, "It don't work."

"Barbara, sometimes things aren't just given to us. We have to work for them. Is there someone you could do an errand for and earn money for your sister's milk or your quarter?"

"Maybe so," she sighed. Nanci waited for her outside the door, and they linked arms as they walked down the hall.

It was discouraging to find an eight-year-old girl who had already decided it did not help to dream, and no one explained that much of life's achievements had to be earned.

That next day the boys were excited about playing baseball with a pro. They watched the sky anxiously to ward off any rain clouds. The girls were going to play a game with me, all except Felicia. She wanted to play baseball, but when she realized that no one minded having her on the team, she decided to play with the girls after all.

The boys managed to walk quietly out the door but ran all the way to the baseball field. Waiting for them by the tree was a tall muscular man dressed in blue jeans, a striped-blue shirt, and a baseball cap. The boys crowded around him and he stood up.

"Wow, man," said Cecil. "How tall is you?" They stared upward at an angular face, blue eyes hidden behind sunglasses and military regulation blond hair dampened by the hat and the sun.

He smiled at Cecil. "Six-five."

"Wow!" they all chorused.

"Okay, let's play ball!"

"Say, my friend," Paul said to Dexter, "you're holding the bat wrong. No wonder you can't hit the ball!"

Dexter watched him change his hands on the bat so that his right hand was on top, and for once, instead of striking out, he hit a home run. Dexter was a hero. His plump body chugged around the bases to screams of encouragement from his teammates.

"Yeah, come on. Run, Dexter! Whoopee!"

"You going come tomorrow, ain't you?" asked Jimmy, an excellent baseball player. A nod brought some shouts from the boys. They talked about "the pro" all afternoon. "Hey man, he sure is cool!"

"Yeah, hope it don't rain tomorrow."

Dexter was not only pleasant, but helpful. I hoped for a home run every day.

Larry still wondered about two "Evans." Appearing at the edge of my desk during arithmetic, he whispered, "Is he your brother?"

"No, Larry, he isn't."

"*Humph.*" He looked disgusted. "I thought I had it figured out." Suddenly his round face lit up and every freckle stood out. I will never forget his triumphant blue eyes. "He's your husband, right?"

"Yes, Larry."

"Hot dog!" he yelled, and the entire class looked at him. "Lt. Evans, her husband."

"Oh," said all the boys.

The girls giggled and giggled.

"He sure is handsome!" said L'Angela.

"Thank you."

The girls giggled some more.

That afternoon we ended our science project on space with a group of astronauts blasting off. We made paper bag helmets and the rest of the outfit was supplied by imagination. I was the home control and monitored their flight. After blasting off, they bounced out of their seats. I contacted them to find out how they felt. Nanci was floating in the air. Edward was going to sleep because it took a long time to get there. Sharon was trying the prepared food. When they landed on the moon, I asked them what they could see, and so on. They planted an imaginary American flag before returning.

Then we talked about their trip. Eric was going to shave off his beard. Most were hungry for a good meal and tired. Besides enjoying it, they learned, during the weeks of planning for their flight, about the moon's surface, weightlessness, preparation for flight, and that the U.S.A.'s landing of men on the moon the year before had been a fantastic achievement. When the bell rang for them to leave, they did not want to take off their space helmets, so most of my class walked down the hall with huge brown shopping bags decorated with dials and knobs over their heads and shoulders.

The next day, Patricia took me aside and said, "I wants to talk to you, Mrs. Evans. My daddy say that don't look like no astronaut outfit to him." She appeared concerned. "He say it just look like an old paper sack."

"Patricia, even though it was a paper bag, it took you to the moon and back."

"Yes, ma'am," she nodded. "Sure enough did!" and she laughed out loud.

Meanwhile, the class also became very interested in the first Earth Day, which took place on April 22. We read the news of the gatherings, rallies, and protests across the country and discussed how it all might affect each of us.

"What can we do to help?"

"What about cleaning up the playground?"

"Yeah, then I won't cut my leg on glass no more," said Jimmy.

"Yeah!" shouted Cecil. And the others all agreed.

So on Earth Day, the children took large paper bags and walked around the playground. It was the first time since I came to P.S. 123 that the playground was not strewn with paper, broken glass, and empty beer cans. The class did an excellent job and was quite proud of its work. Later we talked about the ways they could clean up their own houses.

Edward said, "Do cleaning get rid of rats? My ma got a new pink skirt and she put it on the bed and before she wear it, rats done ate a hole this big." He held up his hands to show the size of the hole.

"Yeah," said Marjorie. "My brother and me killed a rat this big yesterday." She stretched her arms to show a rat the size of a dog.

This discussion interested everyone. They all had rat stories to tell. We wrote some of them down. Then they discussed different things they could do.

"I gonna broom my porch," said L'Angela.

"I pick up the papers and junk. Can't move no car. That in the backyard, too," said Edward.

We talked about easy ways to fix things, and I told them perhaps their older brothers and sisters would be willing to help. The next day, several told me that they cleaned up their yards, and Sharon said, "Ain't no use to clean. It just get dirty again. Last night my dad and his friends throwed bottles and papers back in the yard when they was sitting on the porch." She was angry that she bothered. "My dad, he laugh at me for cleaning up. I get a beating if I do that again."

I told her that her attempts were worthwhile and perhaps someday when she had her own home she could keep it neat. "Yes, ma'am, I sure will. I clean Mama's house already." I wondered if a house of her own seemed a long way away, for she was only 10 years old. Being responsible for cleaning her mother's house and taking care of her younger brothers and sisters convinced me that she never had just been a little girl.

CHAPTER 12

100% Helter-Skelter

A S I PASSED THE OFFICE on my way home that day, Mrs. Black called to me, "Mrs. Evans, where is your self-evaluation sheet? I has everyone else's." That wasn't quite true. She didn't have Maggie's.

I walked back to the room and took the sheet out of my drawer. As I read it, the idea of rating myself for my own permanent folder seemed ridiculous. I honestly thought I was doing the best job I possibly could. Impulsively, I wrote down 100 percent as my total score. Obviously, I did not take the evaluation seriously enough, as my response necessitated a faculty meeting the next afternoon.

At midmorning, Nadette bustled importantly into my room. She had a sheet of paper with all the teachers' names printed on it and the statement: "Teachers' meeting, 3:15." Miss Jenkins's name, the third-grade teacher I replaced in December, was on the sheet. After four and one-half months of teaching at P.S.123, my name was not there. I did not sign the sheet and gave it back. "You supposed to sign it." She pushed the paper back at me.

"Nadette, my name isn't on the sheet, so I can't sign it."

She looked confused. "I was told you has to sign it. Mr. Carter wants it." I employed an answer learned from Mrs. Black, an eloquent shrug. She understood and left. I wondered why Mr. Carter wanted a record of the teachers notified for a faculty meeting. The meeting began on time. All the teachers were there except Ozell Lewis. Naturally, he was reprimanded when he arrived late, but Mrs. Dickson, who strolled in at 3:30, was greeted with nods and smiles. Then Mr. Carter began his harangue that was directed at me.

"Some people don't take these here evaluation sheets serious enough. Now, this here is an important piece of paper. I have been reviewing them and found one teacher who thinks she is 100 percent in all categories." This brought an astonished "*ohh*" from the teachers.

"Yes, she wrote down 100 percent for every area. Now there ain't nobody so good that they 100 percent. Ain't none of you 100 percent teachers. If any of you think you is, well, it ain't so! This here teacher thinks she's so good there ain't no room for improvement. Everybody can always improve. I seen lots of times when she could do better, and then she goes and don't evaluate herself proper like all you girls done."

I waited for him to hand the paper back to me, but he never mentioned my name or gave me the paper. I sat quietly and, preoccupied, watched Mrs. Dickson. She unbuttoned her housedress and fished around for a bra strap, uncrossed her legs, turned and looked out the window. Then she got up, walked across the front of the room and left.

Mr. Carter droned on, "No sir! Ain't nobody perfect, except God, of course. He's perfect but he ain't teaching at P.S. 123." It was a sentiment that I shared and brought a nervous laugh from the faculty. He seemed pleased with his joke and repeated it. The teachers looked at each other and silently tried to guess the 100 percent teacher.

Mrs. Dickson strolled back into the room. The slap, slap, slap of her slippers seemed unusually loud. Mr. Carter was ending his speech. It was 4:10. "Some of you think you know everything, and at least one of you has admitted it. You don't know nothing. There ain't no 100 percent teacher in this here school and don't you forget that. From now on I expect any form to be filled out proper like, and when I send around a sheet for you to sign, sign it! You understand?"

He was perspiring. His face looked shiny in the afternoon sun. His white shirt was damp. His trousers were wrinkled. He gestured to indicate that the meeting was over. I wondered why he did not give the sheet back to me in his office and tell me to reevaluate myself instead of wasting the time of all the other teachers with a faculty meeting. Ironically, I knew that several teachers scored themselves at 96 percent or 98 percent, but apparently that did not upset him.

Mrs. Dickson stood, yawned, and walked over to Mr. Carter. They left together smiling and talking. I overheard several teachers trying to decide who had rated herself 100 percent. "Sure had some nerve," said one fifth grade teacher.

"Yeah," said another. Their voices faded as they walked down the hall. I waited for Maggie outside. The grimness of the building was beginning to sap my good spirits. I have to admit, I was amused that my evaluation sheet upset him. After all, it was given to me to evaluate my own progress. When I received it, I was not told that no one could be 100 percent. That was my opinion of my teaching at P.S. 123. I'm just glad I didn't give into temptation and grade myself at 150 percent for effort. Obviously, I was to rate myself as he wanted me to, which I found fascinating because he wrote that I had not been teaching long enough for him to write an evaluation.

"Well, how does it feel to be a 100 percent teacher?" Maggie grinned.

I laughed. "You don't have any right to say anything. You never handed your evaluation sheet in."

"Nope. And I don't plan to. Come on, let's go home."

Since Mr. Carter had been so upset with my evaluation

sheet and mentioned that he had seen me doing things of which he did not approve, I wondered if he meant playtime. I did not stop taking the children outside. In fact, we continued to go out twice a day. This greatly helped the restlessness in the classroom, but several boys would inevitably lose some time. That Thursday, after leading exercises, I sat on the school steps surrounded by Cecil, Edward, Nicholas, Jimmy, and Jeffrey. We watched the class playing.

One of Maggie's students came over. "Hey, what you do?"

"Sitting," replied Cecil.

"Sitting?"

"Yeah." The boy watched them for a while longer. "We playing a game," volunteered Cecil.

"Can I play too?"

"Yeah," said Cecil. I watched the boy sit down behind Jeffrey. "Yeah," said Cecil. "First one get coal black, win." Cecil was a natural leader. I believed he could convince his classmates to do anything.

I let them play before our time outside was up and reminded them to try not to lose any time from tomorrow's baseball lesson. I watched them hurry to play ball. Cecil took command of his team, Jimmy pitched, Edward went to the outfield, and Nicholas promptly got into a fight with Jack.

As they lined up, I watched the boys talking. Cecil laughed. I waited until they were ready to enter the building. I did not want to have any teacher complain about the noise we made in the halls. Edward stepped up to me. "Mrs. Evans, where'd you get them glasses?" My sunglasses had attracted attention from the beginning. They were huge round circles that hid most of my face. Unfortunately, they continually slid down my nose, especially in the heat. All the boys waited for Edward to tell me what they already knew he would say. As I pushed the glasses in place, he said, "Mrs. Evans, you need more nose for them glasses!" We had a good laugh over that.

That afternoon, Mrs. Williams, the music teacher, was in the teachers' lounge when I entered at 1:45 for my 20 minute break. She was smoking a cigarette. Her voluminous body was wedged into a hard vinyl-covered chair. Wisps of curly gray hair escaped from her barrette. She hitched at her girdle and said, "Sure is hot. Lordy, don't you know."

I opened the only window in the tiny lounge and sat down. "Yes, Mrs. Williams, it certainly is."

"Ain't these kids something?" I opened my eyes and nodded at her. She needed a silent audience. "They is hoodlums, these ones, they is apes! That's what I calls them. They belong in some zoo. I ain't never seen such bad ones as this year. These is the worse I ever did see. Can't mind. Can't sing. They don't belong in school. They belong in jail." Her vitriolic comments startled me. "And stupid. You better believe they is stupid." She grumbled on about the length of time she had been teaching. "Why, I been teaching more than ten years. Live right here in the neighborhood all my life and I tell you The Projects have the highest juvenile delinquency rate in the city. And I has to teach these apes." She groaned, heaved herself to her feet, and walked to the door. Turning back to me, she said, "See you tomorrow, if I don't die first." A typical parting statement that I'd heard before, yet in this context, it worried me.

I closed my eyes again and thought about Mr. Carter blaming all of P.S. 123's problems on white teachers hating black children and wondered what he would think of Aldenia Williams's speech. It seemed from her comments that she hated her own. I could hear her bellowing in the hall, "You there, who do you think you is? Get in here," and the resounding slam of a metal door.

I was not able to teach that Friday and so I left stacks of work papers for the children. Directions were written on the blackboard. Their morning work was on their desks. That Monday, I felt refreshed and ready for another week. When I unlocked the classroom door, I could not believe that I was in my room. The desks were scattered and bunched. The floor was littered with paper and the blackboards were dirty. My desk was completely ransacked. Attendance had not been taken. The worksheets were not used, but the drawing paper I had hoarded and placed in the bottom of the filing cabinet was gone and so were the magic markers. Snoopy's fishing pole had fallen down, and the reading books were strewn along the shelf.

Ida Mae Lee stepped through the bathroom and poked her rouged face around the door. "Your class was just wild Friday!" she sniffed. "That substitute couldn't do nothing with them." She chuckled heartily at the classroom disorder and left.

I wondered what my substitute had done. I had visions of the disorder in Mary Ann Jenkins's classroom and wondered what my students would be like this morning. They wore their usual quiet Monday morning behavior into the school, lined up without fussing, and stumbled into the room. I had not touched anything. There was no morning work. "IS THIS YOUR CLASS-ROOM?" was written on the blackboard.

That morning before reading, they were treated to an Evans lecture on how to treat a substitute, how to help her, and how I expected the room to look, whether I was there or not. A few appeared sheepish. No one could give me an accurate account of Friday's activities.

Sylvia said, "I drew a lot."

Eric said, "They sure was loud."

Kelvin complained, "Yeah and we didn't go outside, neither." They straightened the room, put their desks back, washed the blackboards, picked up the papers on the floor, and straightened the reading books. We both learned something about Friday: they knew they would be held accountable for their actions if I were not there, and I realized again how very superficial their "good behavior" was.

I watched Nicholas that entire day. His arithmetic was not even first grade level. Neither were his spelling or reading skills. Sometimes his writing was legible, but most of the time, it was incomprehensible. He could not follow directions, play with his classmates, or pay attention to discussions. He spent the majority of his time staring off into space. Even when I worked with him individually, he had difficulty paying attention, forgot instructions, and did not seem to retain anything he learned. I could not imagine him working in a fourth grade classroom. His behavior, if possible, would probably be worse, since he would not be able to do any of the work. I asked several times about special education testing in the office and received a shrug. I was determined to have Nicholas tested before the end of the school year and hopefully have him placed in a special education class next fall. I knew that the tests were given by Mrs. Roberts, but she was never in her office and did not answer my notes.

Mr. Carter was too busy to see me about Nicholas. His office door was slightly open and when I walked by, I saw him counting money. The federal lunch sheets were on his desk and the adding machine could be heard as I walked down the hall.

Finally, I caught up with Mrs. Roberts. "Will you be able to test a student of mine?"

She told me flatly, "I am not taking no more testing for this year. I already has too many children to test as it is. You know, it takes a day for each child, besides there ain't room for no more special education children in the county, so he would be placed on a waiting list but remain in the classroom."

I asked her again, "Isn't there any way Nicholas could at least be tested so that he could be put on the waiting list?"

She crossly said, "No. I told you that already."

"Well, could I give him the test?"

"Heavens, no, you don't know how!"

"Aren't there directions written on the test?"

"Oh, no. You just couldn't do that. It ain't allowed." And she walked away.

Nicholas would not be tested that year. I began to think that the next best thing would be to keep him in third grade another year.

As I watched Nicholas that afternoon, he fiddled with two pencils. I saw him break the points against the desktop so that he could go to the pencil sharpener. The first time I let him sharpen them, but not the second time. He scowled at me, digging the pencils into the old desktop, wrapping and unwrapping his legs around the chair. I wanted to whisper in his ear, "Wake up, Nicholas. You are only ten years old and the world is passing you by. Wake up, before it's too late."

I decided to keep him after the others that afternoon, to talk to him again about school and his work. I wondered if he would mind being in third grade next year.

"Nicholas, show me all the work you did today."

He dutifully handed me a wet, wadded up paper ball that was his arithmetic. The two problems that were done, we had done together. His name was written on his spelling paper but neither handwriting nor English sentences were begun. The first-grade phonics sheet I started with him was finished incorrectly, but he had used an ink pen to cover his arms and legs with doodles.

"Nicholas, is this all you did today?"

He stared at me.

"Nicholas, do you know that fourth grade is harder than third grade?"

He continued to stare at me. Then he leaned over to pick a scab on his knee.

"Nicholas, unless you work hard these next two months, you won't be able to go to fourth grade. Do you understand me?"

He stared and then began to fidget, picking at his nose with ink-covered fingers.

"Nicholas, why do you come to school?"

"Don't know."

"Would you like to learn to read and to count?"

"Don't know!" he muttered again.

"I will give you two assignments to do at home. One is the old phonics paper, the other arithmetic. Let's look at them again. Do one on each paper now and then you may go."

He twisted his shirt collar, sucked on a button, and said, "I can't."

"We did these together this morning." I helped him begin and then wrote another note to his mother.

"Nicholas, I must see your mother as soon as possible." I told him what the note said since he was not willing to read it with me and I pinned it on the back of his shirt. "You may go home now." He stared at me, picked up his books, and backed out of the room.

As he left, Dexter came into the room with some filmstrips and books from the library. He enjoyed staying after school to help me, and bustled around with a sponge scrubbing the blackboards, cleaning the chalk trays, straightening the books, and putting out morning papers. Several of the other class helpers had not been able to stay that day, so he did all their jobs. He liked the room tidy. I checked papers and watched him. Even the coat rack hangers were hung neatly and the P.E. closet was straightened. "Thank you for your help. Everything looks wonderful. You worked very hard for the room to be so clean."

He gave me a rare smile and asked, "Can I take a book home to read?" After choosing one carefully he walked outside, but he was back again almost instantly. He said. "You want me to shut the windows?"

"No, thank you. I will. Bye, Dexter." I was delighted with the change in his behavior since December.

That next morning, it rained. The boys were despondent. "Rain mean no Lt. Evans and no baseball." A game of silent speedball with our red yarn ball raised their spirits slightly, but that afternoon the sun shone. We lined up quickly after music and walked outside. They did some exercises and began a game of ball tag. The girls played hopscotch on chalk lines that I drew on the sidewalk. I watched them laughing and talking.

"Mrs. Evans." I turned around to see Mr. Carter coming down the school steps toward me. He gestured at the children. "Mrs. Evans, I has told you about taking your children out to play, and now you is taking them out twice a day! You can't take them outside, and certainly not in the morning and in the afternoon. You just keep your children inside. If I see them outside again, I will come out and bring them in."

I stood quietly and looked at him. I had imagined this confrontation several times. It surprised me that it took four months to occur. Since I had not answered him immediately, he leaned forward and repeated, "You is taking them out twice a day."

"Mr. Carter, this is the first time my class has been out today."

"You wasn't out this morning?"

"No, sir, this is the first time they have gone outside today."

He looked bewildered. He did not ask about yesterday or the day before that. "Oh well," he said, "I guess I owes you an apology. I thought you was out already today."

I responded politely, "Mr. Carter, it rained this morning."

He looked at me thoughtfully, nodded, then turned and went back into the school. It was not clear whether he objected to a morning and afternoon exercise time or to going outside at all.

Later that same week, Mr. Carter came to my classroom door during arithmetic period. He did not step inside but preferred to stand in the hallway. "Mrs. Evans, I want to talk to you about playtime. You can't take them outside again. It is against county policy to have playtime and I will not allow you to take them out. They needs all the time you is wasting to learn reading and arithmetic."

"Mr. Carter, that isn't true. The county does not forbid recess. It is not written in the county policy book, and when I called the school board, I was told that as long as five hours of classwork were completed each day, playtime was fine."

He was angry. "You are working for me, Mrs. Evans, and I don't allow playtime!"

"What about the 15 minute playtime schedule you gave us several weeks ago?"

"Oh yes, well then, I suppose you can have fifteen minutes of playtime, but no more."

"Mr. Carter, the reason I think it is so important to take these children outside is that they have a short attention span. Playtime is an incentive for them to complete their work. Of course, it gives them needed exercise and, as well, a chance to work with others in a group." Before he could interrupt, I continued, "I believe my class is one of the better behaved in the school. The students usually work quietly. They do not disturb anyone in the halls. I believe this is because they have playtime to exercise and to be noisy."

"That is just what I say, Mrs. Evans, they don't need no playtime! I is against helter-skelter playing. They should be inside working."

"But Mr. Carter, the children always play organized games—baseball, kickball, jump rope, relays, and they do exercises."

"You know I am against playtime but you continue to disobey me."

"Mr. Carter, during my interview with you in December, you told me that I could take my class outside for playtime."

"I don't remember ever telling you that. I never say that you could take them out."

"Mr. Carter, you said, 'There is no scheduled playtime, but you may take them outside.'"

He looked at me doubtfully. "I knows I never said nothing like that! And if I did I certainly didn't expect you to spend an hour and to take them out five and six times a day!"

"Mr. Carter, the most time the children have played outside is one half-hour, going outside once or twice in one day."

"That's too much," he said. "I don't want no playtime."

Again I said, "The county allows playtime, and I think it is cruel and abusive to keep children inside, sitting at their desks all day long."

He was furious and shouted, "You work at P.S. 123 and what I says is, no playtime! You understand me, Mrs. Evans?"

I could not make him understand my position. I tried again. "Mr. Carter, I am hired and paid by the county. Its officials placed me at your school. I plan to follow county policies regarding playtime."

He shouted again, "No playtime, Mrs. Evans, and if we can't settle it, I'll report you to the school board."

"If you wish, I will be happy to join you in discussing county playground policy with the school board." I sighed. "I truly don't understand your concern with my P.E. schedule when I bother no one else and am well within the limitations of county policies. I think that it is imperative that children exercise. There are so many other school problems that you could focus on. For example, some teachers show films for two hours a day, every day." He looked surprised.

His parting ultimatum on playground use: "You can't take them out twice a day, but you remember this: I has warned you about playtime. I am against you taking them out." He stomped down the hall. He did not say that I could not take them out for one half-hour or whether it had to be morning or afternoon. And he didn't mention going to the school board.

"Children, you were very well behaved when I was in the hall. I am very proud of you. Mr. Carter has decided that we can no longer have playtime twice a day. He has forbidden it. But perhaps we can find other ways to break up the six hours and forty-five minutes that we spend in school together."

They looked at me dubiously, but I was already planning science experiments, art projects, explorations, and word games that had to be played outside. I knew that was devious and would lead to another tirade, but I could not keep their attention without breaks and could not imagine keeping children inside.

That afternoon, we were notified about another faculty meeting. I groaned inwardly, expecting another playtime discussion. This faculty meeting, however, like so many others, dwelled on well-worn topics: the racial prejudice among white teachers and behavioral objectives.

Mr. Carter continued with the shameful way we were treating the teacher aides. "Now, you all are just loading poor Mrs. Smith with work and not giving Nadette any at all. She is just sitting in the office with nothing to do when poor Mrs. Smith here came to me in tears because you expect her to do all that work. You white teachers will just have to work with us blacks. Nadette wants to do your work too and she is very upset that you don't give her none. From now on, you give all your work to

Mrs. Black and she will give it to the teacher aides. Don't you go giving it to Mrs. Smith. She has to share the work with Nadette. We has to be fair about this, and since you is so prejudiced not to give Nadette any work, this is the way it will be from now on. Understand?"

I don't know why I raised my hand. Maybe it was the memory of Mrs. Smith's tear-streaked face and puffy red eyes. "Mr. Carter?" He looked at me warily. "Mr. Carter, I would like to mention why I gave my work to Mrs. Smith rather than Nadette. Before Mrs. Smith came, I gave my first dittos to Nadette and she returned them two weeks later with one master ripped and the other soaked with copy fluid. She counted incorrectly and gave me too few, and then she wasted half a ream of paper when she ran them off. I really don't need that kind of help. So I just make the copies myself."

Several other teachers spoke up and agreed with me. Perhaps they were tired of his peculiar brand of racial discrimination and annoyed either at his ignorance of the real situation or his purposeful reconstruction of it to fit his race-based narrative. "From now on give all your work to Mrs. Black. I don't want you giving it to Mrs. Smith. We has to be fair about this. After all, we has two teacher aides and we got to use both of them."

It was so humid that my arm stuck to my notepad. I felt rumpled, chalk-dust saturated, and disheveled. He rambled on for ten more minutes about discipline problems, ineffective white teachers, and leaving from teachers' meetings early— Mrs. Potter had just left. "Some teachers think they are something special. Well, ain't no one special here. Everyone is the same." Finally, when I was sure that no one was listening to him, not even Mr. Carter himself, he dismissed the meeting.

That teaching day had exhausted me. I do not like confrontations, even though I prepared for the discussion on playtime for months. I always left faculty meetings resolving not to say anything at the next one, not to voice my opinions, and to accept everything that happened. I vowed to stop caring that Nicholas would never get the special education he needed or that many of my students were being denied the quality education they deserved. I knew I was deluding myself. I would never be able to ignore injustice.

The old green door was hard to open. I pulled harder and was greeted with institutional gloom, the cold stares of the cafetorium workers, the stale food smells, and the building noises. I was determined this teaching day would be quiet and uneventful. I repeated thoughts to myself of avoiding conflicts. Optimistically, I opened the windows, wrote a poem about hot weather on the blackboard, and put a record on the record player. That day, I decided to welcome the children with "Oh What a Beautiful Morning." They enjoyed being greeted with music and liked the song.

"How high an elephant eye anyways, Mrs. Evans?" said Tynetta.

"It high as the building, girl," chided Jimmy. With that question debated vociferously, they left for reading.

I always enjoyed the reading group and believe that a small group of children—12 to 15—is ideal for teaching. They wrote some poetry, listened to some funny poems I had collected, read a story from their reading book, and began to answer some questions when the clock snapped to 10:00. "We have to go so soon?" sighed Steve.

My own class was still in good spirits and quietly doing their language paper when a large black woman barged into my room, dragging Jeffrey behind her. She began formally enough, "I am Mrs. Brown, and this here is my son." I looked at Jeffrey, who was dressed in a white shirt and his good pair of pants. His eyes were big and round.

"Now look here Mrs.—what is your name, anyhow?" I told her. "Well now, Mrs. Evans"—she leaned over my desktop and shook her finger at me. "What this here all about?"

I had no idea what she meant. I pushed back my chair and stood up, but she still towered over me. Jeffrey was staring at the floor. Mrs. Brown wiped her perspiring face on her sleeve and said, "He told me you don't let him in the classroom because he late. Now, what you got to say about that?" She was very angry.

"Mrs. Brown, I have not seen Jeffrey since yesterday afternoon when he left at 3:15."

"You sure about that?" She didn't wait for my reply. "Why you goddamn lying little bastard!" and she hit Jeffrey hard on the side of his head. I winced but he did not cry or move away. He didn't even put his hands up to cover his head. Turning back to me, she said, "Sorry to have bothered you. I should've known better than believe anything he tole me." She slammed the door on her way out.

After that excitement, it was difficult for the class to return to their schoolwork. They fidgeted for 30 minutes, whispered across the aisles, and stared at Jeffrey. He sat at his desk with his head down on his arms.

"Jeffrey?" He did not answer. "Jeffrey, are you ready to talk with me?"

"No!" he snarled.

The children half-heartedly finished their assignments, and we corrected them together, something I rarely did since I felt that it was better to correct each paper individually. During that time, I reminded Kelvin twice not to bother Jeffrey, Nicholas three times to sit down, Marjorie and Jack twice to stop fussing at each other. I wondered if Mrs. Brown had any idea how completely she disrupted the class. We went outside ten minutes early. The morning work was as complete as it would be that day.

As the children ran to their places for exercises, I looked

back at the building and noticed Mrs. Dickson standing at her window watching us. I was tempted to wave at her. I wondered if she would tell Mr. Carter what time we went outside. When I looked again, she quickly moved away from the windows. We exercised energetically. We touched toes, ran in place, hopped, squatted, did jumping jacks and windmills. Even Dexter tried. After running around the field, they scattered to play ball with Lt. Evans or hopscotch with me. Nicholas lost his playtime after ten minutes for fighting with Felicia, but the others seemed to play frantically. I knew the morning confrontation upset them.

After insisting that Jeffrey leave his desk and come outside with the class, I watched him lean against the tree. I tried to talk with him again. "Jeffrey, why didn't you come into the classroom this morning and then get your late excuse? You have done that before." He did not answer. He scowled. I talked to him several more minutes, but he was not ready to respond. Then, I wondered if he had a headache. He nodded when I asked him but refused to go to the office for an aspirin, and instead flattened himself against the tree trunk.

The cafetorium was noisier than usual. Several substitute teachers and the fact that neither Fay Morris nor Millie LeBlanc controlled their classes added to the bedlam. I ate with the boys that day and watched Dexter carefully eat all his noodles and white bread. He traded his hot dog for more noodles. Jeffrey sucked aimlessly on his hot dog and Cecil ate his applesauce with his fingers. "Use a spoon, Cecil." As I got up from the table to get him a spoon, I accidentally hit the corner of his tray and splattered applesauce all over his face, hair, and the front of his shirt.

"Yes, ma'am. I use a spoon!" said Cecil.

"Oh, I am so sorry, Cecil. I did not mean to cover you with applesauce. Here are some napkins to wipe it off." A small glob remained lodged in his hair. He looked startled and funny with applesauce all over him, and I looked so dismayed that the whole table of children laughed loudly. He always used a spoon for applesauce after that. "See, Mrs. Evans, I use my spoon."

The next day was disrupted by tuberculosis shots and the serving of morning orange juice. Since none of the teachers was told about the novelty of morning orange juice, no one appeared in the cafetorium. The cafetorium workers were furious and demanded to know where the classes were. The office then sent Nadette to each teacher to bring the class to the cafetorium, and so the lines were endless, winding around the hall and up to the second floor. The noise was deafening with children shouting, running, and sliding, banging, and thumping into their friends. Some hid under the stairway and yelled loudly. My class watched me watch them and fidgeted but was silent.

The orange juice was a small paper cupful so diluted that only the color proved it was orange juice. The children were not allowed to sit down but were expected to drink it standing over the garbage pails and then leave. It took 25 minutes to get orange juice that morning. Since half of the reading group had not had theirs, they went to the cafetorium to wait ten more minutes. "Do I have to drink it?" asked Steve. "I hate orange juice."

"Yeah. It's awful! Where's yours, Mrs. Evans?"

"Wish I was grown up, then I wouldn't have to drink it either."

I do not know why they decided to have orange juice in the morning. Any breakfast is a good idea, but just orange juice? With this program, morning milk for Edward and the others was discontinued. "We is too busy to be bothered. Don't you send them no more!" The morning orange juice program occurred sporadically, without notice to the teachers, and after five or six more attempts, stopped completely.

That same day, the children received their TB shots. I had reminded them about the shots since Monday, assuring them that if everyone was in school that day, they could play ten extra minutes. That was the only reward I found that all the children would enjoy. We talked about the reason for the shots, the seriousness of the disease, and its effect on their health, and at the end of the discussion, the class seemed to realize the importance of the shots. Then Nicholas managed to change the class mood completely by saying, "Yeah, and them shots sure hurt and you get sick and everything."

"Do they hurt?" demanded Eric.

Fear filled their eyes as I looked from face to face. "How many of you have ever stuck yourself with a pin?" Almost all of them had. "It feels something like that."

"Oh, that ain't nothing," said Kelvin. "Nicholas, you is a scaredy-cat."

Unfortunately, many of the children remembered what Nicholas said and several were absent. They were the ones who would have benefited most from the shots: Barbara, Danny, and Sandy. We lined up twice before they were quiet enough to leave the room. I put Nicholas at the beginning of the line and walked beside him. After their shot, they were to line up again, wait for their classmates, and return to the room.

Mrs. Dickson was helping the visiting nurse. She used the same cotton swab for my first three students before I could stop her and would have continued if I had not asked her to use one cotton swab per child. Luckily, the nurse agreed with me. Mrs. Dickson soon lost interest in helping and went into the office. She was still talking to Mr. Carter and Mrs. Black when my children walked past the office, down the hall, and into our room. She was still there when we left a half-hour later for morning P.E.

Most of the students agreed that getting the shot was not so bad. We talked about fear and how it kept you from doing new things. I asked them what other things frighten them.

"The dark."

"Momma when she drunk."

"Spiders."

Cecil said, "I ain't afraid of nothing. I'm real brave."

"You is too afraid of something, boy," hooted Nanci.

We made a list of scary things and drew pictures of them on paper borrowed from Mrs. Madison. The children hung them on the bulletin board.

That next day, Barbara was in class. "Why were you absent yesterday, Barbara?"

She said, "I was sick, Mrs. Evans."

"Were you sick or did you stay home because of the TB shot?"

"I don't want no shot, so I played sick," she giggled.

"Barbara, after all our talks about the importance of getting the TB shot?"

"I don't want no shot, Mrs. Evans." Her grimy hands left brown marks on my shirt sleeve. She smiled. "You ain't mad, is you?"

I knew that the public health nurse would not visit the school again that year and for the absentees to get their shots, a parent would have to take them to the free health clinic. I sighed when I realized that Barbara and Danny and Sandy would not be immunized that year.

It was almost 2:00 that Friday afternoon. The children were looking at a filmstrip on ocean creatures—"Hey, that a whale"—when I smelled smoke. The room filled rapidly with thick gray smoke. The children began coughing and choking. Looking out the window, I noticed that trash was burning in the junkyard on the far side of the playground. The wind was carrying the smoke right into my classroom. I watched a man add more trash to the fire, including pieces of old tires. Opening the door into the hallway did not help, so we decided to leave the classroom. The children walked down the hall and stopped by the office.

Mrs. Black assured me Mr. Carter was in the building, but she did not know where.

"There is too much smoke in my room to stay. Can't anything be done about burning trash during school hours?"

"You has to ask Mr. Carter."

"Yes, thank you." She watched us walk out to the front of the school to avoid the smoke. We sat in the meager shade from the porch roof. Our eyes smarted and watered. Several still coughed from the smoke, but they listened to the story I read about an old fisherman and the sea. They liked stories. Later, Mrs. Black and Mrs. Dickson watched the class come inside and walk down to the room. The room was still smoky. As the bell rang, the children left hurriedly. After straightening the room and putting out Monday's work, I could not stand the smell of burning trash any longer. On my way outside to wait for Maggie, I stopped in the office. "I would like to talk to Mr. Carter, please."

"Oh, he ain't here now. He gone for the day." She smiled at me.

It was Friday afternoon. I thought about the week: the playground confrontation with Mr. Carter, Nicholas's special education problem, Jeffrey's mother, the diluted orange juice, and the burning trash. I watched Missouri sweep the hall floors as I walked by. The students were outside, lingering around the fence, playing games, or sitting on the dirt, talking. I looked at the front of P.S. 123—the grassless lawn, the boarded windows, the sagging porch roof. I stood outside that barbed wire fence, leaned against Maggie's car, and waited. Groups of students walked slowly past me. They did not seem pleased that it was Friday. Certainly, there was no hurry to go home.

I thought of my students. Would I be able to teach Jeffrey, Danny, Edward, and Sandy enough reading and arithmetic to function in fourth grade? What had I been able to do to help Nicholas's tantrums or Sandra's crying bouts and sicknesses? I wondered about Nanci's and Barbara's growing insolence and continued lateness. My thoughts wandered to other problems—no ditto paper, no art supplies, broken windows, no P.E. equipment, not enough reading books for my advanced group, a broken film projector. Even all of that was not the real problem. The attitude of those in charge was what was most infuriating.

"No playtime. You understand?"

"Sorry, there ain't no more supplies, least wise not for you."

"No, you can't test Nicholas. That's unheard of. I got to do the testing."

"Some of you teachers just refuse to work with blacks. Now this here problem with the teacher aides is just one example."

I knew I should not, but I abandoned myself to unpleasant thoughts.

A little girl in a pink dress skipped down the walk and out the gate. Her black hair was plaited into three pigtails tied with pink ribbons. I had never seen her before and decided that she must be a fourth grader. She carried a library book under her arm and skipped down the broken sidewalk toward me. Stopping beside me, she said, "Gee Mrs. Evans, you sure is pretty!" Her big brown eyes and happy smile compelled me to smile back. I started to say thank you, but she had already skipped away, her pigtails bobbing up and down with each step.

CHAPTER 13

Help from Mr. Nolen?

IT WAS MY WEEK FOR DOOR DUTY. Arriving at 7:45, I put picture puzzles on some desks, number puzzles on others, and wrote morning instructions on the board. At 8:00, I took my position at the south door to ensure that the school was not invaded by students before 8:30. As I stood there, I thought of all the worthwhile things I should be doing in my classroom, like preparing a new science center or making visual aids.

Mrs. Lee popped in and out of her doorway and nodded good morning to me. I watched Missouri saunter down the hall with a mop and disappear into the boys' bathroom. A few minutes later, one of the cafetorium workers walked down the hall and into the boys' bathroom.

Mrs. Lee hissed at me and waved frantically. I walked over to her doorway. "There, did you see that? Did you see that?" she repeated. "If that don't beat all and in broad daylight, front of everybody! Why, they ain't got no morals." My puzzled expression was more than she could stand. "Those two. You just saw them go into the boys' bathroom."

"Sure. They're cleaning."

She hooted loudly at me. "You sure are dumb about niggers! Well, let me tell you. I have known niggers all my life and they ain't cleaning." The bathroom cleaning routine was repeated each day I stood duty, as was Mrs. Lee's statement, "See that? What I tell you?" she would hiss.

P.S. 123 suffered acutely from malicious gossip. Everyone constantly talked about everyone else. Teachers distrusted each other and repeated gossip. Each story contained some truth but was viciously twisted to suit the whims of the teller. It was well known that if you spoke to Fay Morris or Millie LeBlanc, the entire school would know what was said by the afternoon. It was believed that anything Mrs. Dickson saw or did not see, she told Mr. Carter. There were more alliances than an armed camp. The latest rumor was that cafetorium workers were paid to hide in a nearby workroom and listen to the conversations in the teachers' lounge and then report to Mr. Carter.

Occasionally, Maggie and I would laugh about some of the stories on the way home. The favorite stories were, of course, about Mr. Carter's last faculty meeting, his relationship with Mrs. Dickson, his frequent absences, and his constant counting of money.

One day, Fay assured me that Mr. Carter carried a gun with him when he came to school.

"Really, Fay?"

"I am not kidding. He does!"

"Well, did you see it?"

Fay hesitated a little. "No, but I saw the outline of it when he patted his pants pocket."

If that were true, all P.S. 123 needed was a gunfight.

Everyone also discussed who would quit that June. If Fay Morris could be believed, P.S. 123 would be left with Mrs. Dickson, Mrs. LeBlanc, Miss Bernardo, and Mrs. Madison. Succinctly she said, "Dickson got an easy job as Mr. Carter's favorite. LeBlanc doesn't do anything and no one cares. Bernado is too weird to get another job. No other school will take Madison with her arthritic condition."

Most of the young white teachers were leaving for other jobs or because of their husbands' transfers or to get married. At least, those were the paper reasons, but the real reason was that none of them could stand another abrasive year teaching at P.S. 123. Even though these teachers were unwilling to face Mr. Carter in faculty meetings, or write letters of complaint, they did not plan to return.

When interest in the topic of who might return waned, teachers gossiped about other teachers. "Did you know Mrs. Potter walked out today? She went straight to the school board. Last time she went, Mr. Carter rearranged her class and gave her all the problem children. Isn't that dreadful?"

"She told me she takes tranquilizers. I'll bet she's on her way to a nervous breakdown!"

"Did you know that the fifth-grade teacher who left at Christmas gave a full report on P.S. 123 to the school board? She included Mr. Carter's lack of leadership. I heard she is teaching in a private church school, so he did not keep her from getting another job," said Fay.

Occasionally, the interest in gossip disrupted class lessons. Mrs. Lee hissed at me to come to the bathroom's connecting door. She was quite excited. "You won't believe this, but I just saw Mrs. Miller, the curriculum coordinator, and she sure looks pregnant to me"

I shrugged. "Mrs. Lee, I am teaching reading."

"Well, her husband has been away overseas for months now, so it can't be his."

"Mrs. Lee, I really am not interested."

She huffed, "If that's the way you feel, I just won't tell you about the rest that I heard." She stomped back into her own room. In one day, I was told all of the following:

"Mrs. Madison canes her students and sticks them into her closet when they misbehave and Millie LeBlanc's students watched films for more than two hours today. She signed up for every afternoon this week."

"Did you see Ozell? I think he's drunk, smells like it too."

"You know, Bernardo is really weird. Her classroom gives me a headache! All that stuff everywhere, the walls, the ceiling."

"There goes Mrs. Dickson again. She spends more time in the office than in her classroom. You know, she was there at least an hour this morning, leaning on the counter drinking coffee and talking. If she ain't in the office then she is in the hall doing bulletin boards. I'll bet she is on all seventeen of his damn committees. Ha. Ha.

"Hey Evans, heard you got into a real fight with Mr. Carter yesterday out in the hall, and that he threatened to fire you and you said you'd go to the school board."

"You're really not going to believe what I learned today. College degrees can be bought! One of the teachers talked about renewing her degree in the lounge today. I don't know her name. Anyway, she has to send in her money every year so that they will send her a new degree. That's because a few years ago the county decided all teachers must have college degrees, so a lot of teachers who had taught a long time left in June without a degree and returned in September with a B.A. or even an M.A. I guess the M.A. costs more and that way they kept their jobs. The colleges that gave them their degrees demand a payment every year for providing them with a diploma."

The school board was another favorite discussion: "Well, first of all, you should know that the school board is all white. Did you hear about the scandal? A year or two ago the school board lost a lot of school funds. The board couldn't balance its books because a huge amount was missing. Nothing happened, and no one was held accountable! The same school board members were just voted back into office."

"The school superintendent is Junior Jordan. He's a nice guy, used to be a high school coach. Now he's just in way over his head. Did you know that several teachers complained to the school board and an anonymous letter was sent to the newspaper? You know the school board was called about that letter, and Dr. Holstein reported directly to them and nothing much happened. Wonder why!"

It was obvious that the children enjoyed gossiping, too. Typical examples were the stories the children made up when Maggie was absent for one week:

"I knows Miss Stevens done got herself in a fight. She gots a big shotgun wound in her leg," said Carlos.

"No, she been drinking and gots cut up with a knife! Yeah."

The common cold was never suggested. Yet, with the pattern set by adults, it was not surprising to find the same pattern followed by children.

April's heat shortened their attention spans and tempers flared. Restless children daydreamed of summer with each fresh breeze. The frustrations of teaching at P.S. 123 began to outweigh the rewards. Few changes occurred since December. The roof still leaked. The broken windows were still boarded. The plumbing was still faulty. The water fountains either did not work or produced a trickle of undrinkable brown water. The classroom sink leaked and the toilet clogged. The heating system was shut off, but my radiators still toasted the room. Missouri was mystified. "I tell you, Mrs. Evans, there just ain't no way for to figure this. That do beat all." The room was overrun by red ants, wasps, flies, and several other winged creatures I did not recognize. That was in addition to our normal complement of spiders and cockroaches. Without screened windows, this bug infestation was not surprising.

In addition to the building's condition, the school equipment and supplies situation, if possible, deteriorated. Anything that broke was rarely repaired. The paper cutter, the record player, and the overhead projector were all examples. Other equipment , such as the television, the film projector, and the ditto machine, were often in stages of disrepair. There was no more ditto paper for the school for the rest of the year. Each teacher was given one ream of paper to use from April to June. I bought four more reams of paper for my students. Besides the lack of ditto paper, there were no paper towels, no toilet paper, no light bulbs, no pencils or chalk, no magic markers, and, of course, no art or P.E. supplies.

Our lack of books was helped by sharing with other classrooms, but teachers were not allowed to trade books. Mr. Carter said, "Don't want none of the books mixed up." We did it clandestinely, sometimes sending students with two or three books at a time. At the end of June, we returned the books to the correct classrooms.

The lack of supplies and the archaic school building were not all that teachers were forced to face. Each day brought new disruptions. On cue, Tynetta sulked and cried. Marjorie and Felicia insulted each other across the width of the classroom. Nanci and Barbara were late each morning, sauntering in with large grins that were replaced with pouts when I took away minutes from playtime. Jack and Cecil had sporadic tantrums. Dexter, Nicholas, and Jimmy tormented their classmates. Sandra became ill each day by 10:00, and Grandma came to take her home.

The heat made my students sleepy or grouchy. Many of the

girls sat in the shade of the lone playground tree and, by 2:00, several slept in the classroom. Even the teachers were affected by the heat and by the knowledge that two months remained of the school year. Mrs. Dickson spent much of the day planting bushes and flowers in the schoolyard—unattended, the plants soon withered and dried up. Mrs. LeBlanc watched films. Mrs. Lee could not be found for reading in the afternoon, and several teachers spent a sick day at the beach. Many teachers were absent on Fridays or Mondays. Some took off whole weeks at a time. Others arrived late and left early.

Fay complained about Mrs. LeBlanc, and Mrs. LeBlanc complained about the reading program until Mrs. Smith, the teachers' aide, helped her each morning. Mrs. Smith later said proudly, "Why, I actually teach the class, as well as correct all of Mrs. LeBlanc's class papers!"

The office staff was an additional problem. Mrs. Black's obvious favoritism with supplies, her unfairness in doling out copy work to the aides (mine remained on the bottom of the stack for weeks), her inept office procedures, the missing school records for children, and her refusal to stop parents at the office before they reached the classroom all increased the tension.

Many of our problems were caused by Mr. Carter. His apparent lack of interest in the school or the students, his unwillingness to discipline, his hostility to playtime, his refusal to provide the school with adequate books and basic supplies, his derogatory remarks about the teachers, his aversion to demanding that adequate special education or social services or rudimentary health care be provided caused the situation at P.S. 123 to deteriorate.

Teaching in this atmosphere was difficult, if not impossible. I decided to write another letter containing all these complaints and send it to each school board member and to the newspaper. The letter described all the problems at P.S. 123. I hoped to have it signed by a majority of the teachers.

When asked to sign the ten-page letter, Aldenia Williams worried about her retirement. Ozell Lewis and Mrs. Smith were afraid they would be branded troublemakers and not get other jobs. Maggie, Debbie, and Hilda were leaving in June but refused to sign for fear of a poor recommendation. Fay didn't think the conditions were all that bad, and the librarian was content with her situation. Only Mrs. Potter—who had a signed contract at a new school for next year—agreed to sign the letter. Unfortunately, her husband changed her mind by urging her to just accept the P.S. 123 situation since the school year was almost over.

I doubted the letter would have much impact if signed by one white teacher. Was it just a rant by a disgruntled employee, not honest concern for the educational system at P.S. 123?

Another faculty meeting was held that afternoon. Mr. Carter said, "I want you teachers to know that P.S. 123 is out of funds for this school year. This here is the reason for no more supplies. The school gots a debt of more than $500. This here is due to the disappearance of the Coke machine money and some other things," he added vaguely.

He was abrasive and belligerent, stressing again that, "We ain't going have no lack of organization in any way here." He continued, "You teachers handing in those registers late and Mrs. Miller complained about how poor them behavioral objectives is. Some of you teachers ain't taking door duty and the noise in the halls must stop. I wants more orderly cafetorium hours." He paused for a minute and checked the notes he had written on the back of an envelope.

"Mr. Carter," I asked, "What can be done about the burning trash? I am sure that every county has trash burning controls."

Another teacher added, "Yes, it affects my room too, and it is difficult to teach with smoke filling the room."

"I suppose I could find out about that." But he never did. My room was filled with smoke each day that week.

He continued, "I just don't get no cooperation from you teachers. Only one ever volunteers to help is Mrs. Dickson. Why, she has done all that work around the school grounds and the bulletin boards this whole year." Mrs. Dickson stood up and bowed to the group. "I just don't know what I would do without her." We applauded politely.

Mrs. Dickson smoothed her hair, tucked her blouse into her skirt, and beamed. "Thank you, Mr. Carter, thank you very much. You know, I think you is an excellent principal! And I think we should all work hard for you."

"About this here lunch money problem, Mr. Carter ask me to show you how I do it. I keep my lunch money straight by writing little letters by the children's name each day. 'B' if the child bring a bag lunch. 'F' for federal lunch money or free lunch." She opened the register and showed it to the faculty to prove that it was simple enough for even the dullest teacher to comprehend.

"Thank you, Mrs. Dickson, I'm sure that will help these teachers. Now then, I told you before about sending children to my office. I ain't here to discipline children. That is your job! If you teachers can't handle your own discipline problems, then you don't have no right to teach." I sighed, stopped listening, and gazed out the window.

That next day, Sandy came back to school. He had been absent sporadically, returning each time with a note saying, "Sandy sick," signed "Daisy," written on a dirty scrap of paper bag with a pencil. Today Sandy was feeling much better. I watched him as he stood in line. His classmates in front of him would jump or twitch and Sandy would giggle. This also happened when he was at his desk. Eric jumped, whined at him, and moved his desk. Sandy giggled and giggled. He was a tall boy, almost thirteen years old. He combed his hair in a fashionable Afro. A large black comb protruded from his pocket. He had a bright smile and a deep laugh. Mr. Carter warned me the first week of school that "he was a bad one," but I enjoyed teaching him. He worked hard at reading and was now on a first grade level, but most of all, he liked discussions or science.

I watched Sandy hide something in his desk. While working on his spelling, I watched him slip his hand into his desk and pull out a small pen knife. I saw him feel the end of the knife and look around at his classmates, but they were too far away for him to reach. Several were at the pencil sharpener, so I watched him hide the pen knife in his hand and walk toward the sharpener.

"Sandy, put the knife on my desk, please."

"Ain't got no knife, Mrs. Evans," said Sandy.

"Sandy, now."

"Aw, shit!" He looked angry and just a little embarrassed that I caught him. He walked over and put the knife on my desk.

"Thank you, Sandy, you may sharpen your pencil now." We both knew his pencil did not need to be sharpened. I looked at the knife. The blade was filed to a sharp edge. I put it into my desk drawer and turned the key in the lock.

Later, Sandy and I talked about the knife. "Sandy, I cannot give it back to you today. Do you know you could seriously hurt someone with this knife? Why did you bring it to school?"

"Aw, just for fun, Mrs. Evans. I ain't going to hurt no one." He squirmed, looked down, and shuffled his feet.

"Do you understand why I can't give it back today?"

"Yeah, I guess so, but sure is a cool knife." He shrugged. "It's okay, Mrs. Evans, I got more at home."

"Sandy, you must promise me never to bring another knife to school."

"Okay, I promise." I let him join the others on the playground. I watched his bright green shirt as he ran across the field to join a marbles game. He looked like a carefree child as he cheered and laughed with his friends.

The class walked in from the playground and lined up for lunch. Mr. Carter was waiting for me. "Mrs. Evans, you can't take them out no more. Not before lunch. They can't go out at that time again. Understand? Besides, you is keeping them outside too long."

"Mr. Carter, why can't they go outside before lunch?"

"They don't have no time to wash their hands."

"My classroom has no paper towels and no soap. That makes hand washing difficult."

"You got to stop talking at me and start listening. I says no more playtime."

"Would this time be all right if they washed their hands?"

He didn't answer that question. "I talked with you about this here before, and you know what I think about playtime. Someone is going to get hurt, helter-skelter playing like that."

"But you scheduled 15 minute P.E. periods and Mrs. Potter and I decided to switch times. Is that schedule no longer followed?" He never answered but turned and walked down the hall with his hands in his pockets.

I expected that there would be more problems with playtime. Nonetheless, my class washed their hands with cold brown water the next day before they lined up for lunch. The majority of them wiped their hands on their dirty pants or skirts.

That afternoon, the room was again filled with smoke from the trash burning in the neighboring junkyard, and a swarm of curious wasps decided to join the class for story hour. Several of the boys discouraged them, chasing and swatting them with newspapers. "I got him. I got the son of a bitch!" shouted Kelvin.

Beginning with Sandy and the knife, and including Sandra being sick and leaving with Grandma, Felicia sobbing because Jeffrey insulted her, Dexter sulking because he had to give his class duty to another student for the next week, and Mr. Carter's comment about playtime, it was a discouraging day.

I sat by my fan in that empty room with my arm sticking to the papers I corrected. The late afternoon sun warmed my back. I thought about my students and their progress, not always academic—Edward's willingness to play games with his classmates and his participation in class discussions, Jeffrey's occasional smile and his completed schoolwork, Cecil's apologies after a temper tantrum, and L'Angela's lack of shyness with her classmates. Eric, Larry, Billy, and Jack were doing well with multiplication. Sandy and Danny had five words correctly spelled, and Patricia could sometimes add and subtract first grade problems correctly. I was pleased with the progress they were making.

I also thought about Nicholas's learning problems, Sandra's illness, and Nanci's increased belligerence. Each day, Nanci and Barbara were 10 or 15 minutes late, sauntering in, smiling, and slowly taking their seats. Although they lost playtime, it did not improve their punctuality. I already received a warning from Nanci's mother through Mr. Carter. "Mrs. Evans, Nanci's mother don't want her to sit in the sun at playtime no more." Nanci sat wherever I was sitting.

When the tardiness continued the third week, I sent Nanci to the office and then home for a late excuse, a school policy I had avoided until then. Barbara was not allowed to go home since Mr. Carter thought she should not walk the five blocks to her home. I sent a note home with her asking her mother to help Barbara get to school on time.

Nanci returned with an angry mother during reading period.

Mrs. White was thin and intense. Her nurse's uniform was immaculate.

"Perhaps Nanci could help you in the mornings by dressing herself and setting the table for breakfast? If she started to school earlier it would help!" I suggested.

"I suppose so. Yes, I think you're right. Maybe I am over anxious about Nanci." Mrs. White agreed.

"It is important for Nanci to be on time. It is necessary that she follow simple rules. This will help her when she is older."

"Oh yes, I agree. Yes, well, it was nice meeting you. I certainly appreciate your interest in Nanci." Mrs. White smiled and hurried out the door. I thought about mentioning that Nanci had not completed several class assignments recently and was disrupting the class whenever she had the chance but decided to solve one problem at a time.

That day I planned two new, important morning jobs for the class and just happened to select Nanci and Barbara for the duties. They would have to be on time to get their jobs done before reading class. The importance of their new positions intrigued the girls for a few days, but by the end of the week, both were late again. They sulked when they realized that they could not be late and do their morning jobs. Barbara's tantrum was loud. She banged on the desk, kicked the chair, and threw several books on the floor. "Barbara, I am sorry. You will have to be on time tomorrow to get your job done." I sent another note home with Barbara that afternoon asking her mother to come in for a conference.

Nanci laughed and said, "See, I can be late anytime I want." I sent her home again for a late excuse and again she returned with her mother. Mrs. White did not come to see me but went straight to Mr. Carter.

Mr. Carter called me in and Mrs. White yelled at me,

"I am tired of Nanci being sent home. I don't want her sent

home anymore. She is wasting too much class time just because she is a little late. I won't have this happen. I don't like the way she treats my child, standing her in a closet and making her stand in the sun. I told you I didn't like that. Then taking away her class job. You just don't like my girl, always troubling her."

"You just can't teach. No other teacher ever have trouble with Nanci. She is a good girl. You don't know nothing. How dare you put her in the closet, and I already told you before I don't want her in the sun." She shook her fist at me.

While she was catching her breath, I quietly said, "Mrs. White, I have no intention of being screamed at. I came in to discuss Nanci being late and the school policy requiring me to send her home. When you are ready to talk with me, I will gladly come back." I got up and walked to the door.

Mrs. White jumped to her feet and shouted, "How dare you walk out on me! Who you think you is?"

"Sit down, Mrs. Evans," Mr. Carter said sharply. "Now, now, let's try to solve this here problem."

Nanci's mother had not heard him. She was still yelling at me. "How dare you?" she choked. "How dare you? I am not one of your students. You can't act this way with me. I am a nurse."

I can't remember the rest of her tirade. When she stopped momentarily, I explained, "I have never put Nanci into a closet. I have never put any of my students into a closet. I have asked her to step into the girls' bathroom because she was making a scene and I wanted to talk with her immediately. She does sit in the sun with me but she plays in the sun too. There is very little shade on our playground. Unfortunately, lateness is not her only problem. Recently she has refused to do her classroom work, has been insolent, continues to tease several of her classmates, and frequently disrupts the class."

"You lie! I don't believe you. You just don't like my girl. Mr.

Carter, I want her out of Mrs. Evans's class. I want her taught by a black teacher."

Mr. Carter spoke up, "I am sure we can settle this here problem. Mrs. Evans, you send the child directly to the office if she is late."

"That is what I did this morning, Mr. Carter."

"Yes, well, I will talk to her personally." He nodded at Mrs. White.

Mrs. White glared at both of us.

That day, Nanci shoved and pushed in line, pinched her classmates, handed in unfinished work, and refused to correct her mistakes or let me work with her to correct them. I sent the work home with her. She talked back and laughed when she was corrected. She refused to discuss her behavior and seemed to know that her mother would complain about the slightest reprimand. I talked with her numerous times about good behavior. She would grin and giggle and not answer.

Arriving early that next morning, I ran off a number of dittos and unlocked my classroom door as the bell rang. Barbara's mother was waiting for me by the door. "How come you punish my Barbara when you ain't on time either?"

"Good morning, Mrs. Thomas. I have been here since 7:30 working on dittos upstairs."

Mrs. Thomas, a small, plump woman, stalked ahead of me into the classroom. She said, "Well, I don't see why Barbara is in trouble. She ain't never been before."

"Mrs. Thomas, I appreciate your coming in. I wanted you to know that Barbara has been late daily for several weeks. She has temper tantrums, sulks, and talks back when corrected. This behavior is interfering with her schoolwork."

Help from Mr. Nolen?

"I don't know why she doing this. Maybe it is because she playing with that Nanci. I wants you to stop that." She paused. "I wants you to know that I has to take a day off work just to come to school. Don't you call me no more, asking me to come. You just take care of Barbara. That your job." She paused and added, "Don't you take no more of that temper. She got a bad temper, that one."

"Mrs. Thomas, I want to mention that Barbara missed her TB shot. The clinic on First Street is open every day and the shot is free."

"I knows she missed that shot. I done kept her home. I don't believe in no shots. People dies from shots."

"This shot is to prevent Barbara from getting TB."

"I ain't giving no shots to my kids. No telling what they put in them shots. Just trying to kill us!"

"Ah, also the children tease Barbara about being dirty. In this hot weather, she needs to be bathed regularly."

"She get her Saturday-night bath like always. Never need no more."

"Thank you for taking the time to come in and see me. I hope you will reconsider the TB shot. It is very important."

She stared at me. "You keep my girl away from Nanci. All this trouble begun when she started playing with her."

I did not see her again, but from talking with Barbara, I learned that she did not get her TB shot. By her appearance and odor, it was obvious that she was not given extra baths, either.

It was not until the middle of April that Nicholas's mother came to school. One hot afternoon, after months of requests, Mrs. Collins shuffled in. She was an older woman with graying hair pulled into a small knot at the back of her head. Her wrinkled skin and worn appearance, her faded, well-pressed house dress and strap shoes, her humble attitude as she sat with her hands folded in her lap—all of this surprised me. I expected a much younger, more excitable woman. "Me and my husband is worried about Nicholas," she began. "I know he ain't doing so good."

"Mrs. Collins, Nicholas cannot do third grade work. Honestly, he can't do first-grade work. My attempts to get him into a special education class next September have been unsuccessful. Although I work with Nicholas individually, he still refuses to do easy class assignments. Most of his class time is spent doodling on his pants and knees or trying to crawl inside his desk or teasing his classmates. He isn't interested in stories and sleeps through films."

She nodded solemnly. "Nicholas, he play too much. You do what you can. You make him learn! You beat him! You make him learn good. I can't do nothing with him no more." She lowered her eyes and stared at her worn hands.

"Mrs. Collins, it is very important that Nicholas be placed in a special education class where he will be able to learn. However, the classes are filled right now, and children aren't even being tested so they can be put on a waiting list. Please call the special education teacher and request that Nicholas be tested."

"Lordy, no. Mrs. Evans, I can't do nothing like that. Besides, they ain't going to listen to no poor black folk."

"Thank you so much for coming in. I will continue to work with Nicholas individually. Please reconsider talking with Mr. Carter and the special education teacher. Nicholas really should be in a special education class."

"He play too much," she reiterated mournfully. She rose wearily from her chair, smoothed her dress, and thanked me for talking with her. "You learn him good. You beat him if he don't learn." She turned and walked slowly out of the room.

"Nicholas, he play too much," I whispered several times.

Nicholas was going to play his way through life, and his mother knew it.

Waiting in the office to discuss Nicholas and special education with Mr. Carter that afternoon, I overheard him discuss another boy with Mrs. Potter, "Your student don't need special education. Why, there ain't nothing wrong with that child. Anything wrong is your fault." She pointed to his folder and a comment that his previous teacher strongly recommended special education, but Mr. Carter replied, "Just because you teachers think alike don't make it true. He ain't getting special education. You just pass him with good grades so he won't be making trouble in this school next year. Just 'cause he black, he ain't dumb. He's smart in black man's ways."

I sighed. This was not the most opportune time for another discussion on special education with Mr. Carter.

When Mrs. Potter left, Mr. Carter turned to me. "One of my students, Nicholas, must be tested for a special education class." I said. "I just spoke with his mother."

He glared at me. "Ain't no more testing this year. You too late. But I ain't got time to talk to you. I'm busy, already late for a meeting."

That next day was highlighted by: meeting Mrs. LeBlanc in the hall before reading and being forced to listen to her whining complaints about the reading program, Mrs. Smith waylaying me and grumbling over her treatment in the office, not having enough ditto paper to run off several important assignments, settling several stolen pencil disputes, confiscating Jack's marbles that escaped from his desk and rolled across the floor, and finally, Mr. Nolen's sudden and unannounced appearance in the cafetorium.

Mr. Nolen was a small, dapper black man in an immaculate

gray suit with a white handkerchief peeking from his breast pocket. His shoes and fingernails were highly polished. He worked his way around the cafetorium, stopping to speak to several teachers. When he arrived at my table, he announced in a well-modulated voice, "I am Mr. Nolen, the assistant principal for the county. You must be, *ahh* . . ."

"Mrs. Evans," I replied.

"Yes, Mrs. Evans, and how are you enjoying teaching at P.S. 123?"

I looked at him. He was apparently sincere. He leaned forward slightly, waiting for my answer. I still did not answer. So that my lengthy silence would not appear rude, I sipped my coffee. I thought of all the other county officials who interviewed me and how nothing changed. "Frankly, Mr. Nolen, I am not enjoying teaching here at all."

"Oh my," he gasped. He appeared shocked. Was that because I was being truthful and none of the others had been?

"Well, are you unable to handle your students?"

I looked at my tables of students, each staring at Mr. Nolen and me. Their eyes were wide. They flashed looks at each other, "Who's he? Don't know. What he want?" They watched us both. Could they tell I was furious? Without making a sound, they pinched and kicked each other under the table.

I resented his condescending comment. Immediately when a teacher is displeased with a school, the reason must be her own inadequacies. He looked at my students and hastily added, "You don't seem to have any discipline problems. Your class is very well behaved. I would like to talk to you more later—*ahh*— this afternoon?"

I nodded, never expecting to see him again. I assumed this was his way to extract himself from an awkward situation.

I handed out the arithmetic ditto papers, assigned Larry, Eric, Jack, and Billy some multiplication, and started Patricia,

Nicholas, Cecil, Edward, Jeffrey, and Sandy on their assignments when I noticed Mr. Nolen standing at the door.

"May I come in?" He beamed. "Is this a good time to continue our little discussion?" His unctuous voice continued, "Now, Mrs. Evans, you obviously don't have any discipline problems, so just why aren't you enjoying your teaching here? Are you new at teaching? You know that the first year is always difficult."

"No, this isn't my first year. It is my third."

"I see. I see. Well then, why don't you tell me." He appeared uncertain. "Your class is very well behaved." We both stood and watched the class working on arithmetic.

"Thank you. I suppose they are superficially under control, although this is the class that drove their first teacher to a nervous breakdown."

"Oh," said Mr. Nolen. His hands fluttered fretfully. His large ring sparkled in the sunlight. Then he folded his arms across his chest, revealing large ornate cufflinks and said, "Mrs. Evans, what is the matter? I hope you will tell me what is bothering you. As an assistant principal for the county, it is my job to find and solve these problems. And if I don't know what the problem is, how can I help? You may be sure that anything you say will be strictly confidential. And I know that the school board will be interested in your opinions. Please do feel free to talk with me," he urged.

I knew nothing I said would be kept confidential. And I did not trust him to do anything about the problems beyond writing another report. But I was also tired of the teachers who complained constantly and refused to do anything constructive to remedy the problem.

Just then, Sharon came up to us with her paper. "Mrs. Evans, how you do this again?" As I helped her with the problem, Mr. Nolen took out his white handkerchief and wiped his perspiring forehead. Even though we were standing in front of the fan, the room temperature was at least 95 degrees. I watched Sharon sit down and then turned back to him.

"I do not enjoy teaching at P.S. 123 because I do so little of it. My time is spent disciplining students; finding materials, books, and supplies; fixing broken equipment; coping with irate, irrational parents; and enduring racial bigotry from the principal and staff."

He blinked at me, shuffled his feet, and looked confused. "Really, Mrs. Evans? Would you mind explaining?"

Painstakingly, I explained in detail each problem that faced the teachers at P.S. 123. He took out a small notebook and wrote in it. I did not leave him any room for misunderstanding, beginning with Mr. Carter's belittling comments to the faculty. I had heard them so often, I could repeat his words verbatim. Mr. Nolen's eyebrows raised in astonishment.

I also told him that Mr. Carter did not help with discipline, and would not work with social services, special education, or the school nurse to get the services these children deserved and that were available to them. That he was frequently absent, and that he refused to obtain supplies for teachers, berated them for their performances, and showed open favoritism, based on race. I gave him several specific situations that epitomized Mr. Carter's lack of leadership. Of course, I mentioned the deplorable condition of the school building, the leaking roof, the broken windows, the faulty plumbing and heating systems, the unscreened windows, and the smoke-filled room.

He only interrupted once. "Why, the children should be able to bring their own paper and pencils."

"Mr. Nolen, some of these children eat no dinner or breakfast, and many have only the clothes they wear to school. Paper and pencils are expensive items to them."

He looked rather embarrassed and agreed readily. "Yes, yes, of course. I see."

"I am also having trouble with playtime. Mr. Carter does and then does not allow it." He looked puzzled, so I explained. "Some days he thought 15 minutes was all right, but other days he was totally against taking them outside at all. My playtime is always organized. I even bought my class playground equipment, since the school provided none for me to use."

He pocketed his notebook and pen and turned to look out the window. Then he glanced at the classroom walls and the children. They were all working except Nicholas, who had found a green magic marker and was happily covering his legs and arms with green polka dots. I mentioned the office favoritism, the cafetorium noise, our numerous time-consuming teachers' duties, the school debt, and the series of parents invading the class during school hours. Swiftly and concisely, I summarized why I did not enjoy teaching at P.S. 123.

Mr. Nolen frowned, straightened his gray jacket, and folded his arms. "I certainly am glad that I spoke with you. You have told me some very revealing things. Obviously you are an excellent teacher. Your room is very interesting. I can tell just by talking to you that you are concerned about the welfare of these children and certainly have worked very hard to help them." He nodded at me and smiled soothingly. "Do you plan to teach here next year?" he asked and then looked disappointed when I told him that my husband would be transferred. "Well, would you consider teaching here next year if your husband wasn't transferred?"

"No."

"Is it because of the children?"

I wondered how he came to that conclusion after all that I told him. "I would not hesitate teaching another disadvantaged class, but not here."

"But," he persisted, "if things were different here would you consider staying?"

"No. My husband will be transferred this fall."

He nodded several times, clicked his shiny black shoes together, and said, "This has been a very worthwhile discussion, and I am grateful that you were so frank. I shall see what I can do to remedy these problems." He nodded several more times and backed out of the room.

I thanked the children for being so well mannered and told them that their good behavior had earned them a few minutes outside after music. As the class walked down the hall toward music, I saw Mr. Nolen walk into Mr. Carter's office. I figured that the entire conversation would be repeated to Mr. Carter.

That afternoon, trash was burned from 2:00 until it was time to go home at 3:15. I decided to call the county after school to complain about the smoke-filled classroom. The county clerk asked me several questions about the location of the junkyard and the hours that trash was burned. He seemed familiar with the location and said, "A junkyard isn't allowed there, anyhow." I repeated that it was difficult for children to work in a smelly, smoke-filled room. He readily agreed and promised to check on the problem that very afternoon.

Smoke from burning junkyard trash did not bother us again. However, as I walked by the office several days later, Mr. Carter called out, "Mrs. Evans, has smoke been bothering you lately?"

"No."

"See, there now, you is too impatient. Always in a hurry to get everything done. It didn't last long, now did it? Wouldn't it be bad if I called somebody and riled the neighbors?" I looked at him politely but did not answer. I knew that smoke never seeped into his office because he was on the other side of the building.

Help from Mr. Nolen?   227

That next day, during reading, Veronica was acting out a funny poem she wrote when Mrs. Lee threw open the connecting door from the bathroom with such force that it banged against the concrete wall.

"How dare you? How dare you?" she bellowed. Her hands were flailing about in the air. She stamped her foot several times. We stared at her. I did not know what had provoked this outburst and decided that she was irrational. "How dare you use my bathroom? I know you been using my bathroom and I want it stopped. Don't ever use my bathroom again, you hear? Stay out of the bathroom and, you filthy things, you didn't even flush." Her face was red. Her hair was untidy. Then she whirled around and slammed the door behind her.

The entire class was silent. "What was that?" asked Steve.

They look scared. I placated them by assuring them they were not at fault, and the poem continued, but not as enthusiastically as before. I noticed several of them looking at the bathroom door worried it would open again.

After reading period, I walked into Mrs. Lee's room. She was sitting at her cluttered desk, eating cold toast and drinking black coffee. "May I speak with you, Mrs. Lee?" She glared at me and snorted. "I am sorry that you were so annoyed this morning, but very surprised that you would disrupt my class. I hope that you won't interrupt me like that again, and if a problem does occur, you will be willing to discuss it with me between classes."

Attempting to speak, she choked on a piece of toast and coughed. "Look who's talking about being professional!" She laughed hysterically and swept her arm across the desk, knocking several things onto the floor. Then she shouted, "Get out! Get out of my room! Get out of here right now!"

I left quietly, being careful not to slam her door. Because of this last scene, I remembered all her other oddities: her peculiar behavior with other teachers; her belief that people were spying on her; her conviction that the devil made all blacks and that blacks were animals who belonged in the jungle; and her certainty that all the problems in the world were caused by Communism and the devil. I remembered that she always carried a ruler or a pair of black-handled scissors that she pointed at her students. Perhaps my imagination was overactive after the morning drama, but the woman appeared unbalanced. I locked the door leading to the bathroom so that she could not enter my room.

When I saw Mrs. Lee again that afternoon, she spoke to me pleasantly. I believe that she had completely forgotten the morning's incidents.

That afternoon, I decided to take the class outside after music for 15 minutes. Listening to Mrs. Williams's critical remarks and harsh voice always unsettled the children and the classroom was especially hot—I was grateful it was not smoke filled! We exercised, walked to the other end of the playground, and then the class began a game of baseball.

I was surprised to see another class outside. The sun baked the playground dirt until it cracked and a layer of dust settled across the yard. The tree leaned weakly against the fence. Several of the girls clustered against the tree trunk. The heat sapped their energy.

As the children lined up to return to our hot classroom, I noticed a small bump on Danny's forehead. I did not remember seeing it earlier, but Danny always had numerous cuts, bruises, and bumps on his arms, legs, and face.

"Danny, how did you bump your forehead?"

He shrugged. "Don't hurt."

"Cecil done it."

"No, Dexter done it." Those helpful hints from his classmates did not improve Danny's memory.

Help from Mr. Nolen? 229

"Did you fall?"

"Were you hit?"

"Yes ma'am," he answered to both questions.

The slight bump disappeared after I held a cold wet towel to his forehead for a few minutes. "I fine now," said Danny.

After school, a salesman demonstrated a new reading textbook series in the library. It was a programmed reading approach. "Why, this program is so complete, teachers won't have to do anything but hand out the books. All your equipment is right here, and this manual tells you how many pages to cover each day, as well as planning extracurricular activities," the perspiring salesman promised. He wiped his forehead and loosened his tie.

During this discussion, Mr. Carter appeared at the door with Danny, his mother who wore short shorts and a see-through blouse, and Danny's younger sister and brother.

"Mrs. Evans? Mrs. Evans, you come over here. This here is Mrs. Tanner, and she want to talk to you." She stood by the checkout counter in the back of the library, but as I approached, I did not have time to greet her.

She shoved Danny at me and said loudly, "You should be ashamed of yourself, ignoring my son like this. Who do you think you is? Not treating his head and making him miss his bus! I had to drive clear cross town just because of you."

Mr. Carter said, "Mrs. Evans, I has told you before that someone be injured playing outside. You know I is against helter-skelter playing and yet you continues to take them out against my wishes."

"But Ma," said Danny, "Mrs. Evans didn't make me miss no bus."

"Shut up, you." His mother shook him until his teeth clattered.

I noticed that Danny's forehead was cut. The cut still bled a little and the bump was large. "Danny, were you hit again?" I asked. Danny did not answer me. He looked miserable and stared at his worn sneakers.

Mrs. Tanner turned on me. "Don't you make him miss no more buses. I has to drive clear cross town because of you, and why you ain't in your room when I come to talk to you?"

I started to tell her that I was usually in my room until 4:00, but this was a teachers' meeting. I knew she did not want an answer. She pushed her bleached hair out of her blue eyes. "I could sue you, you know," she said threateningly. "I bet my boy has a concussion and you didn't do nothing about it. Just 'cause we poor, you ain't got no right ignoring my boy. He's going get everything just like everybody else. You ain't looking out for my kid. I'm going down to the school board and tell them right now. You ain't no teacher. You ain't shit."

Mr. Carter dismissed me with a terse, "You may go back to the meeting, Mrs. Evans." I heard him say, "I would like to talk to you more in my office, Mrs. Tanner."

The other teachers turned around in their seats to continue listening to the salesman. I admit I do not know what he said. I was thinking about Danny, Mrs. Tanner, and Mr. Carter. I saw Danny's white face, heard his mother's vindictive statements, and Mr. Carter's "You know, playtime ain't allowed."

CHAPTER 14

Confrontation

THE SUN WAS HOT on my wet skin. I floated on my back with my eyes closed. All alone, floating in our apartment building's pool, the library scene reappeared in Technicolor. The images of the people were blurred. Their actions were slowed down and the few minutes of confrontation stretched endlessly.

Danny, poor Danny, his pale skin, shaved head, and thin arms and legs moved by. I knew that the lump on his forehead was much worse than it had been when he left my classroom. His mother's face pressed in on Danny's. "I could sue you, you know!" She smelled of cigarette smoke and her skin wrinkled in dirty creases around her neck. "You ain't no teacher." I had heard that several times since teaching at P.S. 123.

I could not endure the third rerun of this melodrama and, hoping to escape, dove under the water. Clear blue green, silent world, cold against my sun-warmed skin. The rays of light cast my shadow on the bottom of the pool. As I drifted to the surface with my long blond hair floating away from my face, my anger slowly faded. I resented Mrs. Tanner's accusations, her insinuations that I was incompetent, and her accusation that Danny's injury had been ignored. I was not surprised that Mr. Carter agreed with her. I wondered if Danny was hit or fell on the way to the bus. How did his forehead get cut? And what made him miss the bus? Had his mother hit him because she had to drive across town to pick him up?

I felt weary and discouraged. My last few weeks had been difficult ones. I could not avoid thoughts of each incident: Mrs. White and Nanci followed by Mr. Carter's accusations; Barbara's mother; and Mrs. Lee shouting about the bathroom; Mr. Nolen suggesting that it was my fault I didn't like teaching at P.S. 123; smoke filling my classroom along with hundreds of bugs; Mrs. Black's rude comment, "No, Mrs. Evans, your dittos ain't done. No, you can't run them off yourself. Them is Mr. Carter's orders"; no special classes for Nicholas; Sandy's knife; Dexter's sulking; Nanci's insolence; Jeffrey's dense hostility, tantrums, and fights.

The sun licked at my face, leaving a few freckles. The water slapped against the edges of the pool. The sky was very blue, flecked with white clouds. I tucked my arm beneath the water's protective cover. Depressed, I began to wonder why I ever wanted to be a teacher. The faces of my students tumbled, one over the other, L'Angela, Cecil, Tynetta, Billy, Larry, Tanya, Eric, Dexter, and on until each child appeared and vanished. Would I ever want to teach again? A loud voice shouted, "No, no, no!" But a small stubborn voice sighed, "Why, oh why, aren't teachers allowed to teach?"

The injustices of prejudice, favoritism, lack of basic equipment and supplies, and on and on, all detailed in the ten-page letter to the school board members and the newspaper, would be mailed that weekend. I did not know if it would change the problems at P.S. 123, but at least the story was told. The late afternoon sun traveled the width of the pool, lingered briefly at the edge, and then vanished for the day.

Wearily I opened my classroom that next morning. Relentlessly, the sunshine heated the classroom, and stuffy bathroom smells rose from the closed gray door. The small desk fan hummed, blowing several worksheets off the children's desks. The alarm clock clicked toward 8:30. Another teaching day had begun, and another remained in the week. Both passed uneventfully. Only the small cut on Danny's forehead lingered as a reminder.

No parents appeared to disrupt the class. Mr. Carter did not come to school those two days. His office door was shut and the lights were on. The cafetorium workers were slower than ever. No one but my class and Maggie's appeared on the sunbaked playground. The children appeared subdued. I worked to keep them awake, as well as interested. Perhaps P.S. 123's problems had faded with heat exhaustion.

This soporific atmosphere did not calm P.S. 123 the following week. Walking to the office Wednesday afternoon to call Jack's mother because he had thrown another tantrum in class after tormenting Marjorie (with help from Marjorie, of course) and fighting in the cafetorium, I wondered if he had problems at home. I dialed his number and waited for an answer. Nadette was typing a letter behind me. Turning, I looked over her shoulder. The letter she was typing was single-spaced and had several carbon copies. Glancing again, I read "Dear Mrs. Evans." Just then, Jack's mother answered the phone.

"Yes, Mrs. Evans, we have noticed a change in Jack's behavior, too. I will be in tomorrow afternoon."

As I walked out of the office, I was able to read the first typed line: "It has come to my attention that you . . ." Unless I stood behind her and read over her shoulder, I could not read further. Walking slowly out of the office and down the hot, empty hall, I wondered about that letter. Remembering the recommendation,

I wondered what could be addressed to me, single-spaced and covering an entire page.

Maggie and I discussed it on the way home. Paul and I talked about it that night. We decided that the letter would probably be in my box that next morning. It was not, however, nor did it appear that week.

On the following Monday afternoon, I went into Mr. Carter's office while my students were sitting in the P.E. room. "Mr. Carter, I know a letter was typed, addressed to me, and I wondered if I could read it."

"Why, Mrs. Evans, what is you talking about? I don't have no letter for you!" He looked startled by my request. I watched his fingers fidget with paper clips on his desk. It was hot in his tiny office.

Patiently, I said, "I know Nadette typed the letter Wednesday."

He continued to protest that such a letter did not exist. "You must have imagined it, Mrs. Evans. What letter is you talking about? I don't have no letter to you. Now, why would I type a letter to you? I could just talk to you if I wanted!" He smiled at me.

"Exactly. Mr. Carter, I watched Nadette type the letter last Wednesday and I assume she is finished with it by now. Since it is addressed to me, I believe that I have a right to read it, especially if copies are sent to other people."

He became annoyed. "You ain't got no right snooping in my office. What goes on here ain't your concern. How should you know that any letter was written? And even if there is a letter, and there ain't, I ain't going to let you read it."

The chair squeaked when he leaned back. He picked up his pipe from the desk and lit it. He puffed twice but the pipe had already gone out.

I stood in front of his desk, holding a stack of class papers. "Mr. Carter, I was in the office to call Jack's mother for a conference. The letter was in the typewriter beside me."

"You spying on me, huh?" he shouted. "You got no right to be behind the counter in my outer office." It did not occur to him that the telephone was behind the counter alongside the typewriter.

Again I said, "May I read the letter?"

He sneered and then laughed at me. "Would you now! I ain't decided what to do with the letter yet, but you ain't reading it. You got no need to be snooping in my office."

"Don't you think that since it is addressed to me, I have a right to read it?"

"My, you girls sure is curious. That's it, just female curiosity." He grinned widely and leaned back farther.

I spent my entire break time with him and resolved nothing. "Mr. Carter, my break is over and I have to go to my class, but am I to understand that you do not intend to let me read that letter?"

"That's right." He grinned.

"I would like to continue this conversation with you after school."

He was suddenly in good humor, waving his arms expansively as he said, "Sure, you come back then, Mrs. Evans." But he left P.S. 123 early that day, as he had many other afternoons. When I returned, his office door was locked. Obviously, the letter would be sent to whomever he pleased and perhaps placed in my teacher's file, as well. I was angry about the locked door, his laughter, and his obvious intention not to discuss this matter further.

After school that day, I called Mr. Nolen and explained the situation. I told him that I had a right to read a letter addressed to me that would be mailed to others and probably be placed in my confidential teacher's file. He sounded concerned and agreed that I should be allowed to read the letter. Smoothly he said, "I am sure this is all a misunderstanding, Mrs. Evans. Mr. Carter is a very good principal and a fair man." We set an appointment time for the following afternoon.

"Mr. Nolen, my husband, Paul, will also be at the meeting."

"Oh my, Mrs. Evans, I'm sure that won't be necessary, but if you wish."

Nadette appeared at my classroom door the next morning during reading. "Mr. Carter want to see you." I saw Mr. Nolen go into the office as I walked down the hall. Obviously, the meeting was rescheduled. I was certain that he had called Mr. Carter about this meeting and that they did not want my husband present.

"Good morning." Mr. Nolen greeted me cheerfully, and then blandly explained that this was the only time he was available since he planned several out-of-town trips. As I sat down on an old wooden armchair, Mr. Carter sat behind his desk and Mr. Nolen pulled a chair up alongside the desk and sat down, careful not to crease his navy trousers. I was tense, my reflection in the office glass pale. I stared at these two men. Mr. Carter was looking for a match, his short-sleeved shirt open at the neck. Mr. Nolen's blue suit was immaculate but he looked uncomfortably hot. I suppose he was used to air-conditioned offices.

Mr. Nolen said, "Well, let's begin." I realized that he would play the role of mediator.

"Mr. Carter, may I read the letter that was written a week ago?"

"What letter is you talking about? I don't have no letter for you, Mrs. Evans." He sounded uneasy, glanced at Mr. Nolen, and wiped his perspiring face with a Kleenex.

"You know what letter I am referring to."

He looked briefly at Mr. Nolen again. "Well here," and he pulled a copy of the letter out of the top desk drawer. "It ain't important. I don't know why you want to read it. Must just be female curiosity." He started to grin, stopped, inserted his pipe into his mouth instead, and fumbled with a match. The letter was two pages long, single spaced, and signed by Mr. Carter.

My hand shook slightly as I held the letter. I read it slowly and carefully. The contents were startling. Beginning with, "It has come to my attention that Mrs. Evans has been willfully negligent in her teacher duties," the letter contained several direct quotes from Mrs. Tanner, Danny's mother. She said that she had come to the school on numerous occasions to speak with me about Danny but that I was never in my room and the door was always locked, and she was told that I already left for the day. She also said that I purposely kept Danny in until he would miss the bus. She described Danny's injury and insisted that it was ignored, that he was offered no medical assistance, and that the accident occurred through unsafe playground conditions for which I was responsible. Then there were several direct quotes from the county policy book stating that, "All injuries must be reported immediately to the school nurse." There were also several statements made by Mr. Carter that he observed my willful misbehavior, my neglect of duties, and that Danny was injured during an unscheduled playtime. In addition, Mr. Carter stated that I was well aware of the county rules for reporting accidents and was grievously at fault. Finally, the letter ended by stating that such willful negligent misconduct would not be tolerated.

I handed the letter to Mr. Nolen. He read it in a perfunctory manner. I suspect that he read it earlier. I knew it was difficult, if not impossible to have a meaningful conversation with Mr. Carter, so I addressed the majority of my statements to Mr. Nolen.

"Certainly, Mr. Nolen, this is a very important letter that I have every right to read. Depending on exactly what Mr. Carter intends to do with the letter and any carbon copies of it, it could harm my teaching career."

"What carbon copies? That the only letter I have!" He shifted his weight uneasily in the chair and then said, "I ain't planning to send this here letter anywhere. I is just going to keep it on file in my office."

I did not believe him. "Why didn't you give me a copy of the letter last week?"

"Oh, it ain't ready last week."

"It was typed Wednesday, Mr. Carter."

"Well, I don't like your attitude. You ain't got no right coming in here and demanding anything from me. I am the principal and I deserve respect. Besides, you was snooping in my office and all!"

"Mr. Carter, we discussed how I became aware of the letter. I would like to know why you were unwilling to show it to me, when by your own account, it was to inform me of county policy."

He did not answer. At least, not that question. Instead, he started to read the county rule about accidents. "It say right here, all teachers on duty during playground activity must report any accidents that occur. You was on duty and you know about this rule, so you is negligent."

"Mr. Nolen, this letter contains many falsehoods. I am in my room each afternoon until at least 4:00 and many afternoons much later. Of course, you know that teachers are allowed to leave at 3:30. I sent numerous notes to Mrs. Tanner requesting a conference, but none of them was answered. The small bump on Danny's head occurred during scheduled playtime. I did treat it with cold compresses, but there is no school nurse to report to. I was not aware of the county policy about a school injury, but I doubt if a school injury means a small bump. When Danny left on time to catch his bus, there was a small red mark, but the bump was gone. When I saw him with his mother, there was a cut on his forehead and a large bump. And last, it would be difficult for Mr. Carter to observe my neglect of duties when he was never in my classroom."

I looked at Mr. Carter and said, "I work very hard here. My third-grade students are well behaved and progressing nicely. Their reading and arithmetic skills have improved. I even bring my own supplies and books to school. I believe I have fulfilled all my teaching duties."

Mr. Carter growled, "You neglect your duties! You been told about P.E. time, Mrs. Evans. You got no right to take them outside that afternoon. I told you that helter-skelter playing would be sure to get someone hurt and I was right!" He wiped his face with another Kleenex.

"I believe, Mr. Carter, that I have explained this to you. My class exercises first, and then plays an organized game. I do not allow unorganized playtime."

He interrupted me. "I told you no playtime. That ain't your playtime. That ain't your scheduled playtime neither. You got no right being outside." He looked triumphant. Obviously, I was wrong and he would be vindicated in front of a county official. Mr. Nolen sat quietly, smoking a cigarette and listening. He handed the letter back to me.

"Mr. Carter, you have never clearly stated what time P.E. was scheduled. The schedule was changed constantly. Occasionally, teachers swap playtime depending on class activities. I realize that you do not approve of playtime, but you agreed that I could take the children out in December when I was interviewed for the job. Besides, the county does not forbid playtime and only requires five hours of instruction in one day. Since our day is so long, the children could play for one hour, even with twenty minutes for lunch."

I planned to explain the P.E. situation further, but Mr. Carter was highly agitated and interrupted me again. "Mrs. Evans, you just don't listen. You neglected to report this injury, and you was outside during an unscheduled playtime, and so a child was injured, and it is your fault."

I began to explain the situation again, but Mr. Carter interrupted. "Mr. Carter, please stop interrupting me. I cannot answer these questions unless you allow me to explain." That really infuriated him, but Mr. Nolen told him to let me finish. I continued, "These children have a very short attention span and need P.E. time. The situation was not hazardous or dangerous. The class was playing baseball. Danny does not even know how the first bump occurred. It is not possible to report an injury, if there is no nurse to report to. This was not an injury. It was a small bump that was gone by the time he left for home. If you want every bump reported, the teachers will have to be told to do it. None of us are aware of this particular county policy."

"Furthermore, I think it is very unfair to quote Mrs. Tanner. I was not present for her extended conversation with you and had no way to address her remarks." Mr. Carter looked confused. I do not know if he understood what I was saying. "And the fact that this letter was hidden until I insisted on seeing it is even more unjust."

Mr. Carter said, "Well now, Mrs. Evans, you just got to understand this letter. It ain't meant to do anything but inform you of your mistakes. I planned to keep a copy in my desk, and you will have to admit that you had no right to be outside, and that you is responsible for reporting the accident. You know his mother was right upset, took me 15 minutes to calm her down."

"Mr. Nolen, his mother appeared more agitated because he missed the bus than upset over his small cut and bump. I do not know why Danny missed his bus. He left on time with the other bussers."

Mr. Nolen asked to see the letter again, and said, "Well, Mrs. Evans, obviously you disagree with the contents of this letter, so may I suggest a solution?" He smiled amiably. "Why don't you write up your viewpoint of this incident and I will see to it that your letter is clipped with this one. That way both points of view will be expressed." He settled back in his chair, tapping his fingertips together.

I was amazed by his solution to this problem. Mr. Carter thought it was an excellent suggestion. He nodded agreeably. I suspect this had already been discussed.

"That is completely unacceptable to me! I do not intend to refute in writing a letter that should not have been hidden, that is completely untrue, and could possibly ruin my chances of being hired again if it were in my teaching folder."

Mr. Nolen frowned at me, drummed his fingers on the arm-chair, and said, "Well, just what do you want?"

"I want the letter and the carbon copies destroyed."

"Huh," snorted Mr. Carter, "that is impossible. However, that letter will not be put in your folder, but I will keep a copy of it in my office. It is important to have a record of this incident."

"Why Mr. Carter, when the record is false? Why do you want to keep this letter in your office?"

He began to harangue, "You is willful. Your negligence done injured a boy. This here letter is to inform you of your mistakes. You knows it ain't scheduled playtime."

It was so hot in his office and I was so upset that my hands were clammy, my head hot, and my eyes smarted. He ranted on, "You lack obedience! Just because you don't know about the rule ain't no excuse for not reporting it."

I could not stand the tension in that small room. I stood up and walked to the office door. "Mr. Carter, I doubt if the ma-jority of teachers know they should report a small bump as an 'injury' or if they ever do. It is obviously a mistake to talk with you. It is impossible to discuss anything. I will take this letter to the school board now and let them decide about this matter."

It was very interesting that the mention of the school board would bring such an immediate change in the attitude of these two men. Apparently, they did not want the school board to be part of this discussion. Quickly, Mr. Nolen said, "Now, now, Mrs. Evans, you are upset. That won't be necessary. Won't you sit down?" In a very unctuous voice he continued, "I am sure we can solve this problem right here. I am sure we can settle this to please everyone.

"Now, Brother Carter, you know Mrs. Evans is a good teacher."

"Yes," agreed Mr. Carter. He was perspiring heavily. "I has told her so several times!"

"Mr. Carter, you have never complimented me."

He looked embarrassed and did not continue.

"Now Mr. Carter, don't you think, in view of Mrs. Evans's excellent record"—Mr. Nolan nodded at me and smiled brightly—"and since the letter was just to inform her of the situation and she is aware of the problem now, that we could destroy the letter?"

Mr. Carter was not pleased with that idea but agreed. Hesitantly, he held the letter in front of him. "I certainly don't see why you feels this way about this here letter, Mrs. Evans. It ain't meant to injure your teaching career."

"Well," said Mr. Nolen with a placating smile, obviously relieved, "I am sure that you both understand each other so much better now that this has been cleared up. After all, a principal and his teachers should love and trust each other. This is very important for school morale. I am sure you two will just forgive each other and love each other all the more." Fortunately, he did not ask for a group hug. "Shall I just take this letter with me?"

"Mr. Nolen, I would like the letter and the carbons."

"Oh my, Mrs. Evans, we can't allow that. After all, this is official school business."

"Yes, but it was addressed to me."

"Well, certainly you will have no need for this letter."

"If I can't take it with me, I want it and the copies destroyed right here, right now."

"See, see that!" screamed Mr. Carter. "She don't trust me. See that?" He jumped to his feet, knocking several papers off his desk, and ranted incoherently about my poor attitude. I was so hot and weary that I just looked at him. Again, he shouted, "See, she don't trust me."

Very quietly, I replied, "No sir. I don't."

"Now, now, now," said Mr. Nolen in a placating tone. "Why don't you just tear it up, Mr. Carter."

And so, I saw that letter and each of the five carbon copies ripped into small pieces and dropped into the wastebasket. As I watched, I wondered if this would happen again. Would another letter find its way into my teaching folder? I vowed to check my official file before I left the county.

After the letter was destroyed, Mr. Nolen said, "The school social worker will be sent to Mrs. Tanner to explain the situation and a conference will be arranged for you with her."

Neither ever occurred.

We all stood and solemnly nodded at each other. I was exhausted by the tension of that confrontation and, although the letter was destroyed, I did not feel relieved.

It was not until I saw my empty classroom that I realized I was in Mr. Carter's office for two hours. The children were outside on the playground. Nadette was jumping rope and several of the boys were wandering outside the school fence but ran inside after seeing me. I sat down, leaned against the tree, and looked out at the playground and back at the school building.

Maggie walked over and asked about the meeting. As I began

to tell her what happened, Nicholas walked over and stood in front of me. "Mrs. Evans." I did not answer him. "Mrs. Evans," he whined again, "can I go inside the school building?" Nicholas asked that every day, and every day, I said, "No, Nicholas, you can't. You will have to wait until we all go in." Then he would whine and complain, sulk, and pout, but finally run away to play. I stared at him and said, "Hell, no! You can't go in, Nicholas."

He looked surprised and blinked at me. "Okay, Mrs. Evans. Okay." He never asked me again. That time I spoke words he understood.

CHAPTER 15

Those Ponderous
Days of May

I COULD NOT THINK OF ANYTHING ELSE. Again I felt the heated tension in that office, smelled the tobacco smoke, and watched beads of perspiration form, charting new courses on already damp faces. Hours later, I was still angry about that letter, its underhanded inception, the insulting language, the false statements of Mrs. Tanner, the accusations of incompetence, and the charge of willful misbehavior.

The worst was to accuse me of neglecting my duties. That particular statement infuriated me, especially because I noticed other teachers and staff neglecting their duties: Mr. Carter's frequent absences and departures, Mrs. Dickson's lolling in the school office or covering bulletin boards or planting shrubs during school hours, Mr. Lewis's refusal to teach P.E. or take the children outside, Fay's resting her head on her desk and telling the children to do whatever they wanted, Mrs. LeBlanc's daily two-hour film program, Mrs. Washington's unpleasant attitude that fostered the children's hatred for art, Nadette's too-few dittos too late, and Mrs. Black's eloquent shrug to signify "no supplies" immediately after Mrs. Dickson left with more than her share.

I was weary of recounting the examples of incompetence. I never looked forward to the end of a school year until that day. Now I wondered if I would be able to endure P.S. 123 that long. The number of days remaining was small but appeared insurmountable. I spent the weekends dreading Monday. I was angry, frustrated, and exhausted. My idealism was shaken. It never occurred to me that once a problem was noticed, it would not be corrected. I began to realize that many people are willing to accept injustice and endure indignity, and too few care enough to attempt to bring change or fight unfairness. I wanted to shout, "This isn't the way teaching is supposed to be!" The more I protested, the less others heard.

Apparently, the education system did not exist for the children. In fact, they were the last consideration in most decisions made at P.S. 123. I knew some of the administrators had never taught, yet they determined the teaching curriculum and the books. Mr. Carter's indifference to the students was obvious, and many of the teachers were simply filling a vacancy, making some money, living for vacations, and waiting for retirement— all the while hating the children. I also knew from reading the newspaper that politics, and corruption were endemic to that county's educational system. Personally, I knew of inept teachers and equally incompetent administrators perpetuating the system, with the children being the losers.

Added to my distress was the realization that all the school board members had received my ten-page letter—and nothing had happened. There was no official inquiry. There was no change in Mr. Carter's behavior. Even if they did not read the entire ten pages, surely the first paragraph should have elicited comment: "The mood at P.S. 123 elementary school is one of disappointment and frustration. Many teachers, discouraged by the problems and difficulties they face daily and the constancy of these obstacles, have vowed never to return. Others, unable to leave for financial or other reasons, have figuratively shrugged their shoulders at the hopelessness of the situation." The copy sent to the newspaper brought no response, either. Could I be the only person concerned with the students at P.S. 123?

For the remainder of that day, I taught without seeing the faces or noticing the behavior of the students. Dulled by the confrontation, I performed routinely. Assignments were given and corrected perfunctorily. I spent the day closeted within dirty green walls or roasting on a sunny playground. I do not recall discipline problems or delightful comments. That day was washed in gray. It was an unpleasant, dreary existence. Only Snoopy perched at the fishing hole remained imperturbably cheerful.

Eric looked at me carefully that next morning. His sturdy legs were planted firmly in front of my desk and, in a polite voice, he asked me, "Do you feel better today, Mrs. Evans?"

I smiled. "Yes, Eric, I think so."

"Good!" he said, and having settled that question, hurried to the pencil sharpener. Sharon arranged pink flowers from home and put them on my desk. She smiled at me shyly and touched my arm. The children were silent that Friday morning. They watched me curiously. It was a peculiar feeling to realize that I completely ignored them yesterday afternoon. So involved with my own problems, I did not notice the students. I was painfully aware that day how very little the students received in this education system. I was determined not to ignore them again regardless of my discontent with P.S. 123 staff and county administrators.

Problems continued to occur, however, which increased my uneasiness. The days in May moved ponderously and I was unable to hide within the classroom walls. More parents appeared, clashes with Mr. Carter and the office staff continued, and children's tempers flared.

Discipline problems in the classroom centered around the children who were most affected by the heat, lack of breakfast, lack of sleep, or those who had the most disconcerting home problems. Jack ate by himself the remainder of the school year. Each Monday he was allowed to sit with the class, and without fail, each Monday he instigated a fight or food-throwing contest.

Nicholas maintained his usual position in the classroom with some days being more difficult than others. He tormented his classmates, hid their pencils, or broke their pencil points, made peculiar noises, and doodled over his arms and legs. With all that extracurricular activity, he never completed any class assignment and most were never started. Many were sent home with him.

After telling him what his mother said, he was more willing to work with me. I spent as much time as possible with him drilling simple addition and subtraction and basic reading. One afternoon, after a morning of disruption, I put Nicholas beside the door in the hall. The class worked well that afternoon and I was able to see Nicholas from my desk.

Unfortunately, allowing him to go to the bathroom was a mistake. He never returned! I reported him delinquent to the office. That next day he was quiet, but I sent him to the office for being truant the day before. He was returned in five minutes. Naturally, no disciplinary action was taken.

Dexter, Cecil, Kelvin, and Jeffrey were all potential class disruptions. Tempers flared, and at least one of them staged a temper tantrum daily. Nanci continued to be disobedient, gleefully misbehaving and including Barbara in her mischief. I overheard them planning how they would disrupt the class that afternoon but managed to thwart their plans.

Sandra continued to cry, and by 10:00 each day, her grandmother arrived to take her home. I prepared her assignments and sent them home with her. Every note I sent home went unanswered.

Even with all this, I could truthfully say that the majority of the students improved in all areas. The enraged outbursts did not last as long or bring hours of pouting. The students rarely laughed when another was reprimanded and no longer talked back when corrected. They seemed more willing to share and to help than to abuse each other.

Besides a definite improvement in behavior, all could at least do first grade arithmetic and first grade reading. Several boys were learning multiplication and division. The majority of the class could write a letter, recognize a noun and verb, and write coherent sentences. All of the class could print and write script. That last month, I concentrated on those who were making the slowest progress, planning new ways to teach those skills. For those who had already mastered the rudimentary skills, I prepared activities and projects that required some research. Many worked on information that would be important this summer.

For all to benefit, we sat in the stifling heat of the movie room and watched a swimming safety film that I borrowed from the county library. The swimming precautions were simple to remember—always swim with friends, know the places to swim, and so forth. Much of the film dealt with saving a person in trouble. "Don't swim out to save anyone unless that is the last resort. Throw a floatable object or use a rope or a boat." The children watched the film carefully, and when it was over, I asked them about water safety rules. Many remembered several methods. Each one repeated the method they would use.

"I use an oar from the boat," said Larry.

"I just get a long branch," said Jimmy.

"At the beach?" hooted Felicia. "Where you find a branch at the beach?"

"Felicia, what would you do?"

"I just scream and scream. I too scared to do anything else."

"Not me. I ain't scared. I swim out there and save him and be a hero!"

"Nicholas, can you swim?"

"Nope, but I swim out there and save him anyhow. I don't use a branch or an oar. That the sissy way."

Several days later we watched a film on bicycle safety. I watched some of the boys riding their bicycles after school and decided they should learn some riding rules. The class was surprised to learn that bicycles are just like cars. They have to be ridden on the right side of the street. Only Nicholas remained dubious. Only Nicholas refused to learn hand signals. I was concerned that Nicholas would not live long enough to fulfill his new ambition in life—Nicholas wanted to be a teenager when he grew up.

I continued to take the students outside for P.E. Mr. Carter never discussed my P.E. schedule or the fact that my class went outside again. Several more teachers, having watched me go outside since December, also began to take their classes outside. Mrs. LeBlanc, of course, let her children out on the playground without any planned games or equipment while she remained inside. She ignored Maggie and me when we asked her to stop this practice. I did not have the energy or optimism to complain to her, so I included her children in my class's activities during playtime.

During the month of May, the well-established reading routine continued. My own reading group performed well. The students wrote stories and poems, each more intricate than the last. They read the fourth-grade textbook, did phonics sheets daily, read library books of their own choosing, made up stories to tell to the tape recorder, and acted in a play or studied dictionary skills. Several of these activities might be accomplished in one day. The children were interested and eager to learn. They worked quietly and efficiently.

"Say, Mrs. Evans, do you like my new glasses?"

"Yes, Julius. I do."

"Me too. Thanks for telling my mom I needed them. They sure make a big difference."

Unfortunately, at least two other third grade teachers were not as enthralled with the program. Mrs. LeBlanc scheduled two art classes during reading period, destroying the possibility for six other classes to have reading. When I spoke to her, she whined, "But that was the only time I could have art, and anyway, I teach reading to my own class besides what they learn in your room." I admit I was annoyed with her.

"Mrs. LeBlanc, when you schedule art during reading, six other classes cannot have reading."

"Well, they can teach it in their own rooms, just like me." She smirked at me, showing her stained teeth.

"Millie, you must not realize the importance of reading to these children." My annoyance surfaced with that statement. She was furious and probably had a right to be.

"Who do you think you are, talking to me like that? You don't have any right to talk to me like that. I won't stand for it."

"You can't schedule art during reading period unless you intend for your reading group to have art."

Her pale face turned red. "You can't tell me what I can or can't do!"

"If I don't, Mrs. Miller, the curriculum coordinator will. Remember, this is her program." That surprised her.

She muttered, "It still isn't up to you to tell me."

I sighed. "I will send my children to your room for reading at the regular time tomorrow."

If I had not spoken to her, she would have abandoned reading entirely by the middle of May with a month of school remaining. I also knew that no one else cared enough to speak to her.

Occasionally, when Fay Morris had a bad hangover or just was not in the mood, she would send her group outside to play during reading period. Since she had the primer group—Sandy, Danny, Edward, Nicholas, Cecil, and Jeffrey—the boys who needed the most reading help were ignored. I continued to include reading exercises in their special spelling group and heard them read every day.

The first time I saw Mr. Carter after that confrontation over the letter, the children were walking down the hall to music. I was locking the classroom door when he walked by, stared at me, and finally said, "Is you trying to ignore me, Mrs. Evans?"

I looked at him quietly for a long time. The hallway was hot and dimly lit because there were no more light bulbs to replace those that were burned out. He was wearing a white turtleneck, his face shiny from the heat. He stood alongside me waiting, until I finally said, "Mr. Carter, whatever would make you think that?"

Many afternoons, when the temperature rose beyond the tolerable mark, I would tell the children to put their books and papers away. Then I read them a story about an area we had studied that day, or we would have a class discussion or write a class story or poem. I know they looked forward to that time. One afternoon's discussion amazed me. I never had a class of children so uninterested in summer vacation. The majority of them wanted to go to school all summer long and greatly envied the few who were attending summer school. Cecil, Edward,

Jeffrey, Nicholas, and Danny's parents refused to allow their sons to attend. The children dreaded summer vacation and complained loudly.

"There ain't nothing to do," said Kelvin.

"Yeah, ain't nowhere to swim, neither."

"It too hot and buggy."

"I wished I could go to school," sighed Billy.

Sharon said, "I gots to do all the cleaning."

"Yeah, and my kid brother follows me everywhere," complained Jack.

"So, I got to take care of the babies," said Barbara.

"It ain't no fun!" Sandy growled.

"I hate summers!" Eric grumped.

I tried to vary our afternoons by having art occasionally. One enjoyable lesson was bending thin wire into strange shapes. Each made an animal, gave it a name, and then wrote its description. The most difficult part of the lesson was to have the children realize that they could do anything they pleased. Many of them wanted me to help them or describe or name their imaginary beast.

"Mrs. Evan, you help me," demanded Cecil. "What can I do?"

"Anything you want to. Just play with the wire until you like what it looks like."

"But I ain't got no name. You name it."

"I can't, Cecil. It's yours, and I don't know what you want to call it."

"Damn, this here too hard." But he did not slam the wire down and sulk. He tried and finally named his animal "xyz." Then he wrote, "It got 47 legs no head and a long tail."

"See Mrs. Evans, I done it."

"Good for you! You certainly worked hard."

"This here's the best in the class, 'cause I done it myself."

On another afternoon, I brought art paper to school. The children cut geometric shapes to form pictures. They could recognize triangles, circles, squares, and rectangles. Nicholas spread glue all over his face. The children laughed at his antics. He was quite funny. To keep his interest, I set aside several minutes at the end of the day for him to entertain the class. The only stipulation was getting one daily assignment completed. I gave him special papers to do and continued to help him. Sadly, he was happier playing and not working at all.

That afternoon ended with a faculty meeting. I sat in the back, behind Mr. Lewis's huge bulk. Effectively hidden, I watched blue gray smoke rise above Ozell's head and beads of sweat form on his neck. The rest of the time, I looked outside into the heat of the late spring, followed the erratic path of several flies, and counted the petals of a yellow rose on Mrs. Madison's windowsill. The meeting was quite long. I listened sporadically. Mr. Carter droned on. "You teachers ain't meeting your responsibilities. I wants you to sign a sheet swearing that you done read the county policy book and understand it, hear?" I assumed this was the result of my assertion that few knew they were to report an accident to the school nurse. He held up the book and said, "Now, I told you to read this here book last September, and if you don't know none of the rules, it is your fault. Just proves that none of you have teacher responsibility." My attention wavered and I watched Miss Bernardo's nose twitch. She tentatively fanned herself with a test paper.

"And besides that, I have seen you put children in the halls. I told you that you can't do that, but you do it anyway. I don't want it to happen again. If a child goes home, you are responsible, and if he gets hurt on the way home you can be sued! Yes, indeed. I'm taking this here course in law at night. And anything that happen is your fault. You can get sued, you know, and they sue the principal, too." He began to cite several cases in which teachers were sued, but I watched Mrs. Dickson leave the room instead of listening. Her heels hung over the backs of her bedroom slippers. They slapped as she walked to the door. She did not return. "Now if you wants to be careless, you will get sued. So you best be real careful, 'cause if anything happen it will be your fault. I ain't going to get involved in no lawsuit of yours."

On this cheerful note, the meeting was dismissed at 4:20.

Gratefully, I slipped past Mr. Carter and headed to the door. "Mrs. Evans, Mrs. Evans!" He said my name sharply. His voice seemed to cut through the heavy classroom air.

"Yes, sir?"

"You ain't signed this here sheet about having read the policy book."

"Mr. Carter, before I take complete responsibility for its contents, I plan to read the entire book."

"Oh, that ain't necessary."

"Mr. Carter, since ignorance is no excuse for neglecting a duty, I think it is best to read the entire book."

"You can't take this here office copy 'cause that belong to the staff and the library copy is missing. You going sign, Mrs. Evans?"

"Not today, Mr. Carter. I plan to read the book first." I smiled at him pleasantly. As I left the room, I watched several teachers signing his sheet. I heard one of them ask, "What book he's talking about?"

Later Fay Morris told me, "Sure, I signed the paper. Hell, I'm not reading any damn book on policy." I found the missing copy of the county policy book in the library and read it, but never signed his sheet. I never saw the sheet again.

Those Ponderous Days of May   257

That next day, Mr. Nolen joined my class on the playground. He was pleased to see them playing baseball. Arriving too late to do exercises with us, he stood on the dusty clay playground in black patent leather shoes and a gray summer suit. "Those are the metal bars that are partially destroyed and the unused basketball backboards that I told you about." I pointed across the playground. "And the frayed rope swing."

He nodded and then asked, "Well, Mrs. Evans, how is everything?"

I am sure I was supposed to say, "Oh, just fine." Instead I sighed, "Mr. Nolen, nothing has changed at P.S. 123."

Perturbed, he said, "Oh now, Mrs. Evans, I am sure things will change if they haven't already! You just have to be patient, can't expect changes overnight."

I was surprised to see him and wondered about the out-of-town trip excuse that was used to change the meeting time with Mr. Carter. I watched him throw a ball to the baseball players and wondered what he really knew about teaching at P.S. 123.

Mr. Nolen reappeared weekly, peering into my classroom or walking out to the playground. After I called the school board to ask if it were possible to be reimbursed for four reams of ditto paper, Mr. Nolen visited. He was most solicitous. "Why are you buying your own paper?" Again, I mentioned the shortage of supplies at the school and the $500 debt. I also told him that several teachers had reams of paper stocked in their closets while I was forced to buy mine. Of course, he heard all this from me before.

"Why not have the children bring paper?"

"That just isn't possible. They can't afford it." I do not know whether my annoyance was apparent in the tone of my voice or my face, but he hastily retracted his statement and instead said, "I shall see that you have paper. Don't you buy any more."

"Is this special treatment for me, or does the county intend to supply all the teachers at P.S. 123?"

He never answered the question. Instead, he checked his watch, looked horrified, and said, "Dear me, I am late for an important meeting." Hurrying to the door, he repeated, "Don't buy any more paper, Mrs. Evans. The county will meet your needs." As he closed the classroom door, the heavy scent of hair tonic or after shave lotion remained in the room.

My thoughts of Mr. Nolen were interrupted by Nanci screaming, "He's got my pencil. He done ripped my paper." She was yelling at Kelvin.

"That ain't your pencil. Besides, you done it to me first."

The pencil was Kelvin's. Nanci found hers under her desk. I talked with her in the back of the room about yelling in class when others were working and about her arithmetic paper that was not started. She smirked and smirked. Her behavior in the halls was no better. She tripped several girls, pushed one down the stairs, and then ran all the way back from music. "Nanci, please walk back down the hall."

"I ain't."

"You may do it now or after school."

"After school," she mumbled and darted into the room.

That afternoon, I sat correcting papers while she walked the length of the hall. "Nanci, when you think that you have walked down and back properly, I would like to talk with you." She strutted up the hall toward me when Mrs. White arrived.

Storming up the hall, she screamed, "Well, Mrs. Evans, you seem to be having trouble with Nanci again."

Politely I said, "Nanci ran down the hall after music and chose to walk down correctly after school."

"I think it's terrible that all you do is pick on my Nanci. Your treatment of her is awful. You know I don't want her in the sun and you take away her playtime just because she is late. You white folk is all alike. I won't stand for any more of this. Since you are having such a hard time with her, I'm going to have her put in a classroom with a real teacher. A black teacher! I'm sick to death of you white folks."

I never did talk with Nanci that afternoon. She smiled, giggled, and followed her mother to Mr. Carter's office. Later that afternoon, she returned to my room for her books. She was being transferred to Mrs. Madison's class. With a few weeks left in the school year, Nanci would have a new teacher. Mr. Carter never discussed this change with me.

When Nanci arrived for reading that next morning, I sent her back to Mrs. Madison. I did not believe that I should teach her reading if I would not teach her anything else. I sent the reading class work to Mrs. Madison daily so that Nanci could keep up with her classmates, and Mrs. Madison did not have to prepare extra reading papers.

Eager to assure me that she knew nothing about this change, Mrs. Madison met me in the hall after reading that morning. Leaning heavily on her cane, she wiped her face with a handkerchief and said, "Mrs. Evans, I didn't know nothing about this change. I don't want you to think I had anything to do with it. She was put here by Mr. Carter and her mother." She smiled sweetly and walked back into her classroom.

I suppose that Nanci's transfer to Mrs. Madison's room should have given me a deep feeling of defeat. It did not! It was obvious that Mrs. White would not be pleased with anything I did and that she did not believe her daughter was unwilling to cooperate. She believed the problem was my alleged racial prejudice. Nanci was well aware of her mother's attitude toward whites in general, toward me in particular. With this situation, it was impossible to continue as Nanci's classroom teacher. I was pleased that Nanci had a new teacher and hoped her behavior and work habits would improve those final weeks of school.

That same week, Sandra's mother, Mrs. McPeters, and her grandmother appeared for a conference. While Sandra sat in the classroom and cried, her mother said, "Sandra becomes nauseated and runs a high fever at the mention of school. She has been tested by a doctor and by the hospital and there's nothing physically wrong." Her southern accent drawled through the story of Sandra's reaction to being bused to school. "This is such an old school and a black school, too." Her fingers twisted a strand of brown hair. "Why, we brought Sandra over to the school and showed her P.S. 123 last summer, and I told her what a lovely school it was, but she just cried. She was so happy at her old school. Everything seemed to be okay until Christmas time. You know, she really adored Miss Jenkins." Hurriedly she added, "Now, I know she likes you right well, too, but she's just so unhappy. Why, she is calling her friend Sylvia in the morning, and if Sylvia isn't going to school, Sandra gets sick real quick like." I nodded at her.

Sandra's grandmother smoothed her gray skirt and said, "Yes, and Sandra doesn't feel good at first when I come to take her home, but after she stops crying and all, her fever goes down and she plays real nice the rest of the day."

Just then Mr. Carter walked in, listened a few minutes, appeared uncomfortable, and said, "Mrs. Evans, you talk to these ladies and see if you can't handle the problem yourself. After all, you teachers is supposed to handle these here problems."

When he left, Mrs. McPeters leaned over and whispered, "Is he the principal?" I nodded. "I suppose he seemed right nice but I just can't get accustomed to a colored as a principal. A janitor, maybe, but a principal?" She tugged at her tight white pants and continued, "I took a job in this factory to help out financially. Maybe I should stay home, but Sandra is real fond of her grandmother. Do you think Sandra minds me working?"

"Perhaps the real problem is that Sandra is unhappy here," I suggested. "I am relieved to learn that there is no medical reason for her illness." Pointedly, I asked her how she felt about Sandra being bused to school.

"Why, I think it's just deplorable! She went to a nice white school last year. Just walked, you know, and didn't have to be with coloreds. Not that I'm prejudiced, but I don't want my Sandra playing with coloreds. Children are real impressionable, and they pick up such bad habits. Coloreds are so rough too. I keep hearing about the way they tease her and hit her and all that. Surely you can keep them from hitting her, can't you?"

"That happened once, in December when Mr. Carter kept the teachers in a meeting. The classes were already in the building playing. However, the boy was disciplined for hitting her."

"He was colored, wasn't he?" she accused.

"Mrs. McPeters, children do tease each other and some of the teasing starts with Sandra."

"Oh no, I can't believe that. I told her never to talk to them or play with them. I allow her to play with Sylvia or that other white girl but never a colored." I wondered who she meant; there was no other white girl in the class. "Mind you, I'm not prejudiced. I just want them to keep their distance. I was so relieved when she said her new teacher was white. I don't know what I would do if she got a colored. They aren't too smart, you know."

I was surprised that it took months for her illness to appear. With her mother's attitude, it was not surprising that the child was uncomfortable in my class and unhappy at P.S. 123.

"How are Sandra's grades?"

"She is on grade level but has made little progress since December because of her frequent absences."

"I sure am relieved to hear that! Well, the reason I came

today was to ask if it matters if I just keep her home the rest of the year."

"Frankly, Mrs. McPeters, I doubt that it will make any difference."

"Will you send her classwork home?"

"Of course, I will be glad to."

Apparently, Sandra's problem was her mother's attitude toward "coloreds" and P.S. 123 and Sandra's desire to please her mother. Her grandmother stood up and looked around the room. "Lord, this is a horrible place!" She fanned herself with a paper and said, "I plan to take Sandra home with me now."

"Do you intend to send her back to P.S. 123 next year?"

"Oh God, no! If I knew how much trouble this would be, I would have sent her to a private school last year, but it all happened so sudden like that I couldn't find a good private school with a vacancy. No, she is going to the church school next year and Sylvia, too."

Mr. Carter strolled back into the room. "Mrs. Evans, has you set up a psychological test with the school psychiatrist?"

"No, sir."

"Well, I think that is important. Then everyone will know why Sandra is so unhappy in your room. Must be something you are doing wrong."

Mrs. McPeters nodded. "Yes, that's a fine idea. I will bring Sandra to school tomorrow for the tests."

Mrs. Roberts, the same woman who had no time to test Nicholas, spent the morning with Sandra. When the report was returned, it stated that Sandra was very unhappy. She was shy and immature. She was afraid of Mrs. Evans but liked her very much. She was unsure if Mrs. Evans liked her. The report suggested that Mrs. Evans pay more attention to Sandra and her problems and be more concerned with her illness and its manifestations. Also, it recommended that Sandra have a physical exam.

As I read the report, Sandra walked up to the desk. "Mrs. Evans, I guess that you have to be nice to the coloreds 'cause you are a good teacher, but you don't like them, do you?" She stared at me steadily; her blond ponytail bobbed as she leaned over the desk.

"Yes, I do, Sandra. I like everyone in this room."

"Do you like me more?"

"I do like you, Sandra."

"I like you, too, Mrs. Evans. You're a nice teacher."

I remembered the times when Sandra and Sylvia would visit me on the playground holding hands and giggling. We would talk for a few minutes and then they would run off and play. Sometimes, they brought me little presents such as a flower, an old bottle of toilet water, or a broken pin. I remembered too, that each morning when she became sick, I told her that I hoped she could spend the whole day at school because we missed her when she went home. And that she might want to be in class for art or for a story or whatever was planned. Sometimes she would stay—most of the time, though, she went home with her grandmother. She did come to school several times that last month, handing in the assignments that she did at home.

One hot May afternoon, with the temperature almost 100 degrees in the classroom, the children decided to go outside instead of listening to a story. As we walked down the hall past the P.E. room, a locked storage closet was open. Ozell Lewis was conducting inventory of his P.E. supplies. There, stacked behind the locked metal door, were new basketballs, soft balls, bats, playground balls, jump ropes, hula-hoops, rings, and volleyballs. The equipment spilled out of the closet and onto the hall floor. We filed silently by, watching Ozell sitting in the middle of a pile of balls, drinking a Coke, and smoking a cigarette.

"Ozell, have these been here all year?"

"Why yes, Mrs. Evans."

"Why haven't any of these supplies been used?" He shrugged and sipped his Coke. "May I borrow several balls for this afternoon?"

"*Uh-uh*," he grunted. "This here equipment can be used only by the P.E. teacher." I did see Fay Morris using hula-hoops later that day. Ozell was still counting and checking an inventory sheet when we walked back into the building from a game of baseball with the bat and ball I purchased.

"Sure is hot work," he muttered to me. The front of his shirt was wet with perspiration. Mr. Carter joined him and checked the list carefully to be certain that nothing was missing.

CHAPTER 16

Books, Folders, and Test Scores

I WONDERED ABOUT THE P.E. CLOSET. Did Ozell not want to be responsible for the supplies, or had Mr. Carter told him that the supplies were not to be used? It made me angry to think of all the children who had not been allowed outside and who had not enjoyed the equipment already at P.S. 123.

Of course, seeing the contents of that closet, I wondered about the school supply closet. One glimpse revealed well-stocked shelves, reams of paper, and boxes of supplies. I remembered Mr. Carter mentioning in one faculty meeting, "Them supplies is for the next year. There ain't no money for this year's supplies."

Standing at the window, I watched the dirt playground bake in the late afternoon sun. As the children ran across the field, puffs of brown dust curled after them. "Faculty meeting, Mrs. Evans!" yelled Nadette. Before I turned away from the window, I heard the playground gate slam several times. The schoolyard was empty.

"You want a cigarette?" Fay asked.

"No, thanks," said Debby. "I brought my own."

Hilda yawned widely and whispered, "I wish this was over. I'm so tired and hot!" Her blond hair stuck to her forehead. We sat together and waited for the meeting to begin.

Mr. Carter had several notes written on small pieces of lined paper. He picked up each sheet, read the note to himself, looked up at the teachers, and began, "Girls, this here faculty meeting is about books for next year. We has some money coming to us and we plans to spend it all. What books does you think are needed best?" A fifth-grade teacher needed new spelling books. Another teacher mentioned English books.

I asked, "Is it possible to order more reading books so that the reading levels of the children could be met?"

"Does you need more third-grade books?"

"No, sir. I was thinking primer, first, second, and fourth-grade levels."

"Oh, no. This here money is for textbooks. You can't have first and second grade books in third grade. Why, what would the county think of an order for them books? This is a third through sixth-grade school."

I did not ask about ordering easier arithmetic books. Several teachers wanted new science books, but Mr. Carter reminded them of the ABC program.

"Could we use textbook money to buy an RLK, a Reading Lab Kit?"

"What's that, Mrs. Evans?" he asked suspiciously.

"Well, it is a programmed reading kit that allows children in a class to progress at their own rate."

Ida Mae Lee spoke up, "We don't need one of them, Mr. Carter. I got one in my closet on the shelf. I never use it, but it ain't complete. Someone took some sections out once and didn't return them. But we got one." She laughed and added, "It's just sitting on my shelf if any of you want to use it. That is, if you know how."

"Can I go, Mr. Carter? This here discussion don't involve me. I don't use textbooks." Ozell fidgeted with a book of matches.

"No, you can't. You might learn something, though I doubt that!" The two men glared at each other.

The majority of the teachers were not interested in the book discussion. They smoked, looked at their watches, yawned, sweated, and the more industrious ones filled out attendance records.

Mr. Carter looked at the second slip of paper. "Now girls, next I wants to talk on the folders that are due at the end of school. There has to be a folder for each child, and it's up to you to get it done. You has to write comments on the folders for each child and I wants only nice comments. There ain't going to be nothing else on these folders. I ain't going have you teachers read the folders in the fall and only teach the good kids. That ain't going to happen at P.S. 123. I know some of you has difficulty writing comments, so I asked Mrs. Dickson to make up a committee to write comments for you. Then whatever comment fits, you can copy it on these here folders."

Miss Bernardo took notes as Mr. Carter spoke. "Mr. Carter, can you give me an example of a good comment?"

He looked very pleased. "I don't rightly know off hand 'cause I haven't thought none up." He wrinkled his forehead and said, "Is liked by his classmates." Miss Bernardo dutifully wrote it down. I could not believe that teachers were incapable of writing their own comments and that we were forced to take our comments from a standardized sheet drafted by a committee.

Then Mrs. Miller, the curriculum coordinator, spoke up. "Why, Mr. Carter, I think that is a marvelous idea. Now all the children will be treated fairly. I am going to include that in my report to the school board on curriculum." She patted her wig and sat down.

Rufus Carter smiled at her and continued, "You all has to give tests pretty soon. These here tests are for grouping the kids next year. You will get their test scores and group them from there. That way the classes will be closer in ability. You gave this here test in September, so there ain't going to be no trouble using it." Then he assigned special teachers and the teachers' aides to each class. No one was assigned to me.

Mrs. Miller held up a copy of the test so that we could see it. "Now ladies, you know how important this is to administer correctly. Be sure you follow the directions. This covers everything you have taught them this year. We weren't satisfied by the scores in September. So be sure the scores are much higher this time. Last time they was much too low. And you remember, P.S. 123 is a black school and it's right important we do well on these tests. You don't want us blacks to get the low scores."

"Thank you, Mrs. Miller. You heard what she say and you do it!" Mr. Carter puffed on his dead pipe, and said, "Last of all, there is this here speaker, Mr. Frank, who will be talking on programmed learning at the Administration Building Thursday morning. This ain't a required meeting, but I sure wants for you to go. That's a good way to spend a professional day." I had set aside that day to run off a month's supply of arithmetic work papers and make some art projects, as well as begin on the numerous records for the children's folders. I was glad that this meeting was not mandatory.

This was a rare day for me. Earlier, I dropped Paul at the base and had use of our car. I enjoyed having some time of my own, driving the car, and running errands. The windows were open, the sun shone, and the radio played loudly, "The Age of Aquarius," last year's number one hit. How ironic, I thought, with Paul preparing for a tour in Vietnam and me in a war zone of my own. Then I listened to the words:

Harmony and understanding
Sympathy and trust abounding
No more falsehoods or derisions
Golden living dreams of visions
Mystic crystal revelation
And the mind's true liberation

I laughed and turned off the radio. The wind rushing past the open window was heavenly.

"Hi Maggie. No real school today." We both laughed. Maggie and I stood in the shade of the Administration Building waiting for the doors to be unlocked. We saw P.S. 123 faculty members as they walked up to the math center.

"Are you going to that meeting?" I shook my head.

"No? Well, I'm not going either. We can run off all those dittos."

"Do you have enough paper?" Maggie asked.

"I bought more yesterday. It's in the trunk."

"By the way, Maggie, what do you think about the 'committee for nice comments'?"

"Hilarious!"

"I just couldn't believe that everyone else thought it was a great idea. You know, no one was insulted or even amused."

"Yes, I noticed."

By working together, we finished in the math center at the same time the lecture was over. "Maggie, I'll meet you back at the school. I need more teaching supplies, art paper, and felt tip pens." We got into our cars and drove out of the parking lot.

It was a beautiful sunny day, and without any students, P.S. 123 seemed forlorn. As I parked the car alongside the fence, picked up my purchases, and started up the sidewalk to the school, I looked over at Maggie's room. She was hanging out the window and waving frantically. I waved at her and kept on up the sidewalk but she hissed, "No! No! Over here!" and waved again. I crossed the front yard and headed toward the side door. She met me at the door and opened it for me. "I have been so worried! I was afraid you wouldn't be back in time."

"Why? What's going on?"

"Mr. Carter found out that we didn't go to the meeting."

"So?"

"He's livid! I mean really wild. He spoke to me first and now Ann Potter is in there. I was so scared that you wouldn't get back in time."

"I don't understand what he's upset about."

"Well, he said that we didn't go on purpose and so I told him that my car broke down and that you were riding with me, so we couldn't make it on time. I wanted to make sure your story fit mine so we wouldn't get into more trouble."

"Seriously? Maggie, it was a non-compulsory meeting!"

"Now he says we had to go." I just groaned. "Anyway, listen quickly because he is going to be calling for you as soon as he is finished with Ann. I picked you up this morning and had to take the car to the garage. So you called your husband and he came with the car, but by then, it was too late to get to the meeting."

It all sounded complicated, but Maggie's car was in the garage. She had dropped it after we left the county parking lot and taken a taxi to school. I was to take her to the garage at the end of the work day. My mind whirled with the effort to remember each newly fabricated detail.

Just then, Ann Potter came into the room, crying. "He said

that I was a horrible teacher and that he was going to make sure that I didn't get another teaching job and that he was going to count me absent today because I missed that meeting and dock my pay one day."

"You're kidding!" I exclaimed.

"No!" she wailed. Maggie handed her a Kleenex.

"Ann, you already have a job for next year," I argued. "Didn't you tell me you signed the contract?"

"Yes. But what if Mr. Carter calls the new principal?"

Just then the loud speaker in Maggie's room announced, "Mrs. Evans?" and then more authoritatively, "Mrs. Evans! Come to the office at once."

"Listen, Maggie, is this the way the story goes?" and I repeated it.

"Yes, that's close enough." I nodded at her and left the classroom. It was a long walk down that dimly lit hall. I knocked on his door and walked in.

"Mrs. Evans. It about time you gets here. Why didn't you answer the intercom the first time I try to get you?"

"I am sorry. I can't answer you. It doesn't work in my room. That part was removed in March, I believe."

He slumped back into his chair, pushed it away from the desk, and lit his pipe. "Now, I suppose you is going give me that same story about where you was today."

"Where I was, Mr. Carter?"

"Yeah. You heard me announce this here important speaker in the faculty meeting and you knew you was to attend, but you decided to do as you please, as usual, didn't you, Mrs. Evans?" He sneered at me and said, "It ain't no wonder that you has had three different jobs in three years."

"Just what do you mean by that comment, Mr. Carter?"

"With such a bad attitude, you was fired from each one!"

"Mr. Carter, I taught two years in the same school and stopped only when my husband was transferred. This is the reason I started here in December."

"Oh sure, that's what you say!"

"Mr. Carter, did you call me in to discuss my previous teaching record?"

He snapped, "Anyway, you has a disgusting attitude. Always thinking you know everything. That I ain't . . . *ahh* . . . don't know nothing. You better think again, 'cause I ain't through with you yet. You'll be sorry you acted like this, you hear?"

"Yes, Mr. Carter, I do. But you mentioned that the meeting today was not mandatory and I thought it more beneficial to work in the math center than hear a lecture on programmed instruction this late in the year when I do not plan to teach here next year." I paused and added, "There were several other teachers who did not attend the meeting."

"Yes, I know. Mrs. Potter and Miss Stevens. I has already talked to them."

"Yes, sir. But Ozell Lewis and Mrs. Dickson did not attend either." He looked slightly uncomfortable. "Do you plan to dock all our paychecks for one day?"

"Who said something about that?" he bellowed.

"Mrs. Potter. Perhaps you could dock us one hour that we could make up by not taking a lunch hour. Obviously, we are not absent today."

He seemed confused, stood up, and paced back and forth by the window, puffing furiously on his pipe. His jaws bulged from clamping the pipe so tightly. Finally he replied, "Mrs. Evans, I don't like your attitude. You just ain't teacher material. I can't have you openly disobeying my orders, and that is what you is always doing."

"What do you mean, Mr. Carter?" He continued to pace in

front of the window. "Do you plan to dock our paychecks and mark us absent?"

He looked at me for a long time. "No," he muttered. "Not this time, but if this here happens again, you better believe I will."

"Yes, sir. I do believe you."

He glared at me, not thinking my answer sincere, but I was quite serious. I knew the day he docked my pay, I would walk down to the school board and demand a hearing. That day never came.

"Well, what did he say?" Maggie and Ann said in unison. I told them both. We could not believe that all that turmoil occurred because we did not attend a non-compulsory meeting. After taking several tranquilizers, Ann calmed down. I walked back to my room thinking about finishing two new bulletin boards that afternoon—one was about summer fun and safety, and the other was a poem about the future.

As I unlocked my door, Maggie called from her room, "Lisa, a faculty meeting was just announced!" Ann Potter was with her.

I groaned loudly. "Do you think it will be about our absence at the morning meeting?"

"No doubt!"

"If he starts on that, I am going to ask Mr. Lewis and Mrs. Dickson where they were."

"Oh, you wouldn't dare," gasped Ann Potter.

"Yes, I would."

Instead, the meeting was about textbooks for next year. All the allotted money had to be spent and, of course, all the teachers were expected to look at the new books in the Administration Building. Only a few teachers from each grade had done so. Debby, Hilda, and Fay represented the third grade. None of them planned to teach at P.S. 123 next year. The meeting began at 1:30 with Mrs. Miller sitting on a stool and saying, "Okay, what books has you decided on?"

"I want that new English series. These books are too hard."

"No, they aren't," fussed another teacher. "My class just loves them."

A third teacher spoke up, "Certainly the school needs new spelling books."

Several different series were mentioned by the teachers who had seen the new books, and one was selected. The one selected used spelling words in stories only and did not enforce the rules of spelling or use spelling drills. I wondered how children who had difficulty reading would benefit from such a speller. That choice took more than one-and-a-half hours to decide.

"What about new arithmetic books?" a shrill voice asked from the back of the room. "That arithmetic series is too advanced for my group, what with geometry, sets, multiplication and division, and pages of written problems. Besides, there aren't many drill pages."

"That is a very good book," said Mrs. Miller. "I helped to choose it and, as far as I am concerned, no other text can compare to it. Why, it has geometry, thought problems—"

I could not bear to listen and looked out the window. She noticed my inattention and said, "What do you think, Mrs. Evans?"

"I think it is a very difficult arithmetic book, Mrs. Miller."

She snorted. "You must not be using it right." Finally, they voted on new arithmetic books but no workbooks. After that, they discussed and voted on new penmanship books and, finally, new reading workbooks. New third grade level readers were ordered as was an RLK, but reading workbooks were not allowed. Of course, no reading books or workbooks were ordered for primary, first, or second grade reading.

"Mrs. Miller, could we use some of these funds for primer,

first, and second year levels?" I asked when the voting ended.

"Heavens, no. Didn't you hear Mr. Carter? He already told you! This money is just for grade level textbooks." She glared at me, horrified by the question.

Less than half of the teachers bothered to vote. Ozell voted every time. Maggie did not vote at all. She said, "I won't be here next year and I have entirely different opinions on the needs of my students. Besides, I don't know very much about the books they are discussing." After the first few votes, Mrs. Miller did not bother to count hands anymore.

Mr. Carter sauntered in, his hands jingling coins in his pockets. "You decide everything?" Mrs. Miller nodded. "Good. We got to spend all the money whether we need these things or not, elsewise next year we ain't getting as much money."

He looked at the room full of teachers and grinned. "I guess that is all for today, but I want you all here on time tomorrow. Some of you is coming in too late and leaving too early. You will have me thinking that you don't like P.S. 123 and you wouldn't want me to think that, now would you?"

It was 4:30 when Maggie and I left that day, hot and tired. After I dropped her by the garage and she got her car, we met at my apartment. We swam in the sunlit pool, remembering snatches of our conversations with Mr. Carter and the faculty meeting discussions. Maggie was an excellent mimic and soon we were laughing. "Miss Stevens, I is surprised at you. You should know better. I will dock your paycheck if this happen again."

Then Maggie changed her voice to Miss Bernardo's and said, "Mrs. Miller, which books are we voting on now?"

I laughed and added, "Why no, Mrs. Evans, these funds is for textbooks, certainly not for books the children will actually use."

Maggie interrupted, "Do you see any difference between

reading books for third grade and remedial reading books for third grade?"

"Sure," I said sarcastically. "That money is just for text-books." Then I dove into the pool to swim twenty laps. Later, stretched out on towels in the hot sun, Maggie and I talked about education and P.S. 123 until dinnertime.

"I think that teachers in underprivileged schools should get hazardous-duty pay."

Maggie laughed.

"I really mean it. The work is much harder, and with knifing incidents rising—"

"Would you believe that for punishment the kid gets a little talk? A pat on the shoulder? Maybe a week's suspension? What about calling the police?"

I sighed. "Maggie, schools like P.S. 123 won't ever improve if the broken system is allowed to continue."

"Why, what do you mean?"

"First-year teachers always get the worst assignments. Without any experience, they are given the hardest teaching jobs, and of course, they don't stay at these tough schools. They either quit or transfer as soon as they can."

Maggie bit her lip. I feared that I had hit a nerve. She was leaving teaching at the end of the year, but I pressed on.

"What these students need are master teachers, with at least three years of experience. But most importantly, teachers who choose to teach at schools in an impoverished area should receive extra pay for their work. They should stay at least three years, and then be given a choice of their next assignment."

"That would be fantastic."

"Before they ever begin teaching, they should attend summer classes taught by teachers and community leaders who have experience with such difficult settings."

"I needed that. Can you imagine how much easier it would

be if we knew what we do now when we started?"

"That would be the best for the teachers and the students. The students have experienced teachers, and the beginning teacher has an enjoyable classroom experience because she is prepared and knows what to expect."

"That would save a lot of frustration."

We both sighed simultaneously. Glumly, Maggie said, "How could you ever get that idea across to an all-white school board that doesn't give a damn if the roof leaks?"

"I know. I guess I could always run for the school board." We were silent, each pursuing private thoughts of the days to come and the one just endured.

"Maggie, I think teaching is like joining a huge corporation as a lowly vice president, numbering among the hundreds of thousands. It is a prestigious beginning but after twenty-five years, you're still at that same level with no more responsibility than when you started. No one compliments the good job you do or notices an attractive room or attentive children. So, after a while, I bet you don't try so hard. It might be easy not to do much. Did you ever have a teacher who just assigned the next page in each book every day? Then you would correct all your own work with the master sheet? No? Well, I did and I hated it. Every Monday, I did the entire week's work, and then just read library books for the rest of the week. I hid them behind whatever books we were supposed to be working on."

"How dull," said Maggie.

"So what it boils down to is that teachers just stumble along to retirement, never earning new privileges or attaining new goals. After all, we are just classroom teachers and, of course, 'girls.'"

"Oh. How depressing! I refuse to spend my life like that." Maggie sat up in her chair. "You know if women's lib wanted an area of rampant discrimination against women, why don't they pick education? With the majority of teachers being female, just how many do you think are on the school board or are county administrators? Or principals?"

"Several fellows started teaching when I did. They have the same qualifications I have but were paid more, and, after their first year, were picked up for assistant principal or dean of students."

"Sure. There are so few men in education that if you're male, you are almost guaranteed an administrative position."

We had similar discussions before. What galled us most was our inability to improve the situation.

That next Monday, I asked for the folders for each of my students, and Mrs. Black snorted. "They ain't ready, Mrs. Evans. You has to come back."

"May I have all the cards that are supposed to be filled out? I would like to start them now."

"We ain't got enough to give you. You just has to wait." Her hair bristled around her face. She pushed back a strand impatiently and tucked it into the clip at the back of her neck.

I stood in front of the office counter and stared at her. "Do you know when my folders will be ready?"

"I ain't saying." Her voice was cold and sharp.

"Do you have the information forms for the children to take home?"

"Here, Mrs. Evans. Here you is. Just count out what you need." She didn't say it, but I felt she was thinking, "And then leave me alone!" I thanked her politely. She grunted but did not turn around.

With less than a month of school left, the folders were not ready. There were no cardboard folders with each child's name, and most of the forms that were to be filled out were not available. Although it was typical of the haphazard record keeping at P.S. 123, I was still amazed. The information sheets I was given demanded fundamental knowledge that was not currently on file: the child's first and last name, birth date, age, parents' names, immunization record, family doctor, phone number, address, whether the parents were living together, the occupations of the parents, the number of children in the family, and the ages of the siblings. Apparently, much of this vital information was not on file.

I was never allowed to take the records from the office, and it was clear that Mr. Carter disapproved of reading the children's files. It did not take me long to locate and read the files that were there, though. Five were missing, nine more only had names on the cover, and the rest had first-grade tests and grades, plus a notation about whether the child had ever been seen by the school nurse. A few of the students' grades were filled in, while some only had checks or an "x."

That afternoon, I handed the information sheets to my class. "Let us look at these together. You will have to take them home and have them filled out. This is important. I am sure you will remember to bring them back tomorrow. First, we will talk about each section and what is needed. On the top line is your name and address. Please fill that line in." After months of writing letters, all my students could spell their names and addresses. "The next line is for your phone number."

"I ain't got no phone number!" growled Cecil. He looked angry.

"I gots two phones, one upstairs and one downstairs," said Marjorie.

"The hell you do, girl."

"I does too."

"Shut your fucking self!" shouted Cecil.

"Mrs. Evans, do you hear what Cecil say to me? Do you hear? He call me a—"

"Marjorie, sit down please."

"But Mrs. Evans."

"Cecil, if you don't have a phone, just leave the line blank." It was then I realized owning a telephone was a status symbol.

Most of them did not know which immunization shots they had. Sandy and Danny were not sure how old they were. "Gee, Mrs. Evans, I ain't had no birthday for a long time. I forgets how old I is." They did not know if they were born in the state or somewhere else.

When we began the sections on family history, Felicia said, "I ain't got no daddy. I lives with my ma and my grandma."

"Me too," echoed other classmates.

Most of them were mystified about their father's occupation. Patricia offered, "He go to work in the morning and he come home at night."

"Do you know what he does?"

"Nope, he just work."

The children promised that they would remember to have the forms filled out that night and bring them back the next day. Most of them did. Danny handed me his at the door and said, "Mrs. Evans, don't ask me to take home no more forms 'cause my ma ain't going to fill out no more. She was mad and said it ain't none of your business, some of these questions," he stuttered to a stop. He hung his head to one side, watching me.

When I looked through the sheets to be certain that the most important information was included, I noticed my students' ages ranged from eight years of age to Sandy, who was almost thirteen, with most between nine and eleven years of age. Many of their brothers and sisters had different last names, and half of the families were headed by a mother or grandmother. The largest number of children was in Marjorie's family with thirteen, but five or seven was not unusual. The last sheet was Edward's and in the blank marked "sex," Edward's mother had scrawled, "black." I also found that Sandy's mother, Daisy, could not read or write. She made checks in different places and spelled her name differently each time she wrote it. Several parents did not know the date on which they were born, just the year. Some did not know that. With this information, I was expected to complete every form each child's folder was supposed to have for the three years he or she was in the school system. There were yellow attendance cards, orange family history cards, and white identification cards. I also was to enter their grades with a suitable comment on the back of the folder.

One afternoon, during my break, I carried my class folders and information sheets to the teachers' lounge. "Mrs. Evans, where is you going with that?" It was Mr. Carter.

"To the teachers' lounge, sir."

"Why now, that is highly personal information and you can't just take it anywhere you please. You just might be careless and lose it," he sneered.

"I don't plan to—"

He waved his hand, dismissing my comment. "And since you is working on those folders, you remember what I say." I did not respond. "Mrs. Evans, you be sure that everything is complete. Ain't no teacher going leave here or get her last paycheck till all the records is complete, with nice comments too. And you be sure all the grades is filled in."

"Yes, I plan to enter my grades."

"Not just yours, Mrs. Evans. You got to put in all the grades, first and second year too." As he spoke, his hands fidgeted in his pockets, jingling coins together. I could hear the coins jingling as he walked down the hall.

Besides filling out four or five forms for each student, I also began administering the standardized tests that were required for third grade students that year. I attempted to convince the class that the comprehensive test of basic skills was important, and they were to do their best.

"I likes test day," said Cecil.

"Yeah, me too," said Kelvin. "I don't have to do no work."

After reading the instructions carefully and allowing them to begin, I watched Sandy go down each page, blackening in the circles. It took him five minutes to complete a forty-five-minute test.

"Sandy," I whispered, "what are you doing?"

"Aw, Mrs. Evans, I can't do no test like this. This here is too hard for me. I is dumb and this ain't no dummy test. I just fill in the circles like you says and then I get to nap. I sure like test day, then I don't do nothing all day." Sandy had advanced from a non-reader to a first grade reader. This third grade achievement test would only show him as far below grade level.

I knew it was ridiculous to give an advanced written test to the entire class. The vocabulary words were quite difficult and the arithmetic section had many multiplication and division problems. Several of the students would do well. They were able to read the questions, but the majority would do very poorly. Some were too tired to try. Others were immediately frustrated. The entire class was always finished fifteen or twenty minutes before the allotted time.

I watched them work and could guess at the scores. Nicholas tried to work ahead, blackening in circles at random in the next sections of the test. Dexter craned his neck to see what was on Eric's paper. Tynetta spent as much time as possible in the bathroom. Felicia sucked her thumb and twisted her pigtail. Pencil points mysteriously broke and hands fidgeted inside desks.

As I expected, the four highest scores were held by Larry, Eric, Jack, and Billy. These children were doing fourth-grade work. The eleven lowest test scores belonged to Jeffrey, Jimmy, Edward, Cecil, Nicholas, Sandy, Danny, Felicia, Curtis, Sharon, and L'Angela. They were all below second grade level. The remaining eleven students—Dexter, Kelvin, Tynetta, Sylvia, Barbara, Angela, Marjorie, Patricia, Tanya, Shirley, and Sandra McPeters—were at a third-grade level. Nanci took the test in Mrs. Madison's class. It was very frustrating to realize that, with all the advances my students made, they were still—and perhaps would always remain—below grade level. I knew that these children were more capable than this one test showed.

After spending several evenings correcting the tests, I handed them in to Mrs. Miller on Friday. She looked horrified. "Why, Mrs. Evans," she gasped. "I thought you said you was doing such a good job, that you didn't need no help. Certainly not from me! Why, these scores are the lowest in the school."

Then she turned to congratulate Fay Morris on her excellent test scores. "Fay, I am so proud of you. You are an excellent teacher. These scores are so high. Not like those dreadful scores of Mrs. Evans's class. Why, she has some on a first-grade level. Can you imagine?" And she laughed.

"Thanks, I was surprised they did so well," responded Fay.

Fay told me earlier that most of the teachers, including herself, had not administered the tests properly. "Hell, they can't do this test and it doesn't mean a damn thing anyway, so I just helped them. You know, pointed out the right answers." I stared at her in disbelief.

As I turned to leave the room, I met Millie LeBlanc. "That was a lot of work, wasn't it?" she whined.

"What was?"

"Well, you know, adding up all the scores at the end of each test booklet. I don't see why those lazy teacher aides couldn't have totaled them, too. After all, they corrected them."

"Did Mrs. Smith correct your tests?"

"Of course. You don't think I did? That would have taken hours. Sure, she and Nadette corrected all the teachers' tests."

CHAPTER 17

Amen, Brother

THE NEXT TEACHER'S MEETING was announced with a sign in the office window. Mrs. Madison's room was hot and stuffy that afternoon. I sat near the windows hoping for a breeze, but the entire atmosphere was soporific. Several heads nodded and many were supported on bent arms.

Mr. Carter strutted back and forth in front of the room. He repeated the requirements for the children's folders and then continued, "I plans to check your work and if it ain't . . . isn't . . . satisfactory, then you got to do it over. Ain't nobody going get their paycheck until everyone is finished, hear?" He must have been rehearsing that speech the other afternoon when he spoke to me, and I thought he seemed pleased with his performance.

"Now, about this here discipline problem we is having. I can't see no more kids, so don't send them to my office. I is real busy trying to figure this here special summer school program that's going to be at P.S. 123 this year." The teachers woke up at this news since no one had previously heard about it. "And if any of you teachers wants to teach this summer, you better speak to me about it. I'll decide who'll be here, based on your excellent teaching record this year."

I pushed some damp hair away from my forehead and rested my head on my other arm. "But anyway, this here discipline problem, you just gots to learn to control your own class. I has told you from the beginning that any behavior problems is your fault. Take when I was teaching—I never has no discipline problems and I has an integrated class. If I has troubles with any of my students, I sent the whites out of the room and talk to the blacks rough-like. I told them they gots to do good 'cause whitie try to keep them down and make fun of them for their mistakes. I call them 'colored' and 'nigger,' just to shame them. And after a couple of these talks, I don't have no more trouble for the year. Course you white teachers can't do that. You whites just has to learn to love. That's it. You just gots to love your black brother. You gots to stop thinking you is superior!"

"Amen, Brother," said Mrs. Dickson.

That next afternoon as I took my class to music, I met Maggie in the hall. "Hi," she said, "have you gotten your evaluation from Mr. Carter?"

"Evaluation?"

Maggie was slightly breathless from hurrying down the hall. "You know, the one that goes into your permanent record file?"

"No. I haven't."

"He is handing them out today for everyone to sign. I did not do too badly. I really expected worse, but it was mostly threes and fours, and a few fives."

"That's wonderful! You really should be pleased. So one is the lowest and five the highest?"

"Yes."

"I think you did really well. I am so happy for you."

Maggie laughed. "So did he, considering that he has never been in my room or observed me teach."

"You must be kidding."

"No. Oh, my time is up. See you after school."

I did not see my evaluation that day or the next. Finally, one morning as I pushed open the door, Mrs. Black called to me. "Mrs. Evans, come into the office. Here is your evaluation. You got to sign it."

The first thing I noticed was that the numbers were written lightly in pencil. "Mrs. Black, would you mind if I take this to my room? I would like to read it carefully."

"No, that's okay."

"I would like to go over these pencil marks with ink."

"Sure, that's fine."

After unlocking my door and putting down my books, I sat at my desk with a pen and carefully traced his numbers. With one glance, I saw the numbers: ones, twos, and threes. The evaluation was divided into the three categories of professional competence, professional growth, and personal characteristics.

Professional competence was broken into: knowledge of subject matter – 3, room environment – 2, planning for instruction – 2, instructional techniques – 3, class management – 2 or 3. He had put down both numbers. Perhaps he could not decide. I penned in the 3. In the area of professional growth, there were 2s in parent relationships and adaptability, and a 1 for faculty relationships. My personal characteristics received 2s for accuracy, promptness, and personal appearance, but 3s in judgment, communication, and physical health. I was surprised that I had done this well.

It was interesting and ironic to note that only a few months ago, when I received my recommendation, Mr. Carter stated that he could not evaluate me since I was at P.S. 123 such a short time. Two months later, never having been in my room, and never having watched me teach, and never having seen my lesson plans or behavioral objectives—Mrs. Black kept them—he was able to complete fifty detailed questions on my teaching performance. I made a photocopy of the evaluation and returned my signed copy to the office.

It was less than thirty minutes later that Mr. Carter knocked on the door, first rattling the knob to see if he could just walk in. Jimmy opened the door. Mr. Carter pushed him aside and stomped up to my desk. He was waving a new evaluation form, which was also completed in pencil. "How dare you! How dare you!" he sputtered. He was in a rage. "How dare you fill in your evaluation in pen! You ain't got no right to do that! Who told you to do that?"

"I cleared it with Mrs. Black, Mr. Carter."

He stopped a minute, perhaps to catch his breath. "Well, she ain't got no right to tell you that. You just sign this here one. You don't need to read it again. It ain't different!" He handed it across the desk to me. I noticed that class management had been changed to 2.

"But Mr. Carter, it is in pencil. I will be glad to sign it when it is in ink."

"Why you want it in ink?"

"Ink is used for all important papers. I wouldn't think of filling out a check in pencil, and certainly not an evaluation that will become part of my personnel file at the county."

"This here paper has to be in pencil. That is a county policy."

"I am sorry, Mr. Carter, but I will not sign it unless it is in ink."

"It ain't never going to be in ink, you hear? It ain't never going to be in ink!" He was furious with me. "You is the only teacher who refuse to sign her evaluation. You just think you is something special. Well, you ain't. This here evaluation proves that. You ain't nothing. I'll just send your evaluation in without your signature. See what the school board has to say about that."

"But Mr. Carter, I am not refusing to sign the paper. I will be glad to sign it when it is in ink."

"It ain't never going to be in ink!" he shouted, and with that he stomped back out of the classroom and slammed the door.

The children were silent, their eyes huge. Even though I urged them to continue their classwork, they stared at me for a long time. Somehow every teacher knew that I refused to sign my evaluation and that Mr. Carter was furious, yet I had told no one. The next morning, Fay came up to me in the hall and said, "Say, tell me all about your run-in with Mr. Carter."

I looked at her and shrugged my shoulders, and asked instead, "How was your evaluation?"

"Jeez, you won't believe it, but fantastic! I mean all fives! I guess that's because I play up to Mr. Carter, you know, and he likes me. Oh yeah, Mrs. Dickson got all fives too. Hilda and Debby got threes and fours. Millie LeBlanc got all fives. Can you believe that? And she doesn't do a damn thing. Well, toodles! I've got to go find my class." I watched her waddle down the hall.

As Maggie and I left the school that afternoon, I told her about Mr. Carter's scene. "Wow! That must have been something. You really had a lousy day. Gosh, I'm sorry I signed mine. I noticed the pencil and wondered about it. Why, he could change anything he wanted to. Look, after I leave, would you check my folder when you check yours?"

"I may not be able to. It is confidential, but I'll ask."

"Are you ready to leave? I can't believe you're leaving early and Friday is your last day. Have you finished all your reports? Maggie, you only have two more days!"

"Yes, and I wrote some comments on my students. I told it like it is, without glossing over anything. I think next year's teacher should be treated to my opinion."

Maggie laughed.

"I wonder if I can make it through those last two days. Did I tell you about the dreams I have? Well, I keep dreaming that I am in school and Johnny and Carlos are just obnoxious, and in this dream, the teacher—I think that's me—beats them with a belt! Isn't that awful?"

"That's a nightmare!"

"Lord, will I be grateful to leave this school."

"Will you have your master's in education by the end of the summer?"

"I sure will."

"Maggie, that is fantastic."

"It will be great to finish. I only have a few courses left."

"Will you live on campus or at home?"

"Oh, at home, it isn't a far drive at all." As we passed the office she said, "Wait just a second. Mrs. Black, did you receive the leave paper from the school board?"

"What leave paper, Miss Stevens?"

I walked toward the door and stood outside under the porch roof. Maggie was furious when she came out. "Here I am, leaving in a few days and they have lost the leave paper again. That is the second one I filled out for them."

"Mrs. Black lost both of them?"

"No, the school board did. I'll leave without the signed paper if I have to. I don't plan to miss the beginning of summer school classes because the school board keeps losing my leave paper."

She did not have to leave without permission. The school board did not lose her third copy. Her last two days went by quickly, and although I was pleased that Maggie was leaving early to attend university classes to complete her master's, I knew I would miss her. Together we grappled with P.S. 123's unwieldy problems, faced defeat and frustration, and found comfort in friendship. I was also grateful that there were only three weeks left to teach in the school year.

I waited until I was certain that the school board received all the evaluations. Then Hilda and I decided to check our teaching folders at the Education Building. As we waited in the plush, wood-paneled air-conditioned office, I thought of my earlier experiences with Mr. Simpson, the personnel director of the county. I met him when I applied for a teaching job in December. He accepted my application and told me to check in regularly. When I called him the next day with my new phone number, he suggested that I come in for an interview. "I just met with you yesterday, Mr. Simpson." Much to my surprise, when I checked in the next day, I was told that a vacancy was filled because he did not have my phone number. The following day, yet another vacancy was already filled, too.

"Girls, I doubt if you will be able to see Mr. Simpson this afternoon. He is busy."

"We have an appointment."

"Oh, do you? It may be quite a long wait."

I nodded at her. She was a stocky woman, younger than I, with a broad face and penciled eyebrows perched above brown eyes.

"What is your reason for seeing Mr. Simpson?"

I looked at her politely. "We wish to speak with him."

"Obviously," she sniped. "What is the reason?"

"I would prefer discussing that with him." She glared at me and left.

Hilda said, "Why is it that secretaries are so obnoxious?"

"I am sure Mr. Simpson told her to inquire."

"You may go in now, girls." I looked up to see the secretary standing by the swinging gate, holding it open. I thanked her and walked into Mr. Simpson's office. The window behind him made it difficult to see him clearly. The lighting formed a rosy halo around his head.

"Sit, sit down, ladies." He had our folders in front of him on the desk. "Now then, what seems to be the trouble?" He was a short, spare older man with a very pink nose and pink cheeks. Wispy white hair moved with the breeze from the air conditioner.

"We had a little difficulty with our evaluations and wanted to be certain, since they were filled out in pencil, that they were not changed." He nodded and handed them to us. Hilda was relieved that hers was the same. My evaluation had not been changed either.

"Why don't you tell me what this is all about?" He seemed genuinely concerned.

I began to explain. "Mr. Simpson, since my evaluation was done in pencil, I refused to sign it—" But that did not seem to be the best place to begin, so I hesitated and then asked, "Is it a county policy to use pencil on evaluation forms and to evaluate without visiting a teacher's classroom?"

"Good heavens, no! Why, who is your principal?"

"Mr. Carter at P.S. 123."

"Oh. Of course." He leaned back in his chair. "Did I send you two lovely ladies up there? I certainly am sorry. Do let me apologize for doing that." His voice was smooth, almost caressing.

"Mr. Simpson, we were concerned about our evaluations

because they are not fair. You see, he was never in either of our classrooms."

"Oh, well, seeing who wrote the evaluation, I am sure that it won't be considered. Everyone knows that Mr. Carter is the worst principal in the county." I gasped. "Oh yes, Mrs. Evans, we are aware of the deplorable conditions at P.S. 123. Yes, indeed, one of the worst in the county."

"You mean, Mr. Simpson, that you know about the racial tension? The low morale? The deplorable conditions of the building? The lack of supplies?"

"Yes. Yes. Yes. Yes," he answered.

"I was told that two letters were sent to the school board complaining about conditions at P.S. 123. Have you read them?"

His chair sprung up with a snap, and he slammed his feet against the floor. "How do you know about those letters, young lady?"

"Mr. Carter mentioned them in a faculty meeting."

"Yes, I have seen them both," he said.

"Why isn't something done? Why is the school being ignored? Why is Mr. Carter allowed to continue?" I could hear my voice rising with each pointed question. I stopped, lowered my voice, and tried again. "Mr. Simpson, if you know that these things are true, why don't you do something?"

"Oh now, little lady, some things just can't be changed without a lot of problems, and that happens to be one of them. The NAACP would be on us for sure if we tried to get rid of him. Just no way we can fight the NAACP. They'd call in their fast-talking lawyers. Oh, that would be a mess for sure. You know, we just recently integrated. It sure won't do to stir up trouble and have those colored folk yelling about discrimination. Besides, I won't be able to do much after July 1. I am being forced to retire by Superintendent Jordan."

Mr. Simpson continued, "Superintendent Jordan and Jackson on the school board forced me to take Jackson's son, Junior Jackson, as my assistant several years ago, even though he wasn't qualified. Then they voted him a pay raise so that he makes nearly as much as I do." In a confidential tone, Mr. Simpson added, "You know, Jackson and several others control the school board. They plan on making Jim Jackson, his son, personnel director, and then they will have complete control of the county." I was surprised that he was being so forthright.

He sighed. "As you can see, we all have our problems."

"Mr. Simpson," I practically shouted, "why don't you tell your story to the newspaper? The public has a right to know these things."

"I have thought about that, but I am an old man and I have to live here when I retire." He mused awhile, biting the end of his pencil. "Can't say I haven't been tempted to spill the whole mess to the papers." He leaned back in his chair again. "Yes, I am going to retire. Why, I have been personnel director for thirty-five years. That's a long time." He rocked for a little while. "They are accusing me of being incompetent, not tending my duties, but these last few years haven't been easy with young Junior Jackson as my assistant and having to check everything with the school board. Now they want my job, too. Oh, they offered me a small job, but I decided to retire." He closed his eyes and sighed.

So lengthy was the silence that I wondered if he had forgotten we were there. When I looked at Hilda, she looked uncomfortable too.

Just then, he opened his eyes and asked, "What are the conditions at P.S. 123?"

I repeated the long list of problems at the school. He nodded as I talked: racial tension, favoritism, faulty records, lack of books appropriate to the learning level of the students, lack of supplies, problems with P.E., the building's run-down and unhealthy condition. He interrupted, "There shouldn't be any supply problem at P.S. 123—every child in the county is allotted $9.00 for school supplies!"

"Mr. Simpson, I would like to have a newspaper reporter talk to some of the teachers at P.S. 123 and take some pictures. I think the public should be aware of the problems there."

"Yes, well, we mustn't be too hasty. Do you know teachers who would be willing to speak with reporters?"

"Yes, I do."

He lapsed into thought. Perhaps at last something would be accomplished to better the education of the P.S. 123 children.

We rose and thanked him for his time. As we left, the door across the hall was open and I saw Mr. Nolen standing beside Superintendent Jordan's desk. It looked like a very confidential talk. I realized that Mr. Nolen supported the school board's position of "do nothing." He did not particularly care what happened at P.S. 123, but he did want to make certain that Mr. Carter was allowed to bumble along without attracting adverse publicity. Was that why he had been so disturbed when I mentioned speaking to the school board about Mr. Carter's notorious letter to me?

Mr. Simpson's secretary scowled at us. "You certainly were in there a long time. Mr. Simpson has a schedule to keep." She brushed past me and hurried into his office. I glanced back at him and before the door swung closed, saw him leaning back in his chair, his hands clasped across his stomach.

As I crossed the dirt road to the barbed-wire fence, the bussers were just arriving. They waved at me. "Hi, Mrs. Evans. You sure is early today." The sun was already hot on my back as I walked up the cracked cement sidewalk. I noticed several more

Amen, Brother   297

panes of glass had been knocked out of the front door over the weekend.

Walking into the empty cafetorium, I waited for one of the workers to notice me. They were busy with lunch preparations. Finally, one looked up and asked, as she asked every morning, "Yeah, what you want?" Silently, I held up my small lunch bag. She lumbered over to the counter, took the bag, and then slowly retraced her steps to the refrigerator. I was following Mr. Carter's orders—no teachers allowed in the kitchen.

Apparently, the health inspector was not pleased with the condition of the kitchen. Mr. Carter solved that problem by banning teachers from the cafetorium kitchen. The cafetorium workers were not ordered to scrub the walls, floors, and equipment, or to wear hairnets or to get rid of the bugs. Instead, they kept the teachers out.

After closing the refrigerator door, she asked, "Does you have our cups?" I looked at her blankly. "For coffee?" she added. It was so hot in the kitchen that sweat rolled down her cheeks.

"No, I don't."

"You teachers is stealing cups. Ain't going be no more coffee without cups." I nodded at her, swatted at a fly that buzzed by my face, and walked through the screen door into the hall.

My room was damp and warm. The stuffy air rushed at me as I opened the door. The bathroom odor was mingled with the smell of mildew. A forgotten apple attracted several roving bands of ants. I struggled with the rusty windows, opening each one as wide as possible. I wrote some directions on the board beginning with "Choose one!" Then I drew a pair of eyes in the o's of "choose" and listed five activities.

Monday morning silenced my students as they stumbled into my room. Edward pretended to be asleep, walking and bumping into desks and tripping over Cecil's foot. A crooked grin appeared as he found his own desk and sat down. I think he was peeking a little. Sandy was absent and Sandra McPeters arrived in tears, departing soon after with her grandmother. Nicholas settled into his desk, put his head down, and napped.

The children I sent to Miss Morris for reading returned. "She ain't having no reading today, Mrs. Evans. She don't feel like teaching and said for me to tell you that reading groups should stop at the end of May."

I could not believe she planned to waste three precious weeks. I sent the group back to Fay with a note, "There is reading today." I sent the other children to their reading teachers. Slowly my reading group appeared at my door, but 15 minutes were wasted.

Later as I walked past the windows, I noticed Fay Morris sitting on the playground. Her reading class was running merrily over the dirt, trying to swing on the frayed rope and playing leapfrog.

When we walked out to the playground before lunch, I could hear the noise from Maggie's old room. The door was open and a large black woman was sitting at the desk fanning herself with a sheaf of papers. The children were shouting. Carlos was running up and down the aisles. They could not hear the angry voice of their teacher who picked up a short ruler and swatted at children indiscriminately. My class turned the corner, their whispers floating ahead of me onto the playground.

After the baseball game was in progress and the girls were playing a dance game called "Strut Miss Lizzie," Maggie's old class swarmed out the door onto the playground, pushing and shoving each other down the steps. "Come back here," Maggie's replacement shrieked. "Who told you to do that?" Her students had already scattered over the playground.

She walked over to me. "I'm Miss Brown."

"Lisa Evans."

"I never seen such a bad class in all my born days. Lawsy,

they do beat all." She wiped her forehead on her sleeve and tucked her blouse back into her skirt. "I wonder how that other teacher stood them for a year!"

The poor woman looked miserable at the very thought of enduring this punishment for three more weeks. I felt sorry for her. No substitute is ever paid enough to endure what they do. But I did not tell her that Maggie's class was controlled when she was teaching. Several of her boys disrupted the baseball game with a fistfight. "Let me at him. I kill the motherfucker!" Arms and legs were thrashing out from the pile in all directions. Luckily, no one was hurt.

Maggie's class played baseball with mine for months without a single fight. I told them they could not play with us that day and would have to ask me for permission to play tomorrow. The boys were very angry with me. Not only had I disrupted a promising fight, but I also took away their baseball privileges. Lower lips protruded. They muttered and scowled but made certain that I could not hear what they said.

I thought that the cafetorium was like a zoo that day. The animals were fed, and the keepers ran around restraining them in cages, or rather, seated at tables. The classes of Maggie's substitute, Miss Brown, Millie LeBlanc, and Fay Morris were completely uncontrolled, running up and down the aisles, throwing food, and pulling chairs out from under their classmates. The keepers chased after the children, waving rulers in the air and occasionally getting close enough to the children to smack them a few times. Then the chase continued.

At my tables, the children, seeing the chaos around them, emptied the ketchup bottle on their food, sprinkled salt on the table until I took the shaker away, tried to kick each other under the table, and whispered. Edward started the game of making faces. He would make a face and the others would imitate him.

At last lunch was over, and we could closet ourselves in

a hot, bug-infested, but quiet room. My small desk fan barely moved the heavy air. The days would become unbearably long and the children listless or sleepy. Their sweaty hands stuck to the papers. Temper tantrums, sulks, and pouts increased. If possible, the plumbing became less adequate since the water fountain dribbled light brown water, forcing the children to put their mouths on the faucet to get a drink.

The afternoon was spent working on arithmetic and watching a film I ordered: Peter and the Wolf. I played the music for them again in the classroom while several students took turns dramatizing Peter, the wolf and the grandfather. They drew pictures to go with the story, and then the whole class wrote another adventure for Peter. This time, he captured a huge lion all by himself. I wrote the story on the board as each child suggested a new sentence. Several thought their story was more exciting than the original.

That afternoon, another faculty meeting was held. Mr. Carter was in shirtsleeves. He loosened his tie and turned Mrs. Madison's fan so it faced him instead of the faculty. He sat on her stool and reprimanded several teachers for being late. "These here following teachers have been selected to teach summer school: Mrs. Dickson, Miss Bernardo, Mrs. James, and Miss Morris. These teachers has done an outstanding job of teaching this year. They concerned with the children at P.S. 123 and will make this program a success." His selection was not surprising.

He continued, "I don't want you girls asking for no more supplies. What's in the supply closet is for next year. We can't use no more for this year. You just has to make do with what you got now. Ain't no use asking for more paper, 'cause they ain't going give it to you in the office. Just what you need for tests at the end of the year, hear?"

"Next of all, you gots to check all your books in your room. The library need a complete list 'cause it ain't got no list now at all. Mrs. Wilson, you tell them what you wants."

Mrs. Wilson rose slowly. Her hair frizzed around her shiny pink face. "We must have a complete number of books you have by Wednesday, okay? Then be sure the library books are all back this week. Friday the library is closed. I got to get my work done, too. That's simple enough, isn't it?" She sat down heavily. I wondered how she coped with the daily pressure of those 250 pounds.

Mr. Carter left the room while Mrs. Wilson spoke. He strolled back in. "So now you hear what Mrs. Wilson want, and I expect you to do as she say." Abruptly, he changed the subject. "You has to decide who would benefit most from this special summer school, but they has to be 98-01 children. Can't have nobody else, even if they needy. Maybe if there is room later. We don't want no troublemakers or slow learners. Only those who will benefit themselves being here this summer. This here was difficult to get the school board approval. They only did it 'cause they think a lot of my being concerned and thought I was doing a real fine job. Them was the words, girls. A real fine job."

He cleared his throat and continued. "Just 'cause it's getting to the end of school, I don't want to see no lack of discipline. Seems like the school building is getting too noisy. I don't want this to continue. You best remember that, so you stays out of trouble."

He paused, lit his pipe, glanced around the room, and said, "There's been some misunderstanding about the folders, so let me explain it again real simple-like. I ain't going give no paycheck till everyone is finished with their folders, and I plans to check all your work. I wants all them records filled out complete, back and front. Don't use no ink except for the name. They change their address real often and then you gots to cross out and it get real messy, so you has to make a new card. Just put the name in ink. Then on the folder you gots to put the grades and a nice comment. Everybody gots their sheets of comments?" He paused and looked up at the faculty. "I wants the grades from the last two years, if it ain't there. Ain't nobody accuse the school of having an unorganized office. Ain't nobody going say our records ain't right."

Someone asked, "How can I find those other grades?"

"Now, you just call up their old teachers or maybe their old school and see if they don't tell you."

The fifth-grade teacher continued, "But several of my students moved here from another state."

He just shrugged and smiled. "That's your problem, ain't it?"

Fay Morris stood up. "Would all third-grade teachers remain here for a minute?" Fay, appointed by Mr. Carter, was grade chairman for the third-grade teachers, which is an interesting position for a first-year teacher to hold. "Okay, you know that Mrs. Miller wants us to be together, so we have to plan. Any suggestions?"

"Yes," I said. "I propose that the reading groups continue until school is out."

Millie LeBlanc whined, "Oh, you would. You have the easiest class."

Exasperated, I answered sharply, "Well, Millie, you have Mrs. Smith's help for the entire hour." Her mouth flew open. She glared at me and stopped talking. We voted to continue the reading groups.

Then Fay raised the subject of tests. "How do you plan to grade your class?" Several mentioned by specific tests. "Lisa?"

"By their daily performance, as I have all along."

Fay looked at me thoughtfully. "No tests?"

"Not really, just daily papers."

"You correct all their papers?"

"Yes, of course."

"Shit," said Fay. "I might correct all their papers." She laughed out loud. "Well, for those giving tests, do you plan to include spelling, grammar, arithmetic, science, reading, and social studies?" Heads nodded. "Okay then, we should each make up a test and then use it in all the classes. And I'll do grammar. The test will include suppositions, prepositions, and complex sentences."

I interrupted her, "Fay, did you teach all those things?"

"Yeah, I sure did." And then she paused, "Oh hell, I know those dumb kids didn't learn any of it, but I sure taught it." After deciding which test each of the teachers would make up, Fay announced, "I have a message from Mrs. Miller. She wants each of us to write a behavioral objective for a subject area for an entire year."

"What?"

"More work," groaned Millie.

"You know what we do each week, only have it cover a whole year."

"When does she want this?" I asked.

"Next week. Let's decide on the subject areas." I chose health and later that week, wrote a very simple outline, typed it, and handed it in. The goals for the year were ways to good health, with specific areas mentioned. I doubted if it were complex enough for her approval or confusing enough for the school board to accept.

Each day, I waited for a reporter from the *Journal* to appear, but no one arrived. As a matter of fact, no one ever would. I began to wonder if Mr. Simpson decided that the best way to handle me—a troublemaker—was to agree with me and feign interest.

Other newspaper articles appeared, however, that told part of the story Mr. Simpson had related to us. The first newspaper heading read, "School Promotion Due Jackson, Board Member's Son." In a typically dry reporting style, the article stated that Junior Jackson would be recommended for personnel director, since he was assistant personnel director. The newspaper article continued with a quote from Mr. Simpson, "You know, I am the best personnel director this county ever had. Of course, I was the only one."

The morning after reading that article, P.S. 123 seemed dimmer and more wretched than usual. Perhaps part of the lighting was my own attitude, but the major problem was two burned out light bulbs in my classroom. Missouri said, "There ain't no more light bulbs in the school. I done switched all I could, Mrs. Evans." He did take one from another classroom, which helped.

That day included Dexter teasing Jimmy until both were on the verge of tantrums, and Jeffrey and Sandy disappearing after reading, instead of returning to the classroom. When I went to Ida Mae's room to ask about the boys, I found her pounding on the windows and screaming, "You come back here, boy! You little black monkey, you come back here." Her voice was shrill and the windowpane somehow withstood her heavy pounding. The little boy grinned at her and ran swiftly across the dirt to the fence, slamming the gate. "Don't that beat all!" she cried and tugged at her frizzy bangs. "That little black ape has been stealing from me." She rushed over to her desk and said, "Just you look, you look right here. I had fifteen cents in my drawer and now it's gone. That little black bastard, and that what he is before God, I tell you. Just like my momma taught me, 'a nigger is a nigger is a nigger.' Ain't no question about that. Just ain't. No way you can civilize these people. They belong in the jungle, running around without any clothes on. Then they would have an excuse for no morals. No ma'am, ain't no way to civilize them. It's the devil put them on this earth to do his work. They ain't God's children, or do you think it's them Communists?"

She leaned over her desk at me. The sunlight glinted off her glasses, making her eyes look huge. She took them off, wiped the lenses on her skirt hem, and put them back on, saying, "Just you wait and see if it ain't the Communists behind these blacks and that silly black power thing of theirs. Have you seen those horrid fro-fro hairdos? Now, that is the devil's work for sure. Make them look like bushmen!" She sank into her chair, exhausted by her speech.

"Mrs. Lee, when did Sandy and Jeffrey leave?"

"Who?"

"Sandy and Jeffrey. They did not return to my classroom after leaving your room."

"I just sent them home."

"I want my students returned to my classroom, please. There were several things those boys had to do."

"Why you upset over a couple niggers? Seems like you'd be pleased that they was gone."

"Send them back to my room, please."

She shook her head at me. Her hands pulled at the collar of her blouse. "I told you, a nigger is a nigger is a nigger!" she shouted at me as I walked back into my own room.

It was difficult to depend on Ida Mae to teach reading those last few weeks. Many times the boys would come back saying that she wasn't there. The fifth or sixth time that happened, I walked to the office to ask if they knew where Mrs. Lee was.

"Ain't she in her room?" asked Mrs. Black.

"No."

"She got to be here somewheres. Nadette, you seen Mrs. Lee?"

"Who?"

"Mrs. Lee, the reading teacher."

"I ain't seen nobody," said Nadette.

"Well, I wonder where she at," laughed Mrs. Black.

"Maybe Rufus know. Oh yeah, he done left for the day—some principal meeting," said Nadette.

And so, the boys missed another day of special reading class. It was good that I taught them reading daily since they were playing in Fay's class and Ida Mae was vanishing.

That next morning, I was treated to another scene thrown by Ida Mae. She opened my door and then slammed it closed, stamped her foot, and yelled, "So you told the office I wasn't here yesterday! I know it was you. Mrs. Black said so. Why do you care if some niggers miss reading? They're too dumb to learn anyway. Won't make no never mind to miss a few times. You're just trying to get me in trouble. What are you, anyway, some kind of nigger lover?"

I started to talk to her quietly, forcing my voice to be calm and low. "Mrs. Lee, I asked in the office to be certain that the children would be supervised."

She never let me continue. "Don't you go telling on me again, you hear? I work hard, hard as anybody here. I got a right to step out once, without you reporting me." She turned and whirled through the door.

CHAPTER 18

"You Done Good"

THAT NEXT MORNING, a second article appeared in the newspaper, with the headline, "School Board Promoted Member's Son." It appeared on the front page and mentioned that one dissenting vote was cast by a Mrs. Stratton who asked why there were no other applicants for the position. The official answer was that the job vacancy was not advertised because the salary range of $11,500 to $12,500 was too low to attract any other applicants. Mrs. Stratton also mentioned that Jackson's son was not qualified for the position since a master's degree was required. The article ironically stated that Jackson had promised to fulfill all requirements, including obtaining a master's degree. Several other board members spoke on Jackson's behalf, noting the fine job he had done as an assistant personnel director for the past two years. The article then mentioned the discussion of air conditioners, which was the other topic of school board interest that afternoon. I knew that no one would effectively challenge this blatant nepotism.

I remembered the voice of Mr. Simpson, the personnel director, when he said, "They're pressuring me out. They have been trying for the last five years, saying I'm too old, incompetent, and senile. They're going to put Jackson's son, Jim Jackson, in this chair. Why, he's just a schoolboy. What does he know about all this? Sure, his daddy is collecting a few favors. Why, his daddy is going to control the whole county."

The next day, the sun was hot as I walked across the dirt road to school. My thoughts were not focused on the gray clapboard houses or the rusty box springs lying on a broken porch. I thought of that newspaper article—and Mr. Simpson. The barbed-wire fence sagged in the summer heat. I walked past an old man who was curled up against the fence. He had newspaper stuffed into his shoes and an old string was tied around the waist of his trousers. He smelled of whisky and muttered incoherently.

I hurried into the school to find Missouri. He was not in the office or the halls. As I went into the cafetorium, I looked out the window and saw a group of boys begin to shout and laugh. One threatened to poke the old man with a stick. He shuffled to his feet and amid hoots and curses, staggered across the road.

"Yes, ma'am, what you want now?" Missouri looked up from the newspaper. He sat at a table in the cafetorium, reading and drinking coffee.

"Nothing. It's too late." He watched me closely. "He's already gone. I was going to ask you to make sure he was all right."

"Who, Mrs. Evans?" I answered with a shrug. He looked at me, squinted his eyes from the cigarette smoke, and said, "I fixed your doorknob, but that other window is busted and the toilet ain't too good. Nothing I can do about that water fountain or the leaky sink." And then he returned to reading the sports.

My reading group wrote more stories that week. Especially noteworthy were the stories of Willie and Teresa, two girls who were unable to write sentences when they joined the reading group. Their first stories were written about a picture chosen from the picture folder.

Willie wrote:

This is Ann and She 6. She go to school every day one day. She came home for school and found a big rock. She put the big rock in her wagon her wagon has broke down. She went crying to her mother and her mother said I will buy you another one. When father came home Mother and Ann went to the store and bought her a wagon.

Teresa wrote:

This is Brenda and She marry to a sailer. She have on her evening gowns She is going to have a evening party and She got to fix her hair. All of her friends was fix really pretty but not pretty than Brenda. She was the most pretty lady I ever seen. One day She went down town with her little girl and bought her little girl some cloths. When She got downtown her little girl got a Short set, church dress, hat, and some gloves. Brenda got a church dress, hat, stockins, and Shoes. Then Brenda and Susan went to the food store. At the store She got peas, bean, corn, meat, lettuce, candy, meal, rice and everything. The man put it in the bag.

Both Teresa and Willie were very proud of their stories and with many smiles and giggles, read them to the class.

That same morning, I continued a discussion with my own class about the future and what they wanted to be when they grew up.

"Ain't never thought on it," said Kelvin.

"I's going be a teenager when I grows up," said Nicholas, again.

Marjorie said, "I going have babies just like my sisters done. Then I get lots of attention too."

Sandy laughed. "I going get me some wheels and go drinking every night." When I asked him how he would be able to buy these things, he looked perplexed.

Jeffrey spoke up, "I ain't going work no job. I get welfare. Good enough for my ma and grandma. Good enough for me."

Eric whispered confidentially, "I go to college and get a good job."

"I think I'll be a soldier and go fight or something," Billy said.

Barbara added, "I going to be a secretary and make lots of money."

"I never going to work." Nicholas shouted. "I just sit in the sun."

"I guess I be a truck driver like my dad. He make good money," said Dexter.

"I be a nurse or maybe a mommy," whispered L'Angela.

"I ain't going be no nurse," sniffed Felicia. "I going be a maid. That easy work. Nursing work too hard."

I put the jobs they mentioned on the board and added some others. Then they looked in old magazines and found pictures of the jobs. Several children used their extra time to read books on their job choices, and later they reported to the class.

"There are many different jobs that you might have when you grow up," I told them. "Many jobs need extra training and a high school education. Some jobs require you to go to college. Whatever you choose to be, you can be if you are willing to work hard. Sometimes you might be tired or unhappy. You might think it is too much work, but if it is for a job you want, it is worth it. It is important to know the things you like and do well, to think about your future carefully. I always wanted to be a teacher and so I worked hard, and I went to high school, and then I went to college."

Each child drew a self-portrait. Most of the bodies were poorly proportioned. Only a few had five fingers on each hand

and the faces were colored orange or pink. I put their names on their pictures and hung them all on the bulletin board. They wrote a paper saying what they wanted to be when they grew up, and I pinned it alongside their portraits.

Cecil wrote, "When I grow up, I going be rich and I going be fireman."

Larry wrote, "Someday I will be the first astronaut on a star."

"When I grow up, I be a famous baseball player," wrote Jimmy.

Edward wrote, "I like car. I be mekanik."

Patricia came up to my desk and said, "See, there I is all growed up and I is married and has babies! Ain't that right, Mrs. Evans?" I smiled at her.

The children were pleased with their morning's work.

"You going be a fireman?" asked Edward.

"Uh-huh," said Cecil.

"Maybe I be one too."

"But you wants to be a mechanic," protested Cecil.

"Yeah, I be both," decided Edward.

It was a beautiful blue sky day. We hurried outside into the friendly sunshine. The girls played hopscotch, and the boys ran to the baseball field. I noticed Jimmy untying his sneakers before stepping up to bat and walked over. "Jimmy, why are you taking off your new sneakers?"

"Sneakers?"

I pointed to his shoes.

"Them is my new tenny-pumps. I ain't going run in them. I can run fast without them."

"Jimmy, you have to wear shoes. There is broken glass on the ground, and you might cut your feet."

He scowled at me. "I ain't going make no home run." But he put them back on.

We stayed out a little longer than usual. I decided it would be better to be outside than to wait fifteen minutes in a dark, stuffy hall for lunch. When we did return to the building, the other classes had already gone through the cafetorium line and my class walked right in. The last boy in Miss Morris's line had dropped his tray and was cleaning up.

"Where has you been? Why, we has been waiting on you. You is late." I turned around and saw the oldest of the cafetorium workers brandishing a large spoon and wiping the sweat from her face with her dirty apron. "Now you just has to wait for lunch. I is busy. You don't got no right to make me wait. Where has you been?"

"Miss Morris's line has just gone through."

She ignored me. "I has been waiting on you," she grumbled. "Don't you be late again."

"May I have my lunch, please?" She walked slowly to the refrigerator and took out my brown paper bag and then slammed it on the counter with such force that the bag broke.

"Don't you be late again." I added all the minutes we waited in line in the last six months and decided that we could be several days late and the score would not be even.

The lunch that day was macaroni, a thin slice of pizza, corn, a piece of white bread, and a small square of plain red Jell-o. Felicia licked at her Jell-o until I asked her to stop. Dexter ate several helpings of macaroni and traded his Jell-o for more pizza. Edward was always the last one finished since he ate slowly with his arms around the tray, guarding the precious food.

That afternoon, I learned that I was able to place Jeffrey in the special summer school program even though he was not a federally funded 98-01 student. Edward and Cecil had already been accepted. "I is going to summer school," said Jeffrey. "I is going with Cecil and Edward."

"What we do in summer school?" demanded Cecil. I told them all that the program was to include trips to the beach, films, stories, and a daily lunch. Edward chuckled. "I is going school!"

The teacher in charge of the special summer school classes wrote me a note that said, "Anyone who wants a child in so bad to pester me so much, well okay. Jeffrey can come to summer school, Mrs. Evans." Since Jeffrey and Edward were not 98-01 students, it was difficult to have them both accepted. I rewrote the 98-01 list for my federally funded students, adding the children who should have been on the list all along. I wondered if the discrepancies for federal funding would be changed next year.

That evening, another newspaper article appeared. The headline blared: "Forced to Retire, School Official Says, Simpson Charges Nepotism." Mr. Simpson had told his story to the newspaper! I sat down and read the article slowly. Simpson stated that ranking school board officials pressured him into retirement so that the son of a school board member could take his position. He was told that if he did not retire, he would be replaced. "Why, he's been after me since the first of January to let him know when I will retire." Then he added, "This is one of the most glaring cases of nepotism that this county has ever seen."

To refute Simpson's statements, the school board officials claimed that he was grossly incompetent and had been evaluated as such by most of the county administrators. Several other members of the school board, including the Superintendent, Junior Jordan, could not be reached for comment.

I imagined Simpson speaking with the newspaper reporter in his sunlit office, leaning back in his chair and saying, "I fell from Superintendent Junior Jordan's favor about four years ago after a grand jury investigation of Jim Jackson's appointment to the assistant personnel director post. You see, when Jackson was hired for the position, there were seven other applicants, and Jackson was the only applicant who did not meet all the qualifications. All the others had master's degrees. Well, the school board was split in its decision to hire young Jackson—he needed his daddy's vote as a school board member to confirm the appointment. Of course, Jackson voted for his son. You know, I thought we'd handle this like we handled other appointments, but Jordan announced to me that Jim Jackson would start that day. Well, that day was before the school board action on the matter. How about that?"

The newspaper account continued: "The matter was investigated by the grand jury. You want to hear the report? Here's the conclusion—inquiries by the grand jury revealed that the position of assistant personnel director was created by the school board, and the position was filled by the son of a school board member—Jim Jackson. Testimony before this body indicated that eight persons applied for this position, and seven of the applicants had master's degrees. However, Junior Jordan, Superintendent, appointed Jim Jackson, the only one of the eight applicants who did not have a master's degree."

I imagined Simpson shrugging, sighing, his thin voice cracking as he continued, "Junior Jordan and I were good friends, and then this Jackson thing started. I said some things that weren't too complimentary during the grand jury testimony. I guess he got pretty mad, and ever since that time, Jordan would walk right past my office and carry on his business with young Jackson, rather than me. In fact, Jordan had nothing to do with me. You know, there were personnel matters that I wouldn't know about until I saw them in the paper."

Then the reporter interrupted and asked, "Well, about this personnel director appointment replacing you, Mr. Simpson, what about the fact that there were no other applicants for the job?"

"Ha! It was an amusing thing. Everyone knew that they

didn't stand a chance against Jim. So, you know, no one applied. Course the vacancy wasn't advertised much either." With a hint of sarcasm, Simpson added, "I bet the school board votes themselves a nice raise. Why, Jim Jackson's salary in four years rose to my level. He was making $100 less than me when I left on vacation last month. Let's see now, he was making $11,600."

The article dutifully reported that Jim Jackson had no comment to Simpson's remarks. I put the newspaper down.

I thought of Mr. Simpson's story the next morning as I waited for the children to line up and enter the classroom. They fidgeted and scowled. Something was bothering them. That morning I was told some hair-raising tales about the last day of school.

"My brother done told me that there's going to be a riot the last day of school! For sure, they's already planning who's going to get beat."

"Yeah, all the whities!"

"They're going get every last one."

"How are you sure, Sandy?" I asked.

"I done heard them talking. Last year ain't nothing to what's going happen this year. They're going break windows and smash cars up and stuff."

"Who are these people you are talking about?"

"The middle school and the high school kids."

"Yeah, they gets out early and come by this school," added Jeffrey.

"I'm scared!" cried Felicia.

"Me too!" said Sharon.

"I ain't scared of no fight," declared Cecil. "I just whop me some ass and then they be sorry they tangle with me!"

"I'll kick me some for sure!" shouted Jeffrey.

"Who told you all these stories?"

"Our brothers and sisters. They know all about it. Have for a long time too."

"It's going happen. Just you wait and see."

"Yeah, they going beat everybody up."

"Mostly whities get it," clarified Kelvin.

"Whities and teachers," insisted Jimmy.

"Yeah, man they going get the teachers," agreed Sandy.

They stopped discussing this for a minute and looked at me. "You be careful, huh, Mrs. Evans?" asked Cecil, and in the next breath he said, "Oh boy, they is going to be a fight."

And so we discussed the idea that fights do not solve problems. Some children were scared, but others excited. Violence was something they understood.

"I'm going bash me some heads!"

"I'm going to run right home and hide."

"Stupid girl. I ain't going run. I going get me some ass!"

"Ain't nobody going hurt me. Ain't nobody going touch me!"

"I ain't going mess with nobody. I staying out of this."

We discussed this several times before the last day of school. I do not think that I changed any attitudes on the subject of fighting and skin color. But the idea of me being hurt bothered them. Several times, they reassured me: "Ain't nobody going hurt you, Mrs. Evans. I told my brothers who you is," said Jeffrey.

"Yeah, we make sure you ain't hurt."

We also talked about the words "whities" and "blacks." They used the word "whitie" interchangeably with curse words. We talked about the fact that no one could choose what color his skin was. It was already chosen by his or her parents. Why should skin color make enemies?

"Just do," said Kelvin. "I hate whities and Uncle Toms!" Black power symbols appeared on notebooks and were inked into knuckles.

"I don't understand, Kelvin. You say you hate white people but then you tell your brothers who I am so they won't beat me. Why? My skin is white too."

"No, ma'am!" and he shook his head. "You ain't no whitie. We know you. You is Mrs. Evans."

"Kelvin, there are a lot of white people you like, including your friends, Larry and Billy."

He looked at me and said quickly, "Whities the enemy, and you got to hate the enemy!"

For these children, whitie wasn't me or any of their classmates. Curiously, a distinction was made between the white enemy and the white friend.

Later, I overheard Billy, Larry, Jack, Eric, and Jimmy discussing the last day of school. "Cecil says nobody fight unless they has to."

"But if there is a fight, we got some good guys here."

"You can use my bat," offered Larry.

"Okay, remember, you all is fighting with Kelvin's group. We ain't going have no trouble beating them!"

The newspaper editorial for the week stated, "Jackson Elevation Mishandled at Start." The editor's main point seemed to be that the public image of the county was not the best. There were critical audits, unfavorable grand jury reports, and charges of favoritism. It suggested that the tax-supported institution was being run as a private fiefdom. And then the editorial continued by congratulating the editor's astuteness. Four years ago when the assistant personnel position was created, this newspaper asked, "Is this post a stepping stone to Simpson's job?" The editor now accepted his laurels and figuratively smirked, "I told you so." The article concluded that it was a bald-faced but successful attempt to obtain a fairly lucrative job for the son of a board member without the necessity of having to face what might have been some stiff competition.

As I reread the article, it surprised me that several years ago, Jackson had been appointed assistant personnel director without a master's degree and that he still did not have one. It was ironic to note that his new assistant did have a master's degree.

I mentioned the article to several teachers, but none of them were concerned. "Sure, what do you expect?" said Debby. "This whole county is rotten. I can't believe how bad it is, and the kids get nothing. But there isn't any use getting upset about it. After all, what can I do? And besides, I'm leaving in just a few weeks."

Fay said, "Oh, I am sure they know what they are doing. After all, they are the school board, and he is qualified." She giggled. "Sure helps to be the school board member's son, doesn't it?"

Then she changed the conversation to one more interesting to her. "Gosh, you wouldn't believe how many men spent the night in my apartment. They were on the couch, and in the two beds and on the floor. It was quite a party. You know, boy, do I have a hangover. They were still asleep when I got up for work, but I made lots of noise so they'd wake up too. I mean, I have to go to work so the least they could do is wake up. Don't you think so?" she asked.

It was a long day. A swarm of bees invaded the classroom to invigorate the hot and listless students. It was even too hot on the playground. The girls huddled on the school steps and only a few boys played baseball.

In the afternoon, the children ate their fractions. Each was given a chocolate bar, and together we broke it into pieces: one-half, one-fourth, one-third. They counted the number of pieces and arranged them on a napkin.

"Watch me! I eat one-fourth," said Jimmy.

"I'll eat thirds first and save halves for last," decided Eric.

The idea of eating their fractions created a lot of excitement. We had worked with paper and cutouts before this, but the chocolate bars cemented fractions in their minds.

Another faculty meeting was announced at 2:30. I was hot and tired by then. My cotton dress was damp and hung limply from my shoulders. Very few teachers attended the meeting. Miss Bernardo chattered in front of me, and Hilda rested her head on her arm and stared out the window. Fay lit one cigarette after another until the meeting began. Mr. Carter walked into the room, noticed the number of teachers absent, and immediately began to harangue about not attending teachers' meetings. It was unfortunate that those who would most benefit from the speech were not there to hear it.

"When I calls a meeting I expect to see everybody here. Ain't no reason to miss a teachers' meeting. Ain't no one excused. You going get in serious trouble for missing one of these meetings."

Then he changed the subject. "Before any of you can leave this here building next week, this what you got to do. You got to complete the children's folders. Now that means grades, comments, and all the other information. Be sure to use that sheet of comments. Mrs. Miller made them up for you 'cause I wants nice comments and ain't no grade to be lower than C, you hear? You make sure that the folders is complete. Ain't nobody leaving till everyone is finished. I ain't going give no paycheck till I check everybody.

"Now about the school room. You can't leave nothing in the rooms. You got to wrap up all the books and label them so they can be put in the book room. Then they be given out next year. I'll check the rooms personal. Ain't no one leaving without doing their work, understand?"

I wondered why he was so belligerent. His attitude and tone of voice annoyed me. My thoughts wandered outside the window into the bright sunlight. The merciless heat dried and cracked the dirt street. I watched as an old lady, hovering beneath her tattered black umbrella, walked down the middle of the road. Her dress was too small for her bulging body. A bedraggled pink straw hat clung to the back of her head.

Mr. Carter's harsh voice cut through: "And you must hand in all your documents for this year. Testing papers. Record book. Grade book. Everything. You can't keep nothing on your class." It sounded as if he were repeating something he already said.

Miss Bernardo raised her hand and timidly said, "Oh Mr. Carter, I didn't know that you wanted my record book. It is messy. Should I copy it over?" I groaned inwardly at this foolish, well-meaning woman.

"Your record book is messy? Don't you realize the importance of these records? Ain't no one going say this office ain't got records. Ain't nobody going say that. I want all your records, and don't forget you gots to hand in the attendance sheets in triplicate. Ain't nobody going use no carbon paper. Hear? I will check your registers. Nobody getting paid till all the registers is right." He paused. "About the last day of school, I don't want no parties the last day of school. Just be sure it's like a regular school day. If you wants a party, have it the week before.

"Mrs. Evans?"

"I have heard that there will be a riot the last day of school. In fact, there was one last year. My classroom children have talked about it all this week. Are any precautions being taken? Should the police be alerted?"

"I ain't heard nothing about this here topic," he said and wiped his face.

Hilda spoke up, "My students have been talking too. They say last year several cars were damaged and some kids were beaten."

"Now, I ain't prepared to discuss this here topic. But I ain't expecting no trouble this year."

He shrugged off several more questions about the last day of school and ignored another teacher's question: "Well, are we going to be in danger? I would like to know, so that I can be prepared."

"I ain't going to be able to make no statement about this here now. The last thing today is about report cards. You gots to have your students bring in their stamps and envelopes to send home the report cards. We is mailing them home." I was amazed by this decision. "This here is county policy and ain't nobody going to disregard what I says." He glared at me. "Well, that's all for today, except you be sure you get in all these here records."

That next day, the newspaper heading read, "Jordan Recommends Pay Hike for Staff." The article stated that some staff members' salaries would increase by as much as $1,900. This increase would raise the assistant superintendent's salary to $22,000 and, of course, all the rest of the staff would get raises, too.

The teachers, however, who were paid less than in any other county in the state, would receive raises of $200. Actually, the salary range was from $5,800, for a beginning teacher with a bachelor's degree but no experience, to $10,620, for a teacher holding a doctorate and a continuing contract with 15 years' experience. Quite obviously, teaching is not a lucrative job, but altruistic educators discuss the rewards of teaching and chide teachers who believe that they are underpaid and overworked. Such a topic was previously discussed by school board members when a group of teachers complained about their meager salaries. They were bluntly told that a true teacher did not teach for money but for personal reward!

I totaled my personal rewards that next day to see how well I was succeeding. As a class, my students were more cooperative, less noisy, and more industrious than previously. There were no racial problems within the classroom. Stealing was minimal. There were fewer fistfights. Everyone, except Nicholas, had improved in skills. Individually, I studied each student. L'Angela seemed less shy and was doing third grade work. Sandy, Jeffrey, Edward, Cecil, and Danny were reading first grade books. And all of them could add and subtract well. Dexter could subtract two place numbers. Edward, Jeffrey, and Cecil would attend summer school. Sandy did not bring any more knives to school. Tynetta rarely sucked her thumb now, and Jimmy daydreamed less.

On the other hand, I deducted the problems with their parents, the constant warfare with Mr. Carter, the difficulties with other classroom teachers, my poor teacher recommendation, and the fact that Nicholas, Sandra McPeters, and Nanci were all beyond my ability to help. Thus, the balance was not overwhelmingly positive.

That last week the children were extremely well behaved. They seemed to dread the end of school, and interest in their classwork increased.

On Monday, several brought in their stamps and envelopes, but most of the children (Danny, Sandy, Jeffrey, Cecil, Patricia, Curtis, and the list grew longer) told me dolefully that they could not bring in the envelopes or stamps. Curtis's mother even wrote a letter: "Dear Mrs. Evans, Curtis miss school he got his shoes wet and don't have no others to ware. Also I can't afford no stamp or envelop." Curtis looked embarrassed and apologized.

"Could either of your parents pick up the report card at the office?"

He whispered, "They both work." I nodded at him and he sat

down. That day, I collected only seven envelopes and stamps. I needed twenty more.

Late in the afternoon, I called the school board and asked what the county policy was for the last report card. "Just that they can't be given out till the last school day. No, no. They don't have to be mailed home." His voice sounded weary and impatient. "There is no policy stating that a child can't carry it home."

After thanking him, I stared at the telephone and saw Curtis's embarrassed face. I knew that many of the parents would have to buy an envelope and stamp specifically for the report card. I decided to give my report cards out that last day of school to the students who had not brought stamps and envelopes. Daily I reminded the children to bring the stamps and envelopes, but none appeared.

On Tuesday, the workmen tore down the dangerous rusty monkey bars and laid them on the blacktop. The noise was constant. At last, the playground would get a much-needed facelift. They even planted grass. But the basketball backboards were not put up, nor was the broken playground equipment hauled away. Unsupervised children played tag with the water sprinklers, trampling the new grass, and slid down the reclining backboards. When the workmen left, the playground had a rectangular piece of blacktop without white lines for any games and grass that grew erratically, dotting the brown clay with patches of bright green.

While waiting in line for lunch, I watched Mrs. Madison's children stand silently and wondered again how she was able to control them so completely. They acted like a troupe of marionettes, walking perfectly in line without shoving, pushing, fighting, or talking. Billy stood beside me and waited impatiently for the cafetorium to open. "Billy, what does Mrs. Madison do if you misbehave in reading?"

His blue eyes grew round and his mouth flew open. "She puts you in the closet and locks the door!"

"Really?"

"Yeah, and if you bang on the closet door, she will hit you with her cane."

"Has this ever happened to you, Billy?"

"No, ma'am! I am real good in reading. I don't want to be locked up in her closet." I looked at the silent, perfect line and thought how dark and frightening a locked closet would be.

"Good day, Mrs. Evans."

"Hello, Mrs. Madison." She looked especially attractive in a two-piece yellow linen dress, but beads of perspiration formed on her forehead.

"Sure is hot today." She walked painfully into the cafetorium while one of the children carried her tray. I remembered a conversation with her in December when I commented on her well-behaved students and asked what her secret was. "Oh my, I couldn't tell you what I do. Why, I'd get in trouble for sure." If Billy's description were accurate, I understood her unwillingness to share her secret.

The afternoon heat throbbed against the windows, intimidated the slightest breeze, and roasted the classroom occupants. I read them a story of animal jungle adventures. We also worked with straws, making pictures or designs on paper. Everyone seemed pleased with his or her work. A film that afternoon on books and how an interesting story was written ended our day, but the children seemed reluctant to leave.

"Can I take a book home, Mrs. Evans?"

"Certainly, Angela."

"It's my turn to do the boards," shouted Felicia. "You give me that sponge, boy."

"You is the nicest teacher I has ever had," Marjorie said. "Is you going be here next year so I can come and visit you? Ain't never had no teacher stay, so I can visit."

Marjorie's face looked stormy when I admitted that she would not be able to visit me. "But Marjorie, I will give you some paper and write my address on some envelopes. Anytime you want to talk with me, you could just write me a letter."

She looked so excited about this. "I ain't never got no letter before." She whirled around the desks faster and faster until her pigtails stuck straight out from her head, and her ribbons danced. "You really write to me?"

"Yes, I will."

As the last child left that afternoon, the room seemed unusually quiet. Gray clouds brought rain. I watched the sky darken and the rain fall gently and then with more urgency, hastening to soak the parched clay. Raindrops fell rhythmically from the leak in the ceiling. A slight breeze blew several papers out of Barbara's desk and tugged at the orange-faced portraits pinned to the bulletin board.

As I listened to the rain, I worked on the numerous records that were necessary to complete the office files. I already finished the orange, white, and green cards, and tallied the federally funded 98-01 free lunch program children. Mrs. Black looked at me strangely when I asked for the green slip Mr. Carter told us to keep several months ago. No one mentioned it again, and I wondered how he was verifying the federal lunch money program without records.

My last effort was to complete the children's folders. I entered their grades that I already wrote on an orange card and on the report cards. I refused to stuff each child into a regimented comment from the approved list, and instead, thoughtfully wrote a comment of my own that pointed out the child's strengths and progress, as well as areas to improve.

It grew darker outside, and the rain pelted against the windows, leaving puddles on the windowsill and floor where the panes were broken. Each day that week passed slowly. Caught within the rim of a circle, each day rolled into the next or continued from the last, and so the week revolved into musty classroom smells, the last piece of chalk, a missing pencil, and the usual student banter: "Let go my pigtail, boy." "Who you calling boy, girl?" "Get that damn ball. Why is you so slow?" "Look at that. They is going to win this game." "When I grows up, I is going be a mommy just like my sisters done."

And then there was the office's constant badgering: "The orange card is for attendance, the green and white card is for personal history." "Be sure you write down a comment on their folders. Be sure it's from the approved comment list." "Is your behavioral objectives ready for the year?" "I expect to see good grades on these here tests, you understand?"

My mind floated back to my students: "I didn't come to school yesterday 'cause my ma was sick, and I has to take care of my little sister." "Yes ma'am, I take a bath every night." Dirt was crusted around her ears and under her chin. "Ain't no one going do nothing to me. I whop their ass for sure." The wind struck the gray metal door and slammed it shut, breaking the fragile pieces of memories, scattering them across the dirty wooden floor.

The next day was unique. No longer was it a day of beginning or another numberless day sandwiched into the middle, passing without recognition to another equally undistinguishable day—this day was the end. With solemn realization that their lives had indeed spun free from a seemingly unending spiral, a strange pallor settled over the class. Only Sandra and Sylvia stayed home that last day. The children did not wiggle to inner music or hum or play with their pencils as they stood in the morning line. They were silent, entering the room like actors newly cast, but without speaking parts.

Felicia sat in her seat with her knees under her chin, twirled a pigtail around one finger, and sucked a thumb. Jimmy daydreamed. Kelvin fluffed his hair with a big black comb. Marjorie wore her storm-cloud face and scowled at the world. Tynetta made three trips to the bathroom before all the lunch money was collected. Most of them did not respond to several of my stories, nor did our rousing, "Good Morning to You" song invigorate them.

Reverently, they took down Snoopy and dismantled the fishing pond. The vacant orange faces were placed on their desks. Row by row, the books were collected and then wrapped.

"Barbara, where is your English book?"

"I don't know, Mrs. Evans."

"You may have to pay for the book if you can't find it."

"I ain't going pay for no book."

"Please go and talk to the librarian. Maybe she can help you."

"Yes ma'am, but I ain't paying for no book." I watched her stocky body and the defiant slant to her shoulders as she crossed the classroom and walked toward the door. Nicholas did his best to trip her, but failed, and losing interest in that, returned to doodling on his hand with a magic marker.

The booklets with pages of puzzles and stories were enjoyed by everyone.

"Hey man, look. That ain't no right answer."

"Did you find all the animals in the picture?"

As the children wrapped the books, the tape did not hold, spilling the books to the floor.

"Oh, now you done it. You is in trouble for sure."

"I ain't going do no work," declared Nicholas. "I don't have to. This here is my last day."

Finally, all the books were wrapped, and my helpers seemed to glide noiselessly over the floor to their seats. I corrected each of their booklets before going outside. It was a long morning because they did not change classrooms for reading. The other teachers had not wanted to teach reading the last day.

Down the dim hall they walked, whispers hushed, sneakers scuffing impatiently at the heels of their classmates. The line wavered and then burst into the bright sunlight.

"Mabel, Mabel, neat and able," the girls chanted and spun the rope in the air.

Mabel, Mabel, set the table,
And don't forget the
Red hot peppers!
Who will be the highest stepper?
Winds blow hot and winds blow freeze,
How many times did Mabel sneeze?

"Catch that ball, boy."
"Who is you calling boy? You want to fight?"
"Aw, come on. Let's play ball."
"You is just scared to fight. You know I whop you good."
"Hush up and play."

The bright sunlight burned into the back of my head, white-washing my thoughts. I took pictures of them playing. Edward ran over and posed in all of them, raising his thin arms and making a muscle. Behind him stood Dexter with a huge grin on his face. They were excited about having their pictures taken, but mystified why I was doing it.

"You going give them to us?"

Wiggling, squirming, Tynetta asked, "Do I look okay?" The class stood together on the school steps.

"You is suppose to say 'cheese.'"

"Cheese, why you say cheese?" asked Dexter. But the moment was over. The picture was taken—the image captured. They scattered over the playground.

A small group practiced their song, closing their eyes and swinging their hips. They continued to sing.

Ooh child
Things are gonna get easier
Ooh child
Things'll get brighter

Ooh child
Things are gonna get easier
Ooh child
Things'll get brighter

Some day, yeah

It was an excellent imitation of the current hit "Ooh Child" by The Five Stairsteps.

Mrs. LeBlanc's children were let out on the playground. As soon as the last one was outside, she closed her door. Unsupervised, they ran over the newly planted grass, barged into the baseball game, and joined the jump-rope chanting girls. The rest sat and listened to the singers.

Some day, yeah
We'll get it together and we'll get it all done
Some day
When your head is much lighter
Some day, yeah
We'll walk in the rays of a beautiful sun
Some day
When the world is much brighter

After the bright sunlight, the halls were dim. Shapes blurred and melted. Swiftly the line entered the cafetorium. The meal looked like leftovers. "Mrs. Evans, look! Cecil is eating his applesauce with his fingers."

"Cecil?"

"Yes, ma'am, Mrs. Evans. I knows I is to use my spoon, but they didn't give me none."

"Could you use your fork?"

"That ain't as good as my fingers."

I laughed. "You're right. Let me find you a spoon."

When Edward finished eating, we were all ready to leave. After lunch, I read them a favorite story. The heat pressed down heavily. Many small heads rested on arms that afternoon or stared out the open window. A fly's sporadic path caught their attention. They shuffled in their seats, yawned, sighed, and listened to the story.

By 2:00, the heat became crushing, weighing down on the school with a heavy hand. I waited for them to mention the riots they expected that afternoon, but they were never mentioned. There were no older students to harass the children, so we went back outside for a kickball game. The girls did quite well, but the boys won, and after the game, the children were hot and sweaty, so they lined up to drink water.

"Who you pushing?"

"I ain't pushing nobody."

"You is, too."

"I ain't."

"Boys, you will all have your turn."

"He gots too long of a drink."

"I ain't. I just got here."

The line moved slowly past the water fountain as the water trickled out. By the last child, the water did not bubble over the metal rim.

Those last few minutes of the school year, we talked about their summer plans.

"I sure going to miss you, Mrs. Evans," interrupted Tynetta, and she hid her face in her hands.

I lined the bussers up, and those who had not given me an envelope or stamp received their report cards.

"What this for?" asked Danny.

"That is your report card, Danny. Take it home with you today."

"Yes, ma'am."

I shook each hand solemnly. "Have a good summer, Billy." "Goodbye, Larry."

Each in a stately fashion responded, "Goodbye, Mrs. Evans. I ain't never going forget you."

"You sure is a nice teacher."

With the second bell, the walkers lined up. Patricia was dragging a forgotten, but recently found, sweater. Cecil was armed with two black combs, and Kelvin held a stack of baseball cards. Many of them were given their report cards.

"What about me?" demanded Felicia.

"You gave me an envelope and stamp, Felicia. You will get yours in the mail."

"Oh, yeah. I forgot."

Once again, I shook each hand and wished each one a happy

summer. Patricia hugged me. Marjorie patted me on the arm. "Goodbye, Mrs. Evans. You is my bestest teacher."

"I ain't going shake no lady's hand," said Nicholas.

"You is, too," Cecil countered.

Nicholas looked at him and then at me, "Well, okay, but you is the only one who hand I shake."

"Goodbye, Nicholas. Have a good summer."

Cecil looked unbearably gloomy. I smiled. "Goodbye, Cecil. Enjoy summer school." He hesitated and then vanished around the corner of the door.

"You sure there ain't nothing left to do?"

"No, Dexter, but thank you for all of your help."

He stood in the doorway for a few minutes. "Well, goodbye, Mrs. Evans."

"Goodbye, Dexter." Turning, I watched Dexter as he walked down the hall. His bulky body moved slowly around the corner, out of my sight.

Looking into my classroom, the noise of its emptiness clashed in my ears. The walls, devoid of their colorful hangings, slumped into a dirty green to meet the unswept floor. A forgotten paper lay face down. An old coat had not been claimed by anyone. It sat limply in the corner of the closet. The freshly washed blackboards recalled lessons of the year.

"Yes, Sandy, that is the letter 'a.' Good work!"

"Then the elephant put on pink polka-dot pajamas and brushed his teeth."

"Eric, multiply by four, please. That was perfect."

"L'Angela, you keep score for the spelling-word game."

The sound of children's voices drew my attention to the windows. A plainclothes policeman was letting a small group through the gate. They waved when they saw me at the window.

I waved back. Impatiently, the man pushed them through the gates, clanging them shut. The playground was deserted without the afternoon games. The new water sprinkler hiccupped erratically over the arid clay.

I watched Patricia and Sharon walk down the dirt road, arm in arm. "Mrs. Evans, this really an astronaut outfit? My dad says it don't look like none he seen!"

"Mrs. Evans! Mrs. Evans! Can't you hear me? I been calling to you. There's a faculty meeting right now," said Nadette.

The faculty meeting was in Mrs. Madison's room. It was even hotter than mine. Pictures still hung on her walls. It did not look like the last day of school here. Sitting in the back of the room near the window, I wondered if I looked as hot and tired as I felt.

Mr. Carter sat on a stool, snapping a red rubber band. His tie was loosened at the collar. He wiped his forehead with a large handkerchief, stuffed it into his back pocket, and began, "When I calls a meeting, I expect everyone to be on time. This here is a special meeting to talk about some you white teachers. Think you know everything! I just seen a child leaving with his report card. Now, you all know that I told you to get stamps and envelopes to send home these here cards. I says it was a county policy, but someone think she know everything, sending home them report cards. I is sick to death of telling you whities to do something and next thing I knows you ain't done what's right. Some of you just think you is so smart. Why, you think you is smarter than me? Well, you ain't. I knows what the county want and I set the rules. You got to follow them. I ain't never seen the likes of some of you. The way you disregard what you is told to do. You got to do what I says. I is the principal. You ain't. And don't none of you forget that, hear? I ain't never seen the likes, sending home the report cards. Who does you think you is? You whities . . ." He mumbled the rest of the tirade.

He looked as if he planned to continue, but struggling for words, he stopped mid-sentence, shook his head, and snapped the rubber band with such force that it broke. The room filled with street noises, the rustling teachers, and the wheeze of Mrs. Madison's fan.

"Now I want to remind all of you about the records that got to be in the office. Ain't no one going get no paycheck till everyone is finished, so if you is done, you got to help someone else. Remember, I is going check each room myself, so you don't do no sloppy job."

"Ah, Mr. Carter, may I speak to the girls a minute?" Mrs. Wilson pulled herself up. "Some of you haven't turned in all your records and filmstrips and some books are still missing. Now, you know, I have to get my library done, too. So, well, you know." She wiped her round damp face on her sleeve. "I would appreciate it, girls, if you would send back everything I should have, and I still haven't received a book count from several . . ." Her voice trailed off. She took another puff from her cigarette. "And well, you know, I would like to have them. Ah, that's all, Mr. Carter."

Miss Bernardo timidly raised her hand. "Mr. Carter, about those personal history records. Some of the children, I just don't have all that information." She gulped. Her large eyes protruded from her thin face. She sniffed and wiggled her nose nervously.

He glared at her. "You got to get that information. You got to have every record complete!" I was surprised that she continued.

"But Mr. Carter, how do I find that information if the child moved here or the record is incomplete to begin with?" Again, she hesitated.

"Miss Bernardo, your records got to be complete. It is up to you to get that information. I don't care how you does it," he growled at her and turned to the rest of us. "Now tomorrow, just because there ain't no students, I wants you teachers here on time. Ain't nobody coming in late, and you got to stay here until the regular leave time. Ain't no leaving early, neither. You got half-hour for lunch. I don't want you leaving for longer than that, you understand?" Then, after a lengthy silence, he dismissed the meeting.

Missouri was sweeping the hall as I walked back to my room. Blue smoke rose from his tightly clamped cigarette. He paused and looked at me. "Well, this here year is over." I nodded at the fixer of doorknobs, swiper of light bulbs, unclogger of sinks and toilets, retriever of balls erratically thrown, exterminator of creepy crawly creatures—and friend. His body leaned heavily on the broom handle. I smiled and started to thank him. "Don't you give me no thanks, Mrs. Evans. I is doing my job, that's all, just doing my job. I is glad to help. You done work hard yourself now. You done good." With that, he puffed mightily on his cigarette.

"Missouri . . ." I started.

He waved the words aside. "Missouri, heh! My ma done named me Missouri 'cause that's where we was when I was borned." He grinned and shuffled down the hall in a cloud of blue-gray smoke.

My empty room echoed with my footsteps. I closed the windows, staring at the dirty green walls and the empty desks.

"What do you know about the ocean, Sandy?"

"The water ain't good to drink."

"Yes! Dexter?"

"There is a lot of sand."

"Good. L'Angela?"

"You can fish in the ocean."

"How many of you have ever fished in the ocean? What did you catch, Danny?"

"A big fish!"

"Me too!"

"How big, Kelvin?" His hands spread more than a yard apart. Everyone laughed. "Well, maybe this big." His hands were two feet apart. His classmates accepted the revision.

"You can find shells at the beach," offered Angela.

"Yes, you can!" They looked at the things I brought in, and then we wrote a story about going to the ocean, listed ocean words on the board, and labeled our seashore articles.

"Gosh, Mrs. Evans. That was fun! That was almost as fun as going there," Patricia added wistfully.

Determined to leave the thoughts of these students behind, I hurried toward the door, passing Nicholas's empty desk. Oh, Nicholas, the world is passing you by. You are only 10 years old and already far behind. I could see him shuffle his thin legs and wave his arms erratically in the air. "Nicholas, look at me, please." He pouted and squeezed himself into the corner of his desk. "Nicholas, tell me what you would like to learn."

"Ain't nothing," he finally mumbled and scratched his head emphatically. The desk squeaked with his wiggling.

"Nicholas, if one plus two is three, what is two plus two? Look at the blocks. Find two blocks. Good! Now find two more blocks. Very good! Nicholas, what is two plus two?"

He shrugged his shoulders. "Don't know."

"You just counted two blocks and two more blocks. Let's count them together."

"Eight," he guessed.

"No, Nicholas, look again."

He scattered the blocks across the floor. "I tired this!" he shouted and retired to his seat, curled his legs under him, and stuck his head into his desk. Nicholas, the world is waiting for you, and you don't even know it is there!

I closed the gray metal door firmly, and walked down the hall, past the office, through the heavy outer door. The barbed-wire gate clanged shut behind me. The road was empty and quiet.

CHAPTER 19

P.S. 123

T HE ROOM WAS HOT, stuffed with silence—a quiet unbroken by children's voices. I waited for them to appear that day and the next.

"Good morning, Mrs. Evans. How is you today?"

"Good morning, Marjorie. I am just fine. How are you?" She would beam and giggle.

"Look, Mrs. Evans, look this. I found this on the playground."

"You did not."

"I did too. Look, Mrs. Evans, what I got."

The boys were clustered around Cecil. He held a tiny toad in his hand. "You can't have no toad in class. She going make you throw it away, huh, Mrs. Evans."

"Cecil, would you like to show your toad to the class today?"

"What you mean?" he demanded suspiciously.

"There is a big glass jar you could put it in. Then we could all see it and you wouldn't have to worry that it might hop away."

"You mean, I can keep it?" He smiled and smiled. They all had a chance to look at the toad. The jar was passed from one desk to the next. I found a filmstrip on frogs and toads that they thoroughly enjoyed. "There it is! There's mine!" yelled Cecil as he pointed at the screen. He named it Greenie and we wrote a class story about it. He proudly carried Greenie home that afternoon with the name taped to the jar.

I pushed back a lock of hair that persistently drifted into my eyes and surveyed the paperwork I had already completed: the blue health records, the green federal-lunch-program sheet, the orange and white personal cards, the report-card grades, the personal information and comments on the permanent-record file. I still had the permanent-record files to finish. A slight breeze scattered white cards over the floor. Student's name, date, school, grade, teacher, address, phone number, sex, birthday, mother's name, father's name, brothers and sisters, numbers and names, occupation, church affiliation, report card grades for the entire year, A, C, C, B, C. My pen stopped while rounding the B. I stared at those rectangular cards and marveled that each child was neatly packaged in black ink on white cards. Edward, Felicia, Kelvin, Jimmy, Marjorie, Danny, Sandra, Dexter, L'Angela—their lives scattered in front of me.

"Come on, Mrs. Evans, you got to jump next."

Apple, peach, pumpkin pie
how many years before I die?
One, two, three . . .

"You is pretty good, Mrs. Evans, but ain't nobody good as me," and Felicia ran under the rope. "Faster, girl. Turn faster!" Her pigtails bounced with perfect rhythm.

"Mrs. Evans, why is you so nice?" said Marjorie. "Ain't no other teacher nice as you."

"Why thank you, Marjorie. These flowers are beautiful. I will put them in a vase for my desk so we can all enjoy them."

"You like them? We got lots in our yard."

"You like blacks?"

"Why do you ask, Sandra?"

"Why is you nice to blacks, Mrs. Evans? Do you have to be nice just 'cause you teach them?"

"You like me more than blacks, don't you? Who do you like best, me or Sylvia?" Both girls looked at me expectantly.

"I like you both equally."

"Me most?"

"No, Sandra, but I like you as much as everyone else, and I like everyone very much."

"Oh," she said. "Then you like Felicia very much?"

"Yes."

"You like Dexter very much too?"

"Yes."

"And everybody very much?"

"Yes, Sandra, and I like you and Sylvia very much, too."

"Gee, you sure is nice. You is the nicest teacher I ever had, and the most pretty too!"

My pen finished the letter B and climbed the steep slopes of an A. I brushed away a fly.

"Where is Africa? Yes, Kelvin. Good for you!"

"I like Africa films best because of all the animals."

"Hey, are you finished?" asked Fay as she stood in the doorway.

"Hi, Fay, no, not yet."

"Well, when you are, come to my room. I haven't even started yet. I don't think I'll count these books, just make up a number and write it down. They will count them again next year anyway. Besides, that would be too much work. Wow, you sure have detailed comments." Fay leaned over my shoulder and looked at the files. "Where did you find those comments?"

"I wrote them."

"You're kidding. What a glutton for punishment! I just copied them from the list. Some kids didn't quite fit the description, but what the hell." She smelled of tobacco smoke. "Don't forget to come down and help me. Remember, we all have to be finished before we get our checks."

I frowned after her. Considering the time it took to complete several folders that morning, I wouldn't be finished before Friday.

I filled in Edward's folder and wrote his comment on the back. "Edward has progressed remarkably this year. At first, he did not work with the class or play with his peers. Now he enjoys doing both. Beginning as a non-reader, he is now ready for the second primer. Because of his reading level, the written test score is not indicative of his capabilities. Frequent complaints of stomachaches and headaches may be caused by hunger. Edward has a delightful sense of humor and is very playful."

I decided to finish Nicholas's personal file next. I entered his grades, which were similar to those recorded the previous year, and then started my comment. "Nicholas appears incapable of working on a third-grade level. He waited an entire year to be tested for special education, even though his previous teacher also recommended it. He is now on the list to be tested next September. His inability to do classwork has caused him to become a discipline problem. He has difficulty associating with his peers and usually meets problems with temper tantrums, sulks, or fights. It is imperative that Nicholas be tested and placed into a learning situation in which he will be able to function."

"Mr. Carter, Nicholas has to see the county counselor. I am really concerned about him! He is acting strangely!"

"Now, you know she is a busy woman."

"Yes, but this is important. This is the reason she was hired."

"I doubt if it's all that important. You just think so. I knows better."

"Would you like to watch him and talk with him?"

"No, I is too busy for that!"

And so Nicholas, whose behavior and ability to interact with others had seriously deteriorated, Nicholas, who could not do simple addition or subtraction—even with help—or read at a pre-primer level, was ignored.

Wearily, I pushed away their memories, the sounds of their voices. I pushed them back into the deep pocket of my mind and continued to work on the folders. Carefully I filled in the information and the comments until all were completed by 3:00. Some lacked first and second-year grades, others the names of their brothers and sisters or father, and most lacked a telephone number. I placed them on the office counter before leaving that day.

After lunch the next day, another faculty meeting was held. I was barely on time. Mr. Nolen stood beside Mr. Carter at the front of the room. I wondered why he came. His manicured nails glistened and his beige suit looked new. A blue shirt and striped tie completed his outfit.

As if in answer to my silent question, he said, "Good afternoon, ladies. We have always evaluated the principal at the end of the school year, and that is why I am here. These sheets are to be filled out by you. You will rate Brother Carter, a fine principal I might add, on a score of 5 to 1. Of course, 5 is the number for 'excellent,' and no principal in this county has ever received a 1. You aren't expected to sign these."

He passed the papers out. Mr. Carter stood up and, rocking back and forth on his heels, cleared his throat. "Now ladies, you know that I has done a real good job this year. Just remember all the problems you couldn't handle that I took care of. So I knows you will rate me accordingly."

Many of the teachers were finished quickly. If they read the questions, they did not take the time to think about them or to recall Mr. Carter's actions. My paper was handed in last. I rated him a 3 in dress and appearance, but in leadership, executive ability, and discipline, I rated him a 1 or 2.

Hilda had given him 3s and 4s. Fay rated him perfect, all 5s. No one had rated him as severely as I had. When I mentioned several incidents to them, they said, "Oh, I forgot that." Or, "Well, he's not so bad!" Mrs. Williams said, "I was afraid to rate him low. Even if unsigned, he will know."

Mr. Nolen beamed. "Thank you, ladies. That is all for today." Then he turned on a highly polished shoe and strode out of the classroom.

Mr. Carter lit his pipe and noticeably relaxed. "Well now, I am sure you done right by me." He relit his pipe and continued, "Don't none of you forget I wants all those folders in today. I got to see them before you goes so I can check them. I is touring the building, checking the rooms. Most of you ain't done what I has told you. You got to wrap your books and those books got to be the same number as on this here sheet. Then you take the books to the book room, hear?"

Having heard this several times before, my attention wandered, and when I began listening again, he was discussing the summer program. "Don't forget, the only reason that P.S. 123 got this here summer program is because the school board listens to me. They know when I says we need something, that we better get it. Well," he grunted, "you can go back to your room now."

I walked quickly back to my room. Without the children, the school was unbearable. Sometimes I wondered if I would ever leave the hot stuffy air, the dirty green walls, the lifeless playground, the hatred stalking the halls and banging on the inner walls of my mind.

Gratefully, I closed the door and sat behind my desk. I looked at Mrs. Johnson's reading sheet for her reading test scores. Several children skipped two or three reading levels. Four were reading on a fifth grade level—Eric, Larry, Jack, and Nanci—eight on a fourth grade level; five had improved from a first grade to a third grade level; another group included three who had progressed from a pre-primer to second grade six-month level; and Sandy, Danny, Edward, Jeffrey, and Cecil had reached first-grade level from non-reader. The test scores confirmed that the reading program was successful! I know my class benefited by the reading skills I taught in conjunction with our class studies. I wrote detailed information about each child's reading ability and mathematical skills on the back of each folder until it was time to go home.

Time. If time played no more tricks, tomorrow would be my last day. I walked home in the scorching sun, passed clapboard houses, mothers shelling peas on a sagging doorstep, children playing in the dirt road, the family dog asleep in the shade under the porch. "Hey, Mrs. Evans. Hey look, Mrs. Evans!" I waved at the group of children and they walked with me down the road. Time brought me out of their community to paved streets and freshly painted houses, to sweet-smelling rose bushes and green grass. Time had taken me through the invisible boundary into a different world.

I expected the last day to be different, as different as the first day was, but the sameness of that day enveloped me. The barbed-wire fence greeted me, as did the broken sidewalk and the old red brick building. Nor had its occupants changed. The office was littered with papers. Mrs. Black handed me back the pile of folders. "You ain't finished with these here folders. They ain't got all the grades in them, and you didn't put the attendance on them, neither." I took the stack of folders without comment and walked down the newly waxed hall to my room.

The attendance was already written in the register and on the attendance cards. I wrote it again on the folders. As I did, I noticed that Mr. Carter had read or at least looked at many of my written comments. Using a red pen, he drew lines through my comment and printed on top, "Disregard, Constructive statements only are considered." That appeared on Edward's folder. On Nicholas's folder, he wrote, "Disregard any statement that is harmful to student." Quickly I looked through the remaining folders. Five other comments were scratched out. Reviewing each one he censored, I knew I mentioned weaknesses in the child's classwork, such as "is more interested in language than arithmetic," or where I used words such as "procrastinates," "challenges authority," or "is prone to tantrums." But I also mentioned strengths such as "imaginative," "creative," "excellent in sports," "class leader." No principal interfered with any of my comments written on a child's folder before. These notes were for their next teacher.

The grades that were missing were their first and second-year grades, and some of the previous teachers' names could not be entered because the children had moved into the county only this year. Since other teachers had this problem, I decided to ask Hilda what she did. The teachers in the annex were still packing books.

"Oh, there you are. I wondered when you were going to show up." Fay pushed her glasses back up on her nose. I counted Fay's books for her and she wrapped them.

"What did you do about the grades you didn't have, Fay?"

"Oh, I just made them up."

"What?"

"Sure. I just figured that the kid did the same thing those two years as this year, so I just put them in. Maybe he won't check my folders before I leave."

"Yes, he will. He checks them when you bring them in."

"You're kidding. Say, thanks for helping me." She wiped her face on the hem of her skirt. "Just look at me! I'm perspiring like a pig."

I refused to make up grades for these children. I decided to hand the folders back at the very end of the day. Maybe Mr. Carter would not have time to check them before he gave me my paycheck. I did not doubt that he would refuse to give out the paychecks until everything was done to his satisfaction. He threatened it so many times in the last few weeks that I believed him.

As I sat at my desk staring at the folders, I decided to comment on his comments. Taking my pen, I drew a line through his comments and wrote, "As the classroom teacher, I believe these comments to be valid and constructive."

I was behind several other teachers who were returning their records to the office and quietly placed my stack under theirs.

The children's desks were pushed to the edges of the walls. Only my desk remained in the middle of the room, an island floating on an ancient wooden floor. Instead of weeks or days, only hours remained until the end. It did not seem possible that it was here at last.

Mr. Carter called the last faculty meeting that day at 1:00. Sitting in Mrs. Madison's spotless room for one hour, a group of women waited for him. We were divided into two distinct groups, not by age or experience or race, but by our decisions for the future: to stay at P.S. 123 or to leave. The group of teachers who was leaving were young, noisy, and excited. We talked about the future. One teacher was getting married. Hilda was moving to the Midwest. Several were going to find secretarial jobs or go back to graduate school. Not once did we reminisce about P.S. 123. A smaller group of older women sat quietly, withdrawn from each other and from us. I wondered what their thoughts were that day.

Mr. Carter finally arrived in shirtsleeves, tie untied. I wondered if he had called this meeting to thank us, to wish us well—a good vacation, a good future. "Well now, girls, this here is the end of the school year, and I must say you sure made it a difficult year for me. Why, almost impossible! I never had to work with such an uncooperative group of teachers. Some of you girls think you know more than me, going above my head to complain to the school board about problems at P.S. 123 and to be so unprofessional to write letters to the newspaper. Well, if that don't beat all! Course I said this before, all the problems at P.S. 123 this year was on account of you teachers. Some of you was new and didn't know what to do about nothing, and most of you was inexperienced. It takes a good five to ten years to make a teacher. Ain't that right, Mrs. Dickson?"

"Amen, Brother!" She beamed.

"And then there is this here problem with prejudice. I know you white teachers hates those black kids. Why you probably hate me, too! I ain't afraid of none of your hates. You can't get no devil scare on me! The Lord know what kind of job I done this year. Near a superhuman job I done what with all this opposition, and then you white teachers coming to school all dressed up like you was going out on the town. Trying to tell these kids that they ain't nothing. That they is stupid and giving them such low grades just so you keep us blacks down. That ain't going to work no more. We blacks is just as good and just as smart as any of you whites is! You just lucky ain't none of you snatched baldheaded by one of them militant black groups. Course now, they would have had good cause to do it, too."

I forced myself to listen, knowing that this was the last tirade of his I would ever hear. Finally, he dismissed the meeting by saying, "Ain't no one leaving early. There still some of them folders out. Ain't no one going get their check till all the work is done and in the office."

"Mr. Carter, are the paychecks in the office now?"

"Yes, Fay, they is."

I followed the group of teachers out into the hall. I wondered if hell was being forced to continually wait for release. I watched Fay walk down the hall and into his office. She came back a few minutes later.

"Do you have your checks?"

"Sure," said Fay. "I just walked in and asked for them."

"Are you going to finish your room?"

"Hell, no. I'm going home. I don't want that stuff. I don't plan to ever use it again. I'll just let the janitor, what's his name, throw it away." She stuffed her paychecks in her purse and snapped it closed. "Well, see you." She strolled out the open doorway and down the sidewalk.

Several other teachers were waiting in the hall, including Hilda, who was beginning her drive to the Midwest that night. Mr. Carter refused to let her leave early even though all her work was completed. "Hilda, go get your checks. Fay just did and then left!"

"You mean it?"

"Yes. You should leave early, too."

Hilda came out of his office almost immediately. "He barked at me, said he wasn't ready to give the checks out."

"What? What about Fay?"

"I asked him that but he didn't answer."

Finally after waiting another 20 minutes, the group began to file into his office. I had not been inside his office since the confrontation weeks ago, but it was unchanged. The afternoon sun filtered through drawn blinds and a small fan churned through the heavy air. He looked at me and then pawed through his pile of checks, picking up two (one for June and one to cover the months remaining in the school year). As he handed me the checks, he hesitated as if thinking of something to say, or waiting for me to speak. The words were left unspoken. I took the checks and walked out of his office, said goodbye to the remaining teachers, and wished them good luck.

I escaped the physical confines of P.S. 123, never again to be on the inside of the barbed-wire fence, the brick walls, the green classroom—never again!

In a greater sense, I did not escape at all. Rather, I took it all with me. The long, thin arms and legs—"Fuck you!" "I say fuck you!" The hatred, the tension, the favoritism, the bathroom smells, black pigtails tied with different-colored ribbons. "You like my new tenny-pumps, Mrs. Evans?" "Watch me. I is good!" And, "Along came Susie, ten, twenty, thirty . . ." "Who been using my bathroom!" "The fear of God is the beginning of wisdom." "Sandy, great job reading!" "Put the knife on the desk, please." "Now if it ain't Mrs. Evans, how is you doing? Would you stay if there were a new principal?" Cufflinks and fingernails gleaming in the sun. "You is prejudice. You just hates blacks. You thinks we is dumb; well we ain't. We is as good and as smart as whitie." "Amen Brother." "There ain't no supplies, so don't ask." "Nurse ain't coming for one child." "Don't forget, playground time is against county policy." "Hey Mrs. Evans, you nice. Is you going be here next year so I can visit and help you after school?" Memories neatly wrapped, labeled "P.S. 123."

CHAPTER 20

Neither the End,
Nor the Beginning

THE COUNTY LACKED MONEY to repair the roof, the faulty plumbing, and the broken windows of P.S. 123. It also lacked the money for children's books, paper, and supplies, but it did have the money to raise county officials' and administrators' salaries and to renovate their offices. As I waited in the Administration Building, I remembered the article in the newspaper about costly walnut panels, red carpets, attractive leather furniture, and a lowered ceiling to get away from that "old school house look." Despite my well-documented letters to the paper and requests that its reporters interview the teachers, the newspaper never did an article of any kind on P.S. 123 and its sadly neglected students whose parents, after all, were residents, readers, and voters.

I waited for one of the secretaries to come to the front desk.

"I would like to see my personnel folder."

"I'm sorry, but that is impossible! No teacher is allowed—"

I interrupted her. "I realize that I have to look at the folder with Mr. Simpson present."

"Mr. Simpson isn't here. He left at least a week ago. You would have to see your folder with Mr. Jackson, and he is too busy right now. He is on the phone and has a meeting scheduled this afternoon."

"When he finishes his call, please tell him I am waiting for him."

"If you want to wait for him, but it will be quite a while before he is available."

"Yes, I understand."

She glared at me and flounced away.

I sat on a new brown leather chair and watched the office staff. One secretary was putting on fresh lipstick. Another secretary wearing a tight pink sweater finished an apple and tossed the core into the wastebasket. The air conditioner hummed. The room was cool and comfortable despite the summer heat outside. I picked up a magazine on education and skimmed several articles, "Does Johnny Need a Psychiatrist?" and "Is Your Child a Slow Learner?"

"You may go in now." More impatiently, she raised her voice and continued, "Mr. Jackson will see you, but you can't stay long. He is very busy."

I walked past her into his office. A short, thin young man sat facing me. He seemed too small for Mr. Simpson's office chair. "Sit down, Mrs. *ahh* Evans." He read my name off his secretary's note. "Yes, Mrs. Evans. What can I do for you?"

"I thought your secretary would have told you. I am here to review my personnel folder."

"Oh well, now why would you want to take a look at that?" His voice was high-pitched and his manner condescending. A large strawberry birthmark edged the side of his pasty white face.

"My folder?"

"All right. Yes. Yes. I suppose so." He picked up the phone and asked his secretary to bring it in. "Do you suspect something to be wrong with your folder?" Hurriedly he added, "This is most irregular. *Hmm*. Most unusual for a teacher to request to see her folder. You realize I can't actually let you look at the contents, but I can tell you if anything seems to be out of order."

"The last time I looked at my records, I was allowed to go through the folder myself."

"Well." He cleared his throat and looked uncomfortable. "Well, some policies have been changed." He squinted at me. When the folder arrived, he took each sheet out, looked at it, and then said, "Everything appears to be in order, Mrs. Evans." He shuffled all the papers together and placed them back into the folder and closed the cover.

"May I see the papers from this school year?"

He found the application form and the principal evaluation sheet. "This evaluation sheet hasn't been signed, Mrs. Evans."

"No sir, it was filled out in pencil."

He waved it in front of me. "Oh yes, well, no, I can't let you see any of these papers. You see, once they leave the principal's office, they are county property."

"I see."

He leaned back in his chair, tapping his fingers against the arms. "Now Mrs. Evans, please believe me, your folder is in order, but obviously you aren't sure. What is the problem? I see you were employed at P.S. 123."

"Yes."

"And that Mr. Carter was your principal?"

"Yes."

"A fine man!" he said enthusiastically. "Now then, why don't you just tell me what this is about?"

I looked at him quietly. The silence made him uncomfortable. He fidgeted and said again, "Why don't you tell me about this?"

"Good day, Mr. Jackson." I stood and walked out of his office.

As I left the Administration Building that day, I realized the entire school board knew the problems at P.S. 123, but did nothing. The county administrators knew, but did nothing. Mr. Jackson, and before him Mr. Simpson and Mr. Nolen, knew, but did nothing. The newspaper knew, but did nothing. The children of P.S. 123 were locked inside that rusted barbed-wire fence, without hope, without help, and in the words of the old English nursery rhyme, "Thursday's child has far to go."

Made in the USA
Columbia, SC
17 June 2021